Remembering the
Bone House

Remembering the Bone House

An Erotics of Place and Space

NANCY MAIRS

PERENNIAL LIBRARY

HARPER & ROW, PUBLISHERS, NEW YORK
Grand Rapids, Philadelphia, St. Louis, San Francisco
London, Singapore, Sydney, Tokyo, Toronto

First PERENNIAL LIBRARY edition published 1990.

The Library of Congress has catalogued the hardcover edition as follows:

Mairs, Nancy, 1943–
    Remembering the bone house.

    1. Mairs, Nancy, 1943- —Biography.   2. Authors, American—20th century—Biography.   3. Multiple Sclerosis—Patients—United States—Biography.   I. Title.
PS3563.A386Z475   1989   818'.5409 [B]   88-45521
ISBN 0-06-016041-1

ISBN 0-06-091644-3 (pbk.)

90 91 92 93 94 FG 10 9 8 7 6 5 4 3 2 1

For George, again, always

Contents

PREFACE   *xi*

The Way In   *1*

The Port   *12*

In Exeter   *36*

Elsewhere   *55*

"236"   *80*

Sorties   *106*

Lost in Space   *125*

The Farm   *147*

Shelter   *179*

Inside and Outside   *202*

The Desert   *229*

Here at Home   *257*

Not only our memories, but the things we have forgotten are "housed." Our soul is an abode. And by remembering "houses" and "rooms," we learn to "abide" within ourselves.

—Gaston Bachelard, *The Poetics of Space*

In order to protect the privacy of certain individuals who appear in this book, names and other identifying characteristics have been changed.

Preface

I N WRITING a memoir, I have found, the temptation to censor material can grow enormous. Sometimes I have put pressure on myself to omit or prettify details in order to disguise truths about myself I didn't want to face up to or speak aloud. I've been drilled in the rules of polite discourse. I know that talking openly about certain matters—"telling the truth about my own experiences as a body," as Virginia Woolf put it—isn't "nice," especially for a woman. Time and again I've felt myself shrink from the task, and probably I've yielded in ways I don't even recognize. I believe, however, that the proscriptions traditionally placed on a woman's speech foster feelings of shame that lead her to trivialize her own experience and prevent her from discovering the depth and complexity of her life. In defiance of the conventions of polite silence, I've spoken as plainly and truthfully as the squirms and wriggles of the human psyche will permit.

When it comes to censorship on behalf of others, the issues are different. It is one thing to expose one's own life, taking responsibility for the shock and ridicule such an act may excite, and quite another to submit the people one loves to the same dangers. I can't resolve this dilemma to anyone's full satisfaction. But I have tried to keep my focus tight, speaking only for myself. The others all have stories of their own, some of which differ radically from mine, I'm sure. I hope that you'll remember and respect the reality of those differences. In a number of cases, I've changed the names of people and locations.

A word of caution about the first essay, "The Way In": it may not be the best way in for everyone. In it, I meditate on the idea of "memoir," before turning in the following essays to the remembrances themselves, so it is more theoretical than the others. In deciding whether or not to read it, think about how you prefer to enter a house. If you like a formal entry through the front door, pausing in the vestibule to remove your hat and gloves and check your face in the mirror above the umbrella stand, then perhaps you'd like to start with "The Way In." But if you'd rather barrel in through the back door and straight away plunk down at the kitchen table for a cup of coffee, then skip the first essay entirely, or use it as "the way out" instead.

I haven't the space to thank everyone who made *Remembering the Bone House* possible. You'll meet many of them in the following pages. A few who don't appear there deserve special mention, however. Under the tutelage of Sidonie Smith, now at SUNY Binghamton, I began to study and to practice women's autobiographical writing. Through tellings of their own lives, the members of an informal feminist-theory discussion group at the University of Arizona—among them Susan Hardy Aiken, Barbara Babcock, Karen Brennan, Janice Dewey, and Cynthia Hogue— taught me much about the shapes and significances of women's experience and narrative strategies for sharing that experience with others. For her indefatigable encouragement from the first word through the last, I am grateful to my agent, Barbara S. Kouts. Finally, my thanks to my editor, Lisa P. Miles, who has remained, throughout authorial glooms and panics, fresh, amused, energetic, supportive, open to quirky ideas, and quick to reassure. I don't think she's ever smoked a cigar in her life.

Remembering the
Bone House

The Way In

O N A GLITTERING August morning in 1979, at the edge of a salt marsh in Kennebunkport, Maine, I made a psychic sick.

I had never consulted a psychic before, although as a child I had wished I could accompany my mother and grandmother and take a turn having my cards read whenever they went to Salem to consult a woman named Lal. Mother and Granna were two of the least whimsical women I've ever known, smart and pragmatic and as ordinary in their beliefs and habits as two single matrons, one widowed and the other divorced, could be; and I can't imagine what lured them to Lal. But off they went to her, more than once in my recollection and perhaps before, returning deeply convinced of the accuracy of her predictive powers. She told Mother, for instance, that she would remarry—this time a man who changed his coat when he went to work. We awaited a doctor or a dentist, but the man who became my stepfather turned out to be a banker. So much for Lal's clairvoyance . . . until we learned that the bank where Daddy worked required its employees to put on jackets bearing the bank's logo.

Whenever I asked to be taken to Lal with them, Mother and Granna told me I was too young. And then Lal stopped doing readings. She couldn't bear, they said, the accuracy of her insights when they involved disaster. So I never got my turn, and never gave my loss much thought. Then one day over lunch my friend Liz

1

began to tell about a wonderful psychic she'd recently visited, and I felt my curiosity rekindle. "Why don't you give it a try?" my husband asked. (George never does anything weird himself, but he's very good at egging me on.) We were on vacation in New Hampshire, without commitments, and the opportunity to take my children to Kennebunkport, where I'd spent part of my childhood summers, appealed to me. So I took the psychic's number and gave her a call that night to make an appointment.

On the scheduled morning the four of us piled into my cousin's funny green Fiat with the chronic overheating problem and steamed across the state line into Maine. We found the house easily, just across a little bridge on the main road into the village, and George dropped me off. He and the children would drive down to the beach and play for the hour or so I'd been told the reading would take. I felt a little nervous and shyer than usual.

When I went to the door, the psychic, whose name I've long since forgotten, was just bidding good-bye to a reporter who'd been interviewing her for a feature in a local paper. She was very young and very pretty, with dark eyes and smooth, swingy dark hair set off by a delicate white summer dress. She led me through the house into a beautiful kitchen with an antique table and chairs at one end, overlooking through wide windows the silvery green marsh. We sat there, chatting a little awkwardly as I set up my tape recorder, which Liz had recommended I use so that I'd forget nothing. She took a deck of cards and began to lay them out, speaking in a light voice. Having lost the tape years ago, I have no idea what she said—something about airline travel, I seem to recall.

Perhaps a minute or so passed before she put her hand to her forehead and complained of a headache. She tried to go back to the cards, then put her hand up again.

"There's something wrong with my eyes. My vision is so blurred I can hardly see the cards."

"I have multiple sclerosis," I told her as if to offer reassurance. "I have a scotoma, a blurry spot, in my right eye." She tried to attend to the cards again, without much luck.

"I just feel terrible," she said. "I don't know what's wrong. I was feeling fine while the reporter was here. Maybe eating something would help." She took a reddened peach from a bowl on the sideboard behind her and bit it. She laid out a few more cards. "I'm not sure here," she said, squinting as if to focus. "I can't tell what these mean." She seemed reluctant to talk about the cards.

"Look, you don't have to go through this," I said. "I can leave."

"Oh, no," she protested without warmth.

"I'm going right now." I put the tape recorder in my bag and stood up.

"I'm so sorry," she said in a good-girl voice. "Perhaps I'm coming down with something. Listen, my in-laws live in Tucson and I'm going out to visit them this winter. Maybe I could do a reading for you then. Give me your name and address."

"Sure," I said, jotting them down. I'm not psychic, but I knew she'd rather die at this point than lay her blurred vision on me again. I made for the door.

I might be a little more whimsical a woman than my mother and grandmother, but not much. Yet I felt so little doubt that my proximity was causing the psychic's distress that I was reluctant to remain even outside her house. I walked back up the road, across the bridge, and perched on the narrow railing there to pass the half hour or so till George and the children returned for me. I sat in the startling sunshine, almost as bright as I was used to in the desert, and stared into the brown weedy water, pondering why the psychic had not been able to give me a coherent reading.

Kennebunkport has always been a powerful place for me, the most powerful in my world, in fact. My forebears lived there, and my father lies in the small and slightly ragged cemetery a few miles up this road. Perhaps that was the problem. Or perhaps it was my physical condition, an incurable degenerative disease, projected somehow into the psychic's sensitive flesh. Or perhaps she had seen something in the cards so terrible that she couldn't bear to read it to me, couldn't even bear to look at it herself. Although I didn't know it yet, I was already spiraling into a full-blown depressive episode, and by the same time a year later I would be almost lost. Now I look back and wonder whether she sensed this danger. I wonder also whether, if she had seen and warned me of it, I might have handled it better than I did.

As it was, I came away with only a fragmentary tape and a spookiness I couldn't quite communicate to George when he finally pulled up beside me and let me in. We drove on into the village, which I hardly recognized, so gentrified had it become with tourist dollars. We went to my family's house, long since sold and converted into an apartment building. The veranda had been pulled off and the space beneath it cemented to form a barren terrace. The spacious front hall, I saw as I peered through the glass in the door, had been constricted by flimsy blond formica paneling to a tiny square. My children, Anne and Matthew, thirteen and ten that summer, stared at the place vacantly, not even bothering to puzzle out what magic their mother seemed to find in it. They were a bit more intrigued by the cemetery and stood respectfully enough at the foot of my father's grave. But they have all their lives had a perfectly serviceable grandfather in the person of my stepfather, and this one has no significance for them even as a ghost.

After having stopped at the shrines, we drove back into the village and walked around a little. It had all, even the Lyric Movie Theater, been turned into little shops selling mostly tasteful and pricey curios. The River View Restaurant was still there, but remodeled and polished and so popular that we couldn't get a table. We finally found a vacant little restaurant on the other side of the river, in what had been a bait or outboard-motor shop, where we got a late lunch of fried clams before heading back down the coast. That was the end of our pilgrimage to Kennebunkport. I haven't gone back since, and perhaps now I'll never go.

What I didn't know that day, or for a good while afterward, was that I'd begun to write a book. The psychic never said anything about books. Something had shifted in me, like carelessly stowed cargo, skewing my course almost imperceptibly at the first, until I fetched up here in an orange desk chair in front of a word processor on a chilly November afternoon, farther abroad than I could have imagined then. What moved me I'm not certain. In part, I was disturbed by the psychic's refusal, whatever its cause, to "read" my life. Thanks to her denial, something about that life now seemed unreadable, alien, impermissible, as though I'd stepped outside for a minute, the door blew shut behind me, and I discovered that my key no longer fit the lock.

Then, too, there was the puzzle of the lost house, the lost town. A house was here, and a town, right where I had left them, but both they and I had been so transformed by the intervening years that they were, literally, not the ones I knew. The ones I knew were not there. But neither had they vanished altogether. They were perfectly present to me in both waking and sleeping dreams. They seemed to have sunk from their perch on the banks of the Mousam River into the brine of my own cells. I was The Port incarnate, all that was left of the place I meant by The Port, and the only return possible was involution.

* * *

Not long after that day on the coast of Maine, back in the desert soil I've chosen to nurture and chastise me, I bought a copy book and began to sketch some reminiscences of the houses I had grown up in, as part of a preliminary study of women's autobiographical writing. But I didn't get far before other duties claimed me. Then, a year or so later, I returned to the sketches in a workshop taught by a well-known southwestern writer of nonfiction. His response was glum: my memoirs were not readable, he wrote on the back of the last page, "to an ordinary bored, busy, hard-nosed, cynical, weary, cigar-smoking, whisky-drinking, fornicating old fart like—not me!—but your typical magazine or book editor.... Now if you were (already) a famous person this might not matter; but you're not; so it does." Well, I certainly wasn't a famous person. Not only that, but since I lacked the stature or stamina to take up football, and I was too old and funny-looking to pass a screen test, and I was more apt to hang out with the tramps at our local soup kitchen than with Beautiful People anywhere, I hadn't any chance of becoming a famous person. No fame, no life. I put the copy book with its blotchy black-and-white cardboard covers away.

I was, in some ways, a slow learner. At that time I didn't understand the kind of radical questioning that all moral life, but especially life in the ivory phallus, requires. I deferred to the values of the Fornicating Old Fart (let's call him FOF for short) because he'd published a lot of books and I hadn't published any. In this way I remained open to his good advice—that I'd have to make my memoirs readable—but rendered it useless, since I had no permission now to write memoirs, readable or otherwise. What I didn't ask was first, whether the FOF actually represented the audience I was writing for; and second, whether fame was an authentic qualification for a memoirist.

The answers to these questions unfolded for me slowly. I began to recognize that, in fact, nine-tenths of the literature I was familiar with had been written for FOFs—but it had also been written *by* FOFs, of which, by dint of my gender, I could not be one. This literature forms what is known in conventional feminist parlance as the patriarchal literary canon, still firmly entrenched after centuries. So, if typical magazine or book editors were FOFs, I was going to have a tough time getting published, no matter what. I could, of course, choose to write in the persona of an FOF; some women slipped by the gatekeepers of current literary taste that way. But I could also, thanks to the bravery and honesty of women writing before and beside me, choose not to.

As for a memoirist's fame, it's a requirement attached to the moldy definition of autobiography as the self-reporting of "the great deeds of great men." By this definition, no woman could ever compose a "life." Yet the earliest extant autobiography in English literature was dictated by a woman (illiterate, of course), fifteenth-century Margery Kempe; and similar claims have been made in other literatures. And women, whose access to fame has always been severely restricted, though notoriety has been more commodious, have continued to excel at autobiographical writing—memoirs, notebooks, letters, journals—to the present. Isak Dinesen wasn't famous when she wrote *Out of Africa,* although, as it turned out, *Out of Africa* has made her famous. She needed to make some money, her African coffee venture having turned financially disastrous, and she was desperately homesick for a land and a life now permanently lost to her. The strength of that yearning, which sings on every page, has touched more readers than any "great" man's memories of his "great" conquest of the Dark Continent and its peoples.

That the FOF and I have fundamentally different attitudes toward life (what one does day after day) and "a life" (the report one makes on the outcome of what one has done day after day) is clear from his demand that I conduct my daily affairs so as to attract public attention for my distinctions; then I will have something "worth" writing about, a "life" even an editor will look at twice, a "life," that is, which will sell. Now, I don't object to selling books, but neither have I found the prospect of selling them a motivation for writing them. The only motivation that works for me is the desire to contact others, to share my experiences with them, to stir them to recognition of the similarities that underlie their experiences and mine, to illuminate and delight in and laugh over the commonplaces of human life. To this end, I *can't* be "a famous person," standing out from my audience, declaiming publicly my distinctions as, say, a fabulously wealthy automobile company president, a multiply reincarnated actress, a venerable Speaker of the House of Representatives. I want my "life," in reporting the details of my own life, to recount, at the level beneath the details, the lives of others. No modesty is entailed here—simply the desire to celebrate the private rather than the public world of human habitation.

I took a long time to free myself of the FOF's notion that one merits one's memoirs through acquiring fame and to develop the divergent sense of purpose I'm describing. What returned me to my "life" wasn't a sense of this freedom and development, however. It was an accident of intellectual messiness. Because my thoughts are easily scattered, I try to read and assimilate one book at a time; but if another comes along to intrigue me, I'm apt to sneak a peek. Thus, while I was working my way through Gaston Bachelard's phenomenological study *The Poetics of Space,* a new translation I had ordered, *The Newly Born Woman* by the French feminists Catherine Clément and Hélène Cixous, arrived in the mail and I found myself shuttling back and forth between them. Suddenly the two collided in my head, houses and female sexuality tumbling and tangling into the autobiographical project I wanted to do: a feminist memoir.

The body itself is a dwelling place, as the Anglo-Saxons knew in naming it *banhus* (bonehouse) and *lichama* (bodyhome), and the homeliness of its nature is even livelier for a woman than for a man. Bachelard speaks of "inhabited space" as the "non-I that protects the I." Woman may literally become that inhabited space, containing, in Cixous's words, "a thousand and one fiery hearths" of erotic desire and experiencing in childbirth "the not-me within me," thereby becoming the non-I that protects the I of the unborn child. Still, forced to function as man's Other and thus alienated from her self, "she has not been able to live in her 'own' house, her very body. . . . Women haven't had eyes for themselves. They haven't gone exploring in their house. Their sex still frightens them. Their bodies, which they haven't dared enjoy, have been colonized." Through writing her body, woman may reclaim the deed to her dwelling.

The reverberations of these texts have coalesced for me into the project of exploring my own "felicitous space," to use Bachelard's phrase, the houses where I once lived and where, time collapsing through dreams, I continue to live today. I return to them, reenter them, in order to discover the relationships they bear to my own erotic development and thus perhaps—because I'm ever aware of my self as a cultural, not merely a personal, construct—to feminine erotic development in general.

Admittedly, "eroticism" has a more global meaning for me than language in its present state permits. This dissonance between idiosyncratic meaning and meaning that everyone can agree upon causes me problems with all the good-hearted people who inquire after my new book with much the same solicitude they might summon for my ailing puppy or my recently widowed mother-in-law. "An erotics of place and space," I tell them, waiting for the wince, the furrow, the grin—the responses vary, but plainly they all assume that I'm writing "a dirty book." Well, maybe I am. I mention my body, certainly, quite a lot, even its secret places. Here and there I kiss, stroke, press, squeeze, even engage in sexual intercourse. Not as often, though, as I lie in bed, run across a playground, eat favorite foods, listen to the radio, tease my sister, roll in new snow. All these acts, happening to me as a body, shaping my awareness of my embodied self, form my erotic being. It is that process I'm seeking to capture and comprehend: how living itself takes on an erotic tone.

For a woman saturated to the bone in Calvinist tradition, such an exploration necessitates the healing of a classic Western patriarchal bifurcation: body/mind or body/spirit. I grew up in the belief that my intellectual-spiritual life, reflective of my "true" self, was separate from and superior to my life as a body. My body's appearance, which preoccupied me, was dismissed as beneath my concern: "Handsome is as handsome does," I was told whenever I seemed to think well of my looks. Its urges were denied, or at least deferred: I was "saving" myself for marriage, when I would "give" myself to my husband, the reward for which seemed to be not physical bliss but spiritual satisfaction at having him appreciate my "purity." As an adult, apparently, my bodily life might begin, and I suppose it did, at least in sexual terms. After I was married, I deliberately masturbated for the first time, so I must have believed myself entitled to my body's sensations in a new way. But I got through two pregnancies and childbirths, several sexual affairs, a couple of serious suicide attempts, and the onset of a devastating degenerative disease locked almost entirely in my head.

My body, of course, was going through all these experiences, whether "I" was holding my "self" aloof from it or not. Fortunately, one simply cannot *be* without being a body. One simply *is* inches of supple skin and foot after foot of gut, slosh of blood, thud of heart, lick of tongue, brain humped and folded into skull. And it is as a body that one inhabits the past and it inhabits one's body: "But over and beyond our memories, the house we were born in is physically inscribed in us. It is a group of organic habits," Bachelard writes. "After twenty years, in spite of all the other anonymous stairways, we would recapture the reflexes of the 'first stairway,' we would not stumble on that rather high step. . . . The word habit is too worn a word to express this passionate liaison of our bodies, which do not forget, with an unforgettable house." Whether or not I permitted myself to think of my self as a body at some earlier time, I cannot deny the identity today. That identity offers my only means of entering and literally making sense of my past.

The search for lost time necessitates spatial, not merely temporal, recall. As Bachelard tells us, memory "does not record concrete duration"; rather, "we think we know ourselves in time, when all we know is a sequence of fixations in the spaces of the being's stability. . . ." We can impose a grid of time onto our memories, much as we sketch lines of latitude and longitude on a globe, a useful device for knowing when or where we are in relation to some event or spot used as a reference point. But the memories won't yield up their freight in response. For that we have to let go of lifelines and plunge into the multiple modalities—sensory, emotional, cognitive—which have encoded the past and will release it, transformed, into the present. To this end, I prefer to work in the fragmented form of essays, each concentrating on a house or houses important to my growth as a woman. Each house contains its own time, of course. But in emphasizing the spatial rather than the temporal elements in my experience, I attempt to avoid what critic Georges Gusdorf calls, in "The Conditions and Limits of Autobiography," the "original sin of autobiography" (and, one might add, the outstanding feature of phallocentric discourse in general)—that is, "logical coherence and rationalization."

To avoid these qualities, their reassuring rigidity and muscularity beloved by all of us who are products of the ivory phallus. To abandon the phallic narrative structure inculcated there: exposition, complication, climax, denouement. To refuse its critical questions: What does this mean? Why does it matter? To embrace the past as "meaningless," as "matterless," without "worth" in an economy based on the scarcity of resources, on the fear of running out: of reasons, of memories, of precious time. To seduce the impatient reader boldly: *Here, let's take our time. We've got plenty more where it came from.* To dare to dally. These are the risks of a woman who experiences her past—the past in which she lived as a body, which dwells in her body still—as a bower.

When we were children, we formed an enclosure of hands linked into arches and sang:

> Go in and out the window.
> Go in and out the window.
> Go in and out the window
> As you have done before.

Writing my past as a body enacts that circle game. I invite you through my openings because I have been schooled in hospitality: you, my strangers, my guests. *Mi casa es su casa.* "Writing," says Cixous, "is the passageway, the entrance, the exit, the dwelling place of the other in me. . . ." Writing itself is space. It is a populated house.

In the houses of my past which I write about, I often felt alone; now, in writing about them, I am never alone. I cannot write my self without writing you, my other. I don't believe literally that, in writing my "life," I am writing yours as well. On the contrary, I feel certain I am not. You didn't get bitten on the foot by red ants when you were four, did you? You didn't sing "Lullay, Thou Little Tiny Child" in the fourth-grade Christmas pageant? Your baby bunny wasn't chewed up and swallowed, hind legs last, by your Irish setter, Pegeen? You don't eat the same thing for breakfast every morning of your life? You're not still scared of the dark? These are my details. And heaven knows I have enough trouble getting them straight without keeping track of yours as well.

In fact, this is one of the problems that pursues and daunts me in autobiographical work: I can never get the details right to the satisfaction of everyone who shows up in the telling. The French philosopher Maurice Merleau-Ponty comments that "all action and all love are haunted by the expectation of an account which will transform them into their truth." My mother's expectation in particular! She wants to check over my essays to make sure I've told things as they "really" happened this time, since I missed the mark mightily in an earlier book. Others who find themselves presented here will no doubt wish the same.

But the past, that ramshackle structure, is a fabrication. I make it up as I go along. The only promise I can state about its "reality" is that I "really" remember (reembody? flesh out anew?) the details I record; that is, I haven't deliberately invented any of them. But on the whole I haven't sought historical accuracy. Instead, I have tried, in Merleau-Ponty's words, "to give the past not a survival, which is the hypocritical form of forgetfulness, but a new life, which is the noble form of memory." In these terms, I can't even tell my own truth, much less anyone else's. I can only settle the problem in the manner of Clément's sorceress: "She is true because she believes her own lies."

And yet, in a deeper sense of the word, I hope that I've spoken truthfully about all our lives. Because I think that my "story," though intensely personal, is not at all private. Beneath its idiosyncracies lie vast strata of commonality, communality. I don't see how anyone engaged in self-representation can fail to recognize in the autobiographical self, constructed as it is in language, all the others whom the writing self shelters. The not-me dwells here in the me. We are one, and more-than-one. Our stories utter one another.

Think, for example, of your houses: the one you live in now, if you have one, and the ones you have inhabited before. I am writing a book about your houses. You never lived in a yellow house on the coast of Maine? No matter. You have had such a house, perhaps a long time ago, not perhaps your chief house, the one you spent the most time in, but the one that you return to now most frequently in dreams, whether you remember them or not, a locus for you, inexplicably, of mystery and desire. I will write about the yellow house. You will read about your house. If I do my job, the book I write vanishes before your eyes. I invite you into the house of my past, and the threshold you cross leads you into your own.

The Port

i

J dream of old, decaying houses. Some exist only in dreams, although they may, by appearing there more than once, begin to feel like home. Others, having crossed over with me from my waking life, possess a different sort of familiarity, a sense that something beloved, once lost, has been redeemed. What they all share, in general, are their size and decrepitude. My task is not merely to inhabit but to rescue them.

Of all, the one that recurs most faithfully is the yellow house on the coast of Maine, vast and dark, vaster and darker than it was even in real life. Sometimes there are dozens of rooms just in the ell, where there were really five, or on the third floor, where there were six: all in a shambles of broken furniture and damp bedding. Sometimes the stairway to the third floor is so clogged with old clothing and broken toys that it's impassable. Occasionally the house has been chopped up with cheap paneling into so many units that I can scarcely tell where the rooms originally lay. But no matter how dreadful the decay, I glory in possessing this house at last, and I set to work restoring it. Usually, I've already finished a couple of rooms, and my heart is high. The dreams of this house, though often somber, are never sad.

I have surely lived in this house more years of my sleeping life than in any other. Its grip on this level of my consciousness puzzles me, because I spent far less of my waking life in it. I never lived in it as I did in other houses, and my visits seldom lasted longer than a few days. I certainly wasn't born here at the edge of the fishing village we seldom call by its formal name, shortening it, with the sense of entitlement nicknames confer, to The Port. By synechdoche, the house is The Port as well: the place of arrival, of refuge. In fact, I haven't any suitable birthplace. Thanks to World War II, I am a native Californian, an incongruity that perhaps troubles only a thirteenth-generation New Englander. Growing up among relatives whose roots proudly clutch thin and rocky soil, I'm *embarrassed* to have been born in California, as though I hadn't got properly born at all. My father was born in Greenfield and my mother in Salem, Massachusetts; my husband, at the Boston Lying-In; my children, in Bath, Maine, and Waltham, Massachusetts; they're authentic people, born where they belong, not accidents of war.

At forty-three, returning to Long Beach to speak at a conference, I stare from the seventeenth floor of the Hyatt Regency down at the city and out at the snowy mountains beyond, and for the first time it occurs to me that one might authentically be born a Californian. Too late for me, though. I'm permanently estranged from my birthplace. It doesn't shelter my dreams, waking or sleeping.

For some reason, my soul chooses for a birthplace a dwelling where it has never literally been at home. Perhaps that itself is the core of its magic for me: that I don't belong here, that this space is untainted by the tedium and trivia of my ordinary existence. The Port forms an absolutely separate plane. The people living here I seldom see anywhere else. They're like characters in a book or a film, who gesture and laugh as soon as I step into the frame but freeze, like the sleeping villagers of *Brigadoon*, when I step back out; even my father very nearly comes to life. No wonder I return and return in dream. The capacity to dream beyond the facts of existence into their significance enables us to remember a true past, one that simultaneously reflects and illuminates experience. I dream my self into being at The Port: a child capable of falling in love forever with a house and its environs. Long after the structure, passing out of my family's possession, is altered beyond all but the most superficial recognition, I will persist in such dreaming.

At forty-five, I no longer know which of the details I can retrieve from my past are memories and which are daydreams, and, to be honest, I no longer care. I have lost any reverence I may once have had for the "facts," and with it any genuine belief in them.

Not long ago my mother told me a version of an incident from our past which was simply wrong, though at earlier times she'd told it accurately enough. For some reason, she'd suddenly revised the tale, "dreamed" it differently. I started to correct her, in that habitual manner children have of setting their parents straight. Then I shrugged. If I'd told her my version, she wouldn't have believed it. She'd have thought I'd forgotten what "really" happened. But what "really" happened, I understood suddenly, is always irredeemable. One thing happened in the world she dreams and another in the world I dream, that's all.

The past itself is an oneiric house: the house we were born in. You can't get into it in real time, or in real space, for that matter, the way you can climb into your car and drive through the city streets and pull into your driveway and (provided you haven't forgotten your back-door key) open the sliding glass door and, shooing the puppies out from under your feet, step inside. There's no place to go to get to the past. Better stay, comfortably, right where you are.

Nor can you "relive" it, even in imagination, if by that you mean reexperience it exactly as it occurred. You are now another person. The person of the past is gone. Because of the experiences you think of as in the "past," the person of the past has been transformed into you, knowing what you know. The past exiles you from itself. You may live the past, however, even though you can't relive it. You may live it as often as you like, but only as your present self, the one sitting (comfortably, I hope) right where you are. The one who knows what you know. Each time you enter it, you build it anew.

Here's what I know, this time in.

ii

The Port makes me possible, because my parents meet there when they're thirteen. The house belongs to Daddy's grandparents, Bunty and Grandfather. Even though they have four children, and the eldest of these, my grandmother Garm, already has four children of her own, they have room for summer boarders. Through a mutual friend, my grandmother Granna learns of the place. In the throes of an unpleasant divorce, she's crippled by migraine, and the doctor has recommended a rest, a change, so she brings her three children—who will be my Aunt Jane, my Uncle Robert, and my mother—here. While she lies in a shaded room at the front of the house, the children clatter with Daddy and his siblings out the back door to play croquet on the wide side lawn, gather wild strawberries in the field that stretches all the way to the river, canoe up the river past the golf course with a picnic lunch.

Through stories and reminiscences, especially those of Aunt Jane and Daddy's sisters, Aunt Sadie and Aunt Nora, and through snapshots as well, fragments of this time will survive in me. I will know about Sally and Pat, the Irish setters, mother and son, stealing Mary-the-black-cook's Sunday roast; about the itch and sag of woolen swimming suits; about Petsy-dear, another summer boarder, the daughter of a ritzy dress-shop owner and a toy salesman, who tags after the other children and whines if she gets mud on her skirt or burrs in her white ankle socks; about the way the eels Daddy has caught in the millpond writhe as they hit the spitting fat in Mary's pan; about skinny, pimply Henry Maling, who fancies my slender mother with her pouting lips and pale hair. Who fancies my father. Who fancies her. Part of the power The Port has over me lies, surely, in the ghosts these tales evoke, especially the young ghosts of Jack and Anne, without whose summer romance I could not be.

At thirteen they don't make eternal vows, of course, or for many years to come. In high school, Mother has a boyfriend, a serious one, serious enough so that when Daddy proposes, Darren tries to talk her into marrying him instead; serious enough so that, more than fifty years later, long married to others, they will remain friends. Daddy has girlfriends, too, one a wealthy socialite—quite a catch. But while Mother is at Wheaton and Daddy at Annapolis, they spend more and more time together, winters as well as summers, and by the time the navy permits young Ensign Smith, commissioned in haste on December 8, 1941, to propose, Mother is eager to board a train from Boston to San Francisco and become, in a sky-blue suit that matches her eyes, a war bride.

Before my birth, I'm a boy. Junior Junior. I will be startled by this fact forty-five years later while reading a handful of letters written by my mother to her mother during my gestation. "Jr. Jr. is a very active baby I should say, even without previous experience," she writes. "He seems to squirm constantly. Most interesting to watch the queer bulges he makes." "He kicks like h— and is getting huge." "I sure wish my Mama could come out to Long

Beach . . . in August to see him." I'll always have known, of course, that my parents wanted a boy. What parents, at least of their generation, didn't? But knowing their preference isn't at all the same as hearing myself referred to, in a dozen or more letters throughout several months, as a boy in fact, huge, rugged, lusty: he. It's as though I discover an existence hitherto secret even from myself.

What I turn out to be, after a labor lasting from Tuesday night till Friday morning, is "the funniest looking, skinniest little bundle of humanity you ever saw," "all bones," with "Jack's mouth, and she wrinkles her forehead exactly as he does!" Not a boy, but at least my father's daughter. "Your face was the size of a teacup," she'll always tell me, the metaphor rendering me inanimate and fragile, like one of those antique dolls with soft bodies and painted porcelain faces. "Long feet. *Long* fingers. A mop of light brown hair." She shows me a ring of it taped into the pink leather baby book. Slowly calling me, each time, into being.

As for Junior Junior, they can always try again, they say. And say again after Sally's birth. In the last letter of my meager handful, written from Guam less than four months before Daddy's death, Mother writes teasingly that if her brother and his wife don't hurry, she'll "come home and produce a grandson" before they do.

Like all children, except perhaps orphans, my memories begin before I have the capacity for remembering, coded for me in the tales adults, and Mother in particular, recount over and over, joined in time by stuttering images that gradually become surer, more continuous, until I can say on my own: "I remember!" Before that self-creative moment, a tomato rolls out of a shopping bag and, crawling to it, I bite firmly through the skin, my face, bigger now than a teacup, screwing comically at the spurt of tart juice. I have to be hospitalized with rheumatic fever, and an undetected allergy to sulfanilamide nearly kills me. While Mother is pregnant with Sally, I dash away, Mother lumbering in my wake, and so Daddy buys Mother a leash to keep me on. For Sally's birth, I am sent to Garm, who is so charmed by me that at the end of three weeks Mother and Daddy have to insist a little sharply on getting me back. Left alone to take a nap, I smear Mother's lipstick all around my mouth. Delighted by the effect, I call out from my second-floor room to my parents, who are sitting at the end of a long lawn. From that distance they can see only a gash of red, and so they rush in, breathless and terrified and then, of course, very, very cross, the way people get after they've had a bad scare. When Daddy calls all the way from the South Pacific, I can't think of anything to tell him except that I ate corn for dinner.

Adults provide the texts for their prereminiscent children. But the children must tease out the subtexts for themselves, without being told, as a rule, even that this task exists, let alone how to go about it. Some learn about it more quickly than others. I, for one, take a very long time to decipher the drift of the tales of my earliest life: I am the "difficult" child. This is not at all the same as being a "bad" child, though I am occasionally bad as well. Rather, the difficult child is the one who deviates from the family's (and possibly, though not necessarily, society's) most cherished values, which in my case tend toward the Yankee conventions of thrift, diligence, restraint, discretion, modesty, a cheerful though undemonstrative disposition, and, as soon as we're old enough, a vote for the Republican ticket.

The families whose confluence I am produce a difficult child in each generation: Aunt Jane in Mother's, Aunt Sadie in Daddy's, me in mine, Matthew in my children's. Matthew's may be the most complicated role of all, the difficult child of a difficult child, a double deviant. Is it by accident that we're also the artistic ones—the writers, actors, photographers, rock musicians? Perhaps not. The practice of art does demand a certain willingness to take risks—the gamble that one can make, out of nothing, something—which is incompatible with the solid Yankee business sense that informs our familial values. In a family in which everyone practices—or at least admires—art, the budding banker might function as the difficult child, I suppose.

Part of the reason I will fail until middle age to recognize my structural role as the difficult child is that I assume, on the basis of my own experience, that every family has one. The role is as natural to me as having five toes on each foot, and I pay it about as little attention. Maybe, in fact, most families do have one, but not all. The man I will marry is, because of the stillbirth of his one brother, an adored only child. Even without his unusually compliant nature, he'd have had a hard time getting his parents to project on him the troublesome qualities characteristic of a difficult child. Given just one chance, they had to find in what they got the fulfillment of their ideals, or go unfulfilled. Nor, of course, did he have anyone to receive his projections. One of the reasons he may readily adopt my family's evaluation of me, and find me problematic himself, is that I provide his lack: I function as George's difficult sibling.

iii

I remember: Being waked in the dark at Garm and Pop's house in Exeter and driven, against a red horizon turning gold, to Logan Airport. Lying in a ship's berth, shielded from the lighted cabin by a draped towel. The voices of Mother and some other women fret because my sister has a fever. Sometimes we go to a dark room to watch cartoons. Mother perches me on a railing and points at a green hump against the sky: "That's Diamond Head." We fly in a plane with no seats, only benches. Even wrapped in a man's coat, I shudder with the cold.

With this trip to Truk, an atoll in the South Pacific, I begin to store my past for myself. Because my memory is almost exclusively eidetic, my past is essentially mute and still, an album of colored photos, some badly faded, or, at its most animated, an old home movie rather than a Hollywood production: no dialogue, only an occasional stutter of sound; just a few frames to the second; bits missing where the film, brittle now, has snapped and been spliced. I may not know what anyone is saying, and I certainly don't understand much of what's going on. But I can always see my surroundings and sense my location within them. I am always in place.

In the whitewashed Quonset hut on Truk, my young father is still alive. I don't think of him as "young," of course, or even as "father." I don't "think" of him at all. That kind of reflective consciousness of others will come later, too late to include him, after his death, perhaps in part because of it. Later, trying to bring it to bear on him, I'll find myself working from an almost maternal perspective, my own children fast approaching his age on Truk. A handsome young man, I'll know from pictures, short and sturdily built, and very bright, his academic record suggests. *But was he also witty?* I'll want to know. *What did he like to talk about? Did he like to read books? Which ones? What ambitions did he harbor? Did he love me?* I can get this kind of information from Mother and others who loved him. But that's not the same, of course, as hearing from him.

Just once, I'll sense who he was to himself, when Mother

lets me read his proposal of marriage, a long, thoughtful explanation of what life might be like for the wife of a naval officer. Here he's alive, a young man talking earnestly to the woman he loves, and in the absence of tape recordings, this is as close as I'll ever get to the rhythm and timbre of his speech. I weep and weep.

"Oh, I shouldn't have given it to you!" Mother says, shaken as always in the wet face of emotion.

"No, no, it's all right," I try to reassure her. "I'm not upset. I'm only crying because this is the first time in my adult life I've heard my father's voice." Mother looks dubious. For her, I think, tears are never good. But I'm thrilled to have heard my father speak, however briefly. Later, Mother gives me his other letters, which I keep, wrapped in plastic, in the commode in my bedroom. She wants to take one out before anyone reads the rest, and I don't want to lose any of them, so I simply don't read them. Still, I like having my father's own words nearby.

On Truk, Daddy's voice is muffled, the way grown-ups' voices are. He whacks open a green coconut, giving me a sip of what he calls the milk, cloying and translucent, nothing like the milk my mouth has expected, and laughs as I screw up my face. Crouched under a leaky tarpaulin with the women and other children, I peer out at him and the other men in the bow, dressed in blue shirts and trousers soaked with spray. When Sally throws up, I clamp my hands over my mouth in horror, wanting to go outside with Daddy, but of course I can't. Our little dog, Petey-Puss-the-Platypus, goes mad—dogs often do in the tropics, they say—and Daddy swings me up onto a piece of furniture for safekeeping. The house is filled with the rumble of men's voices, which must contain orders and plans, as he and his friends prepare to track her into a mango grove and shoot her.

More vivid than Mother and Daddy in that Quonset hut, its tin roof resonant in every afternoon's rain, are our native servants, Yoska and Sistem, slender brown teenagers dressed in soft, pale cotton, with bare feet. I want bare feet, too, but Mother is afraid of hookworm, so I always wear sandals. Yoska and her friends take us and some other children to a nearby grove to pick mangoes. Sometimes they stand in front of the mirror on Mother's dresser, pulling their long, straight, dark hair across their faces and giggling. Mother finds this behavior quaint, but I don't think much of it, since Sally and I often make faces into mirrors and giggle, too. I'm much more impressed by the quantities of toilet paper Yoska uses, huge white handfuls of it, as though it were some kind of treat.

Sistem takes care of the house and yard. When I'm supposed to be taking a nap, I lean out of my bedroom window and hiss, "Sistem, get me a coconut." He scales a nearby palm swiftly with his bare hands and feet, brings down and breaks open the fruit, and gives me some of the pieces. Though I hate coconut milk, I love to nibble this white sugary meat off its fibrous rind. Once during naptime he takes me from my bed into my parents' bedroom, pulls off my panties, and rubs my genitals with his brown penis. Although it doesn't hurt, I'm puzzled and aroused. I don't know what he wants me to do, but the only use I know for down there is to make tinkle, so I urinate a little on his penis. "No, don't do that," he says in his soft, accented voice, "don't do that."

Somehow I know (does he tell me?) that this is a secret event, so I never tell anyone. Indeed, I can't tell anyone, because I forget it. In psychoanalytic jargon, I suppose I repress it. (Like Freud's Dora and her kind.) Whatever the mechanism, it simply vanishes until I become sexually active many years later. It seems as though I can't think of it because I lack the lexicon in which it can be expressed. Once I become conversant in sexual intercourse, it will make sense, literally, and it will speak itself quietly but emphatically back into my memory. Aha! I will say. So that's what *that* puzzle was about. The process of remembering: fitting each piece against another until the pattern leaps out.

We move to a three-family Quonset hut on a barren hillside on Guam. When Daddy pulls up in his jeep every afternoon, all of us—Sally and me and the big Labrador retriever named Rochester—tumble onto the porch to meet him, Mother close behind. Later he strides, wrapped in a white towel, from his room at one end of our unit to the bathroom at the other, singing "The Battle Hymn of the Republic" in a lusty baritone. Sometimes he bathes us and puts us to bed. One morning when Mother is sick, he even gets us ready for Sunday School by himself, taking us in to Mother to show off, two little girls in starched pinafores and sandals with smooth hair and the breakfast washed off our faces.

At the other end of the Quonset hut lives tow-headed Kurt. The three of us like to paddle our feet in the ditch across the street, which fills during every afternoon's rain with warm brown water and squishy mud. Once we even take off our sunsuits, making our mothers very cross. Kurt has something like Daddy's, only littler, of course, because he's a very little boy, younger than me. I think it's called a *deeny*. We have other friends, too, Judalee and Buz. Sometimes Mother and Daddy take us to parties, at one of which I address an admiral as "Admirable"; at another, I take a healthy swig of Mother's crème de menthe, which knocks me straight over backward onto my duff. Mother loves these two stories, so it won't matter that I can't remember the incidents themselves. More often, they leave us behind with Mrs. Crab, who isn't crabby at all, though you'd never know it from the way Sally bellows when Mother and Daddy walk out the door. I beg Mrs. Crab to make us baking-powder biscuits, which Mother never does, letting me help roll out the fleshy dough and cut it into circles with a jelly jar. I adore these hot, salty rounds crumbling on my tongue. Better even than coconuts.

One night, just before Christmas, on the way back from driving the babysitter home, Daddy blacks out and runs his jeep off the road. A nurse driving by notices the accident and stops, but he's already dead. His injuries aren't severe, and the doctors speculate that he died of a cerebral hemorrhage caused by a blow on the head at work earlier in the day.

Someone, but not my father, must come to our door in the middle of the night. Someone must say to my mother, "There's been an accident. . . ." I sleep through. All my life I will try to conceive what that nocturnal visit meant to her, how she must have felt, but I can't, not "really," not even, for that matter, by analogy. Some events belong only to the person who experiences them. No one ever knocks on my door and mutters, "George . . . accident . . . dead." I am spared, happily and for the moment, what my mother knows.

Women, most of them strangers to me, fill the house. At night they take turns sleeping on a cot set up across from mine. I've been given a calico kitten named Muffin for my birthday, and I like to swing her in the sling of mosquito netting which forms between the frame the netting hangs over and the mattress where Mother tucks it in. One night the sling sags lower and lower, until Muffin hits the floor softly with each arc. Thud. Thud. One of these women comes in and takes her away, chiding me for hurting the kitty. I hate her. I remember nothing else about the days following Daddy's death, not even my hysteria when Mother tells me we are "going home."

Daddy has gone to heaven, she has told Sally and me. Having been to Sunday School, I know about heaven. It's up in the sky, where God lives. But it's *up in the sky over Guam.* If we go somewhere else, we'll leave Daddy behind, in the sky over Guam. I won't go. No, no, Mother soothes, it's all right, heaven is up in the sky everywhere, and Daddy will be up there wherever we move. I acquiesce. From now on, Daddy will float along above me, as though at the end of a tensile tether, up there where I can talk to him inside my head as he watches whatever I do. He never appears, never speaks, but I'm sure of his presence. When I'm bad, he's sorrowful, I know, but he goes on loving me. He didn't leave because he stopped loving me. Why did he leave? He had to. Because of the accident. "Our Father, who art in heaven," I pray every night. God and Daddy. Up there. Wherever I go.

Mother and Sally and I ride in a little boat through the dark to a plane sitting on the water, where we put on orange Mae Wests. We lie in a narrow bunk, Mother and Sally in one direction and I in the other, my face at Mother's feet. "Stop kicking each other," Mother says in a tired voice. I wake in a twin bed in a white room in San Francisco. We sit on prickly green plush and press our faces against the wide window of our Pullman compartment, staring and staring at a landscape entirely white and gray and brown until we arrive at the place in it which will become home.

How Mother survives this voyage I will never be able to imagine. I never see her cry, and nobody else does, either. Shortly after we get back, Daddy's refrigerated body arrives at 5:30 on a bitter morning. Aunt Sadie goes to the station in Exeter with Mother, who wears a brave red outfit, to meet the train. Sally and I don't go to the funeral, but when we're older, Granna will tell us of Garm's insistence on an open-casket funeral. So Mother must have to look at her husband one more time, sealed under glass, a macabre Sleeping Beauty in a tale that permits no magic kisses. Afterward, he's taken to The Port and buried.

iv

Perhaps this too is why The Port holds such power for me. Here, if anywhere, Daddy "lives," in the untidy little cemetery shaded by dark pines where one is still permitted to raise square monuments of gray granite; to plant cedar or juniper or euonymous and, on Memorial Day, red geraniums; to tend the plants, trimming a straggly shoot, picking off a blossom gone by, throughout the brief Maine summer. Under our family's stone dwells my father, at his feet a plaque reading "John Eldredge Smith, Jr. 1919–1947. World War II" and an American Legion flag, brilliant and crisp each Memorial Day, steadily more faded and tattered by sun, wind, rain, snow, and thaw until the next Memorial Day. I can depend on him in a world where it seems, as I spin through childhood, through adolescence, I can count on little. Daddy is fixed, permanent.

Beside him lie Grandfather and Uncle Phil. I often stand staring at these three graves in a row and think about Garm, losing father, brother, and son within a year. I wonder how she has survived—how anyone could withstand—the depredations of old age, tuberculosis, accident. Only after many years will I recognize that I, too, have survived a loss, and not necessarily intact. The depression and multiple sclerosis awaiting me will suggest that changes at the structural level have already occurred by the time I learn to forgive Daddy for abandoning me without even saying good-bye.

I visit my father at least once a year, usually more often. I like the cemetery: the narrow dirt road winding through; the names, grown familiar over the years, carved into the headstones; the squat, windowless brick structure with the green door, which for a while I think of as a mausoleum until I realize it's probably a tool shed. But I never know what to do here. Although I feel somber and remote, I also feel a feverish need to grieve, as if grieving were an activity like capturing the flag or rehearsing an anthem in junior choir. If Daddy were alive, I'd want to do something for him—bring him the newspaper, say, or make him a cup of tea—but there really isn't anything he needs here. Once, on a November day the color of ashes, Sally and I scurry around gathering pine cones and arranging them in a discarded green metal florist's container to decorate his autumn-sere grave. That's the most we can ever do.

Daddy also "lives," in another sense, back down the narrow asphalt road toward town, in the huge yellow frame house next to the Second Congregational Church, where several generations of my family have spent their summers. Daddy grew up among these people, and they all speak of him frequently, warmly, casually, as though he were for the moment somewhere else but still real for them, a boy and then a man with a dense history woven into theirs: Jack earning pocket money picking blueberries; Jack the future naval officer going fishing in a sixteen-foot outboard motorboat, seasick the minute he got beyond the breakwater. If families tend to designate difficult children, they also have golden ones. My daughter will be one of these. My father was another. Beloved throughout his life, he is burnished to perfection in death.

Some of the glitter scatters onto me, gilding my difficultness in a confusing way. "Her eyes are as blue as Jack's," they say. "She has a widow's peak like his." If I say something clever, they exclaim: "How like Jack!" I am thrilled by this identification, of course, wanting nothing more than to be my father's daughter. But as time goes on, I sense it as a burden, too. My task is to embody all Daddy's excellent qualities so that they won't be lost, with him, from the world. I'm not at all certain I'm equal to this task. But if I'm sulky, or clumsy, or lazy, I'll prove myself an unworthy vessel, and everyone will mourn. At The Port, then, I have to bear myself very, very carefully, as though I were spun from glass.

I love the house here as though it were an entity, a living and active presence, aloof but benign, its being in a tension of desire with my being, a body other than but like my body. Not that I don't think of it as a structure of wood and plaster and glass, but that these substances seem to me to serve as well for making a desirable being as do bone and blood. The passion that I feel for this house will mold my relationship to every other space I occupy, just as my passion for a dark-haired, slender boy named James Hopper will teach me how I'll be with men. First love.

I love the mass of the house, the square three-story front with a long two-story ell behind. The side porch, dusky behind a heavy screen of wisteria, with its green-painted furniture of wicker and wood. The vast, light-flooded kitchen with the cream-colored enamel stove at one end, the enamel trestle table in the middle where Auntie B makes pies from the little green windfalls, wormy and sour, we children collect under the apple tree outside the back door, and the big round table in the corner where we gather for lunch and dinner on all but the most formal occasions; also the two side kitchens, one for storing and preparing food, the other for washing up. The heavy Blue Willow dishes and the cobalt glassware, row upon row, in the dish closet.

I love the shadowy dining room, too, a jumble of dark furniture, white crocheted doilies, silver candlesticks, painted china serving dishes, where a dozen or more of us once gather around platters of red steaming lobsters, bowls of potato chips, ears of corn heaped in pyramids under dish towels, saucers of butter melted to yellow liquor with white flecks floating in it, pies with thick blueberry juice crystallizing on their brown crusts. We eat noisily, filling pots with lobster shells and corncobs. This is the only meal I know in which the more you eat, the higher the table is piled. The hallway outside fills with the peculiar thick yellow sunlight of a late afternoon in summer as my appetite subsides and I float, stupid with surfeit, on the sleepy conversation around me. I love the living room, with its dark woodwork, oriental rugs, chunky furniture, and especially the glass-fronted bookcase with the elephants on top, carved of mahogany, their tusks real ivory. Not the shiny horsehair sofa, though. I love the wide, polished stairs in the spacious front hall and the narrower side stairs with the landing where Phineas almost peed in his sleep, thinking he'd made it a few feet farther into the bathroom.

With a sense of abundance, of excess, which no other house confers, I count fifteen bedrooms. I never sleep in them all. In a bedroom in the ell, Sally and I bounce on the iron-frame bed, something we're never allowed to do, and when her head strikes sharply under my chin, one of my lower teeth flies out. Terrified, I run howling into Mother's room, certain that the ruin of my body is upon me. She laughs—perhaps the first but certainly not the last time she'll laugh at what she calls my "dramatics"—and assures me that teeth always fall out of five-year-old children. I stop crying, but a certain uneasiness about my body is never allayed.

Later, in the front bedroom overlooking the river, having come down with some sort of aching and queasiness, I lie in the big double bed and memorize the exotic birds on the wallpaper while the others leave on a jaunt, the first of the hundreds, probably thousands, of hours I spend alone, ailing mildly, while the rest of the world goes off for some fun. Mother brings me, for consolation, a pair of enameled scatter pins in the shape of fawns. I don't wear them much—they drag my blouses and dresses out of shape—but I keep them in my jewelry box a long time. Still later, my cousin Louisa and I, groggy with heat in one of the little bedrooms up under the roof, sleep till past ten o'clock, when her father, my beloved Uncle Dick who used to be a Texas Ranger, wakes us by dribbling water from a drinking glass onto our sweaty faces. On my last visits, after Bunty gets too weak to climb the stairs, Garm and I share the large room with the heavy oak twin beds that Bunty once shared with Grandfather.

As with all desirable entities, I fear the house as well as love it. The cluttered, dark back kitchen and the steep, narrow stairs climbing into the ell above. The bathrooms: the little lavatory off the back kitchen and the cavernous white bath with the claw-footed tub and marble sink on the second floor between the main house and the ell, where I'm constantly in danger of hearing a rap on the door and having to whisper, humiliated, "Just a minute"; and the one on the third floor, private enough, but furnished with an old-fashioned toilet whose chain I'm afraid to pull. The dark walk-in closet in the ell, and the bedrooms behind it, which belong to Daniel and Phineas—boys' rooms, messy and smelly, the privacy they shelter forming one more mystery in my obscure and baffling child's world.

v

In memory, in dream, I am mostly alone in the house. Indeed, I lead a singularly solitary existence for someone growing up in a large family bound tight by the ties of blood and obligation. Although I can call up reminiscences of people, often vivid, they do not come spontaneously as do the images of the house itself. It is as though the landscape and architecture of my past exist, sometimes in great detail, sometimes only impressionistically, but permanently; they are empty, however, unless I people them deliberately. Otherwise I wander through them as a solitary dream-dweller.

More than a trick of memory is involved here, I suppose. For although during the years of my visits to The Port I am attached to the people in my life—passionately attached to some of them and fiercely dependent upon the adults among them for approbation and affection—I never feel any real connection between them and me. "I" am different from "Nancy," and "I" am some shadow-creature nobody knows: observer, recorder: eye, ear, hand, tongue. And, indeed, I make this separation true. Early on, I develop a clear sense of what I think others expect of me, and since my interior life violates those expectations, I become secretive about it. Thus, I can believe in others' affection for and approval of Nancy, but inasmuch as she's not I, they are hopelessly beyond my reach.

Does this make sense? I can't ever tell. All I know is that people never penetrate the veiled consciousness that earns me the label "dreamy" (though it isn't dreaminess unless life itself is, after all, a dream). Places do. I can establish a direct relationship with the slant of sun across a rug, the smell of blueberry bushes or mud flats, the scratch of sand inside a wet bathing suit, pale creamy oatmeal in a blue-and-white bowl, hot and sweet. These things speak to me as people do not.

All the same, I can't possibly be always alone, whatever memory will insist. Not in a house, however large, as full of family and guests as this one. Not in a family as gregarious as mine. Not as a girl, who shares household chores like making beds and scrubbing carrots and holding skeins of Bunty's yarn while she winds them into balls, and who is expected to exhibit social graces: shaking hands firmly, speaking clearly but briefly when spoken to, serving iced tea to Aunt Amy, she of the great wet kisses, and Uncle Earl in lawn chairs out under the apple tree. Daniel and Phineas have more scope. They live here all summer and they're boys, so they're bound to wander off on their own errands. Having no errands of my own, I accept the errands of others. And even though I feel awkward and shy in company, I'm glad to be integrated into the bustle of life here, feeling that, as one of Jack's girls, I really belong.

At the heart of this lively household are my great-grandmother, Bunty; Bunty's younger daughter, Auntie B; and Auntie B's sons, Daniel and Phineas, just older than I. In the winter, they live in Puerto Rico, where Uncle Paul works for a soft-drink company, and sometimes they joke with one another in Spanish. Mother, Granna, and Grandma Virchow sometimes speak German, but they never sound like they're joking. The people here are always joking, in English too, in ways that both shock and charm me. One night, I'm lying on Auntie B's bed with her and Phineas, listening to their mixture of serious talk and banter.

"Did you fart?" Phineas asks her suddenly.

"I did *not!*" she denies righteously, and the two of them collapse, squealing, and roll around on the bed. I don't think I've ever heard "fart" spoken, certainly not by a son to his mother. My mother would wash my mouth out with soap. Even words I hear people say all the time, like "stink," are forbidden where I live. My world is circumscribed by linguistic dangers. But Auntie B and Phineas don't even seem to notice. They're talking about something else now. They seem at ease with one another, like friends.

Maybe this easiness, this affectionate familiarity of equals, alarms my mother. She doesn't seem to like to have me at The Port, at least not without her, though she permits me to accompany Garm while Pop is in Florida on his business trips, which I finally figure out is the code phrase for drinking binges. Mother says that Auntie B is too lenient, turning the boys into spoiled brats, letting them run wild. Wildness, bad enough in boys, is disastrous in girls, I gather. Later, I will see that at the heart of all her care for me is the conviction that she must protect me from catastrophe, and Auntie B never seems to feel the same mission. She permits the boys a kind of freedom far more unacceptable to Mother than any brattiness.

On my last visit to The Port, the summer I turn fifteen, when Pop returns from his annual business trip to take Garm back to The Cottage, I plead to stay behind for a few days. "No," says Mother when Auntie B telephones to invite me. By this time I really am a difficult child, overwrought and volatile, and at her refusal I sob and sob. Phineas, my darling Phineas, now a handsome college student, hugs me and then, taking the telephone from his mother, persuades mine, however reluctantly (I neither know nor care), to extend my visit until Saturday.

Phineas's authority over my mother seals his glory in my eyes, though he rather forgets about my presence, in the self-absorbed manner of almost adult men toward worshipful girls, for the rest of my dearly bought stay. No matter. I adore him anyway, all the more because I've so often been told how, as a little boy, he adored my father and was so jealous that he wouldn't even speak to my mother when they were first married. And he is unfailingly, if abstractedly, kind to me. He takes me to an art gallery and an auction. On a drive along the coast, he shows me St. Anne's, a lovely little stone Episcopal church. I get the feeling he's Episcopalian, though I can't think how in my stalwart Congregationalist family, and I want to be one, too; and later I will be one, for quite a while, until I go the whole route into Roman Catholicism. A little farther up the coast, he points out the house he'd like to have, a tall weather-beaten place perched on a bluff above the sea. Years later, closing my eyes, I'll still be able to see it, a dark gray hump against the pale gray sky and middle gray water, and I'll want it with the fierce appetite that one reserves for lost or unattainable objects: a house I've never lived in, a house that may for all I know have blown from its precarious position into the waves.

In the same final summer, Phineas salvages a small catamaran and a three-horsepower motor from the junk accumulated over the years in the long carriage house out behind the kitchens. It could even have been my father's. Even though I've been to sailing camp twice now, I've never thought about having a boat for myself. Phineas patches the boat up, paints it gray, rigs a platform in the stern for the outboard, and tinkers with the motor until it chuffs and sputters reliably. Then he enters it in the River Festival parade. Gathered on the bluff above the river, we spy him putting along, in a floppy straw hat, the stern of the little boat sinking lower and lower under the weight of the motor and shipping water. Hearing our laughter from a great distance, he waves through the gathering dusk. Under my amusement, and my anxiety that he really will go down before the parade is over, leaving only the straw hat circling on the water, lies awe at the mysterious power that has enabled Phineas to patch a boat enough so that it doesn't sink entirely for the duration of the parade, to make an engine run, above all to go along the river under the laughing eyes of the whole town. This power springs in large measure, of course, out of freedom from the fear of catastrophe, a freedom unlikely to accrue to my mother's daughter, but I don't yet know that.

If Phineas serves as a romantic idol, Daniel provides both everyday companionship and some grounds for Mother's catastrophic thinking. Just eleven months older than I, he's a handsome boy, handsomer than Phineas, with dark brown hair and a cleft in his chin. My father may have looked a good bit like him as a boy; after all, their mothers were sisters and their fathers cousins. Looking at a photo of him at forty-five, I'll have the startled sense that I'm seeing how my father would have looked in middle age: a heavyset, graying naval officer with crinkles of laughter around his eyes and mouth. In boyhood, Daniel can use his handsomeness to good advantage. When I'm a mother myself, I'll have to admit he was spoiled.

In the first years, Daniel and I, though thrown together a good bit, refuse to have much to do with each other. He's got a hideaway at the top of some closets at the back of the carriage house. Sometimes cars are parked here, though visitors leave theirs in the wide gravel space between the house and the church. Mostly, it's a tangle of dinghies, outboard motors, paint cans, lobster traps, old tools, fishing gear. And, in the rear corner, Daniel's sacred space.

"Please, Daniel," I beg through the slammed door, sniffing in the heated smells of mildew and rotten wood and turpentine with my tears. "Please, please," I dance. It doesn't occur to me to thrust my body in after his, permission or no.

"Nyah," he jeers. "This place is mine, and I say NO GIRLS."

Later, after his attitude toward girls has softened, he lets me into another secret space, the attic. The air here is hot and still, the dust suspended in it as though in amber. The dry smell of it eats my breath so that I can only whisper. We stare somberly, without recognition, at rickety tables, broken lamps, an old steamer trunk, some brownish snapshots, a wicker baby carriage. In Tucson, all but the oldest houses lack both cellar and attic, and so my children will grow up without knowing how houses can literally embody the not-quite-discarded past in mysterious jumbles like this one.

The summer of my twelfth birthday—just after, while staying with Aunt Jane and Uncle Kip in Boston, I menstruate for the first time, and Jane gives me a belt and a pad, and we all walk down Mount Vernon Street to an Esplanade concert, me stiff and bandylegged from the unfamiliar bunch of bloodied cotton between my legs—Daniel kisses me. Afterward, in a fever of excitement and revulsion, I try to avoid him, but of course I can't. The next night, he and Sally and I cross the street to play on the short, soft, dense grass outside the post office. (Where was Sally when I got kissed that first time? I'll never be able to remember.) Daniel chases and catches and falls on top of me, struggling for a kiss.

"No, Daniel!" I shriek over and over, rolling and wrestling. "Sally, help!" To Sally it's only a noisy game. "Help, help!" Excited by my frenzy, she shrieks too, giggling, as she tails along behind us.

Another summer, Daniel comes into Bunty's room, where I'm alone in one of the twin beds, and kisses me a number of times. Now I don't resist. I'm wearing tailored pajamas, white cotton with stripes of pink flowers, and Daniel puts his hands up under the loose pajama top, stroking the beginnings of breasts on my bony chest. Later, I'll find that in the beginnings lay the endings, that what Daniel stroked was about all anyone would ever get to stroke. But now they're new and tender and fraught with possibility. After all the romantic novels I've consumed, I must know that they'll be touched. But sitting there in the dark, with Daniel's hard boy's hands clamped over them, I feel appalled and sad, as though I've given something up without return.

During my last summer at The Port, our cousins Jimmy and Beth come for a visit with their mother, a thin, arthritic, querulous woman who sits in one place knitting all day, ignoring her own children and everyone else's as best she can. Their presence changes the sex games Daniel and I have been playing. We can't include Jimmy, our age, and Beth, a couple of years younger, and still keep one another as partners, since they would then have to make love to each other. Actually, in terms of incest, this would be the purer arrangement, because Jimmy is adopted and thus unrelated to Beth by blood, whereas Daniel and Beth are first cousins. But we don't know about such distinctions. The fact that Jimmy and Beth have been raised as brother and sister is plenty to make even their holding hands unthinkable. So Daniel takes Beth and I take Jimmy.

We climb to one of the bedrooms on the third floor and lie, four abreast, on the double bed. There are six of these bedrooms, on either side of a narrow hallway with a window at each end, letting in some light but not much air. Tucked up over the eaves, these rooms, with their slanted ceilings and small windows, are dim and cramped and stuffy, though pleasantly furnished in what will one day be pricey antiques. Tourists who want a room for the night can have one of these for two-fifty. When they're empty, visiting children often get them. For getting away from grown-ups they're perfect: two tall flights of stairs and the length of the house from the center of grown-up activity, the kitchen. Here we lie, our heads like four peas on the pillows, making out two by two in the yellowish light of the bedside lamp, talking to one another between clenches.

Despite my sexual naïveté, I can tell from the first kiss that Jimmy has had a whole lot less experience than Daniel. Except for long kisses and breast-touching, Daniel and I haven't done much. He's never touched me below the waist, and I've never touched him at all. We haven't even stood or lain close enough together for me to feel his erection; or perhaps we have and I just haven't recognized it. But the alarm and dismay that I feel kissing Daniel tells me that he knows what he's doing, far better than I do. With Jimmy I feel not a twinge. Maybe their backgrounds account for the difference, Daniel growing up in Puerto Rico, Jimmy raised in rural Tennessee. But their natures are different as well. Daniel has the cocky confidence of a handsome boy who can count on winning his own way; Jimmy, plump and buck-toothed, is shy and deferential.

Although making out with Jimmy is a relief, I'm bored. He doesn't start a flame in my heart or anywhere else. I'm also worried about Beth, only my sister's age, in Daniel's knowledgeable clutches. But she's a chubby, pallid girl, almost as querulous as her mother, and I don't know her well enough to express my concern. So I leave her to her own devices, never learning whether she shares my sexual unease. Maybe not. Even if we were intimate friends, I wouldn't know how to ask. Girls just don't seem to talk about such things. About sex, yes, a little. But about being afraid of sex, no, not in my experience.

vi

Daniel and I do not spend all our time in steamy clinches. On the contrary, he is out of the house most of the time and I am in it, scrunched down into the cushions of the living-room couch behind a book whenever I get the chance. This posture reflects an ambivalence in my approach to the world. I really do love to read, to enter realms where life is both more shapely and more passionate than anything I've experienced. I also prefer to remain inside the house, inside a book, because there I feel safe, certain of where I am, unlikely to get disoriented and stray in some strange direction or to encounter anyone with whom I'll have to make conversation, in which I always feel stupid. But I retreat into the pages just as much to mask the fact that I haven't got anything else to do. I lock myself in because I feel locked out of life's larger possibilities.

Occasionally, however, Daniel takes me along and introduces me to the wider life of the town. One summer he has a job at the Lyric Movie Theater, an old board structure painted green, just before the bridge out of town. I go down and watch him sweep up squashed cardboard and popcorn kernels. I can find my way there on my own: past the church, down a steep bank, across a vacant lot, past Smith's Market, where handy children are often sent on last-minute errands—another quart of milk, some sugar for the pies—and Weinstein's Produce, dark and fruity, and the Red Dragon Gift Shop. When he's older, Daniel works behind the counter at the River View, on the opposite side of the street, cantilevered high out over the riverbank. Here he teaches me to call the kind of frappe I like, with chocolate syrup and vanilla ice cream, a "black-and-white frappe," raising my sense of worldliness another notch. Later, even more worldly, I'll discover that in other parts of the country "frappes" are called "milkshakes," except in Providence, Rhode Island, where they're called "cabinets." People in Rhode Island put vinegar on their french fries, so what can you expect?

My final sojourn at The Port ends, fittingly, with a family festival. I don't know it's my last, of course. I'm fifteen, and I think that the places and events and people I cherish are fixed forever, as though my love were a seal of amber. Auntie B has a wonderful scheme for next summer: all of us—me, Daniel and Phineas and their cousin Boo, Jimmy and Beth, too, if they like—will get jobs and live at The Port together. I know perfectly well that Mother would die first, but in Auntie B's spirited presence, I let Mother fade for the moment. I think only of the weeks and weeks I could spend at The Port, really live here, the way Daddy did when he was my age.

Instead, I will return only fleetingly. For Garm's burial in the fall. Four years later, for Bunty's funeral and burial. Before I finish college, Auntie B and Uncle Paul will be dead as well. Almost by accident, I see Uncle Paul just weeks before his death, when George and I find ourselves in the area on a bright summer afternoon. After visiting Daddy and Garm, we go to the house. I've heard it's been converted into apartments and Uncle Paul is living in one. Daniel too, while he finishes college, but he's out the day we stop. Uncle Paul lets us in the side door. The hallway's been blocked off, and we turn into what used to be the kitchens. This both is and isn't the space I remember, and the disjuncture makes me dizzy and sad. Uncle Paul and I hardly know each other, since he was usually working in Puerto Rico during my visits, and we don't find much to say, though later I'll learn he was touched that we came. He can hardly speak anyway. Throat cancer.

I know none of this on my last night at The Port. My pleasure in the festival is unalloyed. It doesn't matter that the event has nothing to do with me. I happen to be there, and my family characteristically opens itself to incorporate whoever chance drops at their door, rather like an affectionate amoeba. This summer, Daniel has been working again behind the soda fountain at the River View, and Phineas and Boo have had real jobs waiting on table at The House on the Hill. The three have saved the pennies from all their tips in a fat glass jar on the chest of drawers beside Bunty's rocker in the kitchen. Daily the jar has grown heavier, and now, at summer's end, the money is to be used for a gala steak dinner at The House on the Hill, Phineas and Boo sitting regally instead of scurrying, sweaty and fiercely smiling, between table and kitchen.

Just in time, Phineas's fiancée has arrived for a visit. Emma is a pretty Midwestern college girl, with a small low voice and floating red hair. I think her terrifically brave to have flown all the way from Chicago to New England to be with the man she loves. She spends the first day lying on the cot in the kitchen. She has diarrhea, they say, quite common after such a trip. No one seems concerned. But I, with my horror of being ill in strange places (and I will almost always be ill in strange places), regard her with a mixture of distress and respect. She seems so calm.

In spite of my romantic dreams about Phineas, I feel little jealousy. Love, which Phineas and Emma have grasped, has so far eluded me, and I suffer badly from its lack, but I can't really imagine having it for myself. I stand outside their relationship in the age-old posture of the child with her nose pressed to the bright window of the Red Dragon. A few years later, when I do have love, I'll spend a weekend with Emma and her baby, Lily, in a bright, bare apartment in a spacious gray-shingled house in Newport, while Phineas is at sea and my fiancé is at Officer Candidate School. I'll admire and yearn for Emma's domesticity, but I can't imagine having it. Even later, of course, I'll have that, too.

Twelve of us have gathered for the dinner at The House on the Hill. I've never been to such a place, suffused with light, green, gold, white: candles and linen and flowers on the table, plants in the windows, a steady glisten on china, silverware, water goblets, windowpanes. We sit at a long table. Phineas and Emma and Boo order drinks. Scotch for Phineas. I vow that as soon as I grow up, I will drink scotch. And I do, for a while.

I want so badly to be grown up.

Before going back to the house, some of us drive along the coast for a while. The moon is full, glittering on the ruffled black water. Later I lie in the twin bed in Bunty's room, the dark house breathing quietly around me, behind my eyelids the glint of candle flame, of moon flame: festival lights.

In dreams the house, through some mysterious transaction, has become mine: rooms and rooms of it, more space than I could possibly need or fill, all mine to do with as I wish. I will make it beautiful once more. I will open its rooms and draw in everyone I love. It is the house of abundance, of excess, of enough and more-than-enough. In its shelter, I can lack nothing ever again.

But of course, outside of magic, I could never really own it. I can't imagine what I'd have to pay to acquire it, even if it's still standing, but I know it's more money than I'll ever get together. And then the cost of restoration, even if restoration were feasible. . . . Even if I managed all this, I could never use it. How would I furnish it? Everything's gone, who knows where: the Blue Willow dishes and the cobalt glasses and the table for twenty, the horsehair sofa, the iron bedsteads, the wicker baby carriage in the attic. How would I populate it? Most of the inhabitants have moved up the street to the cemetery, or scattered to Arizona, California, Florida, North Carolina—places far, far from The Port. They wouldn't come back for me.

No, I'll never get the house back, not if by "getting it back" I mean holding a deed, owning a key, crossing the purplish shade of the porch to enter the side hall, slamming the screen door behind me. I must content myself with another kind of possession altogether. My task is to house this house, which has vanished from the waking world, as it once housed me, to grant it the deed to my dreams. In the biochemical bath of my own body, through multiplex processes even neurophysiologists don't yet understand, I preserve and perfect the yellow house on the coast of Maine. As long as I do so, I get to dwell in it immemorially.

In Exeter

i

IN THE FIRST dream I remember, Mother, Sally, and I huddle in the open front window of Mother's bedroom, next to her dressing table with the silver-backed brush and comb and mirror and the little flacon of Chanel No. 5. In the street far below us stands a truck with an open tank of boiling oil on the back. I can see the oil, as pale and lucent as maple syrup, with reddish-orange flames, nearly transparent, dancing on its surface. Some force I can't identify demands that the three of us leap outward from the window into the tank of oil, where we will surely die.

By the time of this dream, I'm at least five, possibly older. I have years of dreaming behind me. Yet this is the one powerful enough to mark itself out in memory as the first: a nightmare about crossing the boundary between inside and outside in an involuntary transgression with lethal consequences. However you're inclined to interpret the house—as maternal body, prehistoric cave, the self's shell, or practical shelter against New England's harsh winters— the fact is that by this time I've decided against leaving home.

This house I mustn't leave on pain of death is the one at 17 Prospect Avenue in Exeter, New Hampshire, where we live for five years after Daddy's death. It is not, despite its presence in this dream, an oneiric house. In the years after leaving it, I will seldom find myself, awake or asleep, suddenly within its walls. This is not to say that it lacks essential powers for stirring or shaping me. All my houses have such powers. But in it, unlike the house at The Port, life goes on and on and on, shaped by routine and, increasingly, obligation. Here I develop that ability to concatenate events which characterizes human consciousness and makes "daily life" possible. If, in future years, I will not be able to remember feeling happy in it, the fault may belong less to the house, less even to the inarticulable grief of a small girl abandoned without warning by her father, than to my dissatisfaction with prosaic life. The plodding rhythms of prose—noun + verb, noun + verb, noun + verb, each event spun out from the one before it and spinning another out in its turn, endless, linear, unemphatic—feel all wrong for me.

The house itself provides a perfect setting for the practice of everyday life: the left half of an ample but graceless, elderly side-by-side duplex on the edge of respectability demarcated by Prospect Avenue itself, which runs along the top of a hill. To the east lies the Exeter Hospital, a small brick building on wide grounds; to the west, along streets rising perpendicular from one of the main thoroughfares, Portsmouth Avenue, shabby houses teem with noisy children who say "ain't." Mother enunciates our address clearly, stressing the "Avenue" so that no one can mistake our location for one lower down.

I, too, have to practice saying my address clearly, in case I should ever get lost. This is the first place I've ever lived where getting lost is mentioned as a possibility, if not an option. And I do once sort of get lost, wandering down the Swayze Parkway, where I've been forbidden to go because it's A Very Bad Place, the sort where Very Terrible Things Could Happen. I don't think any such Thing happens to me on the Swayze Parkway, however, and since my own mother finds me, I don't even have to come up with my address. I keep it handy in my head, nonetheless.

At 17 Prospect Avenue I am safe. In all other places lurk incomprehensible dangers, one of which rises perilously close, just at the end of Prospect Avenue: a high silver cylinder from which, on windy days, blows a cold spray. This is the Water Tower, and Sally and I have been enjoined under penalty of death never to set foot on the short drive leading to its base. I understand the death part, but not how I might get that way. No one explains that I'd have to walk up that dirt drive, climb the ladder that clings to the tower's side, and topple over the edge into the dark, dark water within. I think that one day, as the result of some misdeed of mine (but I have no idea which one, or even what sort), the silvery skin will rupture, sending a suffocating gush of water over the heads of Sally and Mother and me.

Run inside where it's safe.

Above the long set of rooms that hold our daytime lives lies another for the night. From the landing at the top of the steep stairway between the living room and the dining room, a step up to the right leads into Mother's room, another to the left leads into ours, and beyond to the bathroom, another bedroom, and finally the sun porch we use as a playroom. On the landing, holding a deck of cards, Sally has one of the temper tantrums that are her truly spectacular gift and she tumbles down the stairs. When, still bellowing, she hits the floor of the hall below, the cards spray from her hand across the dining room and *all the way out into the kitchen.* Mother instructs me, as always, just to ignore her, but how can anyone, in all fairness, "just ignore" the agent of such a prodigious feat?

We're not supposed to play near or on the stairway, of course. But we like to stuff our legs into our pillowcases and ride our pillows the length of the stairs: bump/whoop, bump/whoop, bump/whoop. . . . We do this while Betsy Kulick is babysitting us. She lets us do anything, even bounce on our beds, and never makes us mind. We hate to have her come. Our regular babysitter is Janice Wright, who, being Garm and Pop's next-door neighbor, has known us since we were babies, before we ever moved to the Tropics. Her firmness, like Mother's, rescues us from our frightening unbridled selves and enables us to sink back under our covers, our heads and not our duffies on our pillows, into the safety of sleep.

In the windowless bathroom with a wrought-iron register in the floor, useful for spying on grown-ups after bedtime or for dropping marbles through, we brush our teeth with Dr. West's Tooth Powder and fight, dancing with our hands clamped over our crotches, about who gets to use the toilet first. Then we jump into bed. Mother comes in to read us a story. Even after we can read by ourselves, we like to listen to her low, lisping voice. Our room is small, and of course a route through it has to be kept clear for Mother to get to the bathroom, so our twin beds are shoved side by side into one corner with a narrow space between, not even big enough to walk in, which we call the Little Crack. Mother sits on the inner bed, and we cuddle against her, one on each side, to see the pictures. Sometimes, like when she reads "The Search for

Small" in *The House at Pooh Corner*, she laughs so hard that she chokes and we have to pat and soothe her till she can go on.

After Mother leaves, we're supposed to go to sleep. This can take a long time, during which we go off to Thinking Land. Some nights, especially in summer when it's still light, we don't even try to go to sleep. Wakefulness can lead to trouble. Once, while sucking on her favorite marble, Sally begins to make weird noises.

"Gggghhhh!" she gags. I begin shrieking for Mother but choke myself in a fit of giggles.

"Gggghhhh!" says Sally.

"Hehehehehe!" I reply. Mother clatters up the stairs and bursts into the room just as Sally sits up and the marble shoots from her mouth across the room.

"It's not funny!" Mother shouts at me. I know it's not funny. I'm not sure why I'm laughing. If I don't, maybe I'll die of terror.

Another night, Sally and I push out the screen of our window and climb onto the roof that covers the porch and part of the dining room. It's dusk of a late spring evening, the maple tree in front of the house is already leafed out, the air gray and dense and sweet, and as I dance the length of the roof, Sally behind me, I feel as though, if I leap straight out, I can fly into the rustling shadowy branches.

"Girls, come in now." Mother's voice, unusually quiet, tugs me down. If I'd danced much longer under the reaching arms of the maple, I might really have jumped. The spring air, the smoky light, the whisper of leaves have made me feel light and queer, out of myself, free of gravity. "Come on in." Later she'll admit that her peculiarly reasonable tone was born of the fear that if she shouted as she felt like doing, she'd scare us straight over the edge.

Innocent, docile, we scramble back through the window, and she spanks each of us with a ruler on our pajama-clad duffies, the only time she ever uses a *weapon* instead of her bare hand. Then she brings a hammer to nail the screen into place. She doesn't have to do that. We're good girls. Once punished for something, we're seldom inclined to repeat it. But she can't figure that out for herself; and lying in our beds, stung and smoldering, we're not about to help her out. Anyway, she needs the nails for safety. The world threatens us at every turn, and there's only one of her to protect us.

Her voice holds the same sort of controlled calm when she

finds Sally and me playing doctor with our friend Jessie. We usually play in the bushes outside, taking down our underpants and using twigs as rectal thermometers, our crotches pulsating as our anuses tighten around the rough wood. We never touch one another "down there" with our hands, and I for one never touch myself either, at this or any other time. But the slip of knitted fabric, the air on my naked buttocks, the shoving twig make me shiver ecstatically. On a rainy day we try this activity under a blanket in my dim bedroom, but Mother comes in and sweeps the blanket off.

"What's going on here?" she asks. She doesn't paddle us, though. She doesn't even tell us not to do it again. We just know that our bodies are off limits. We never do it again.

Here is Mother's genius: to cool frenzy with a word.

For a while, a lab technician at the hospital named Betty rents our back bedroom, but then she marries a gangly redheaded man named Art and goes to live with him in Maine. Rather than look for another boarder, Mother decides to give the bedroom to me. Maybe I've said something to make her think I want a room of my own. Or maybe she decides by herself, too soon, that I'm ready for a private space. In any case, I'm miserable in it, alone, without Sally's plump, warm, reassuring fingers to reach for across the Little Crack, her drowsy voice telling me to go back to Thinking Land and thence to sleep.

It's a long, dark room above the kitchen, with a green rug and a single bed against the far wall, next to the playroom. In there, one night, I hear a heavy sound, between a thud and a crash. A giant is lumbering around, I'm sure. The playroom is a jumble of dollies and dollhouses and doll furniture and doll clothes and doll dishes, which Mother endlessly, fruitlessly exhorts Sally and me to clean up, and part of me knows that the sound is probably the toppling of some overbalanced heap of toys: a tea set on top of a trunk on top of a rickety wicker table, perhaps. But the rest of me recognizes a giant's footfall. Thereafter I lie rigid night after night, my back against the wall, my body swaddled in bedclothes no matter how hot the night, my limbs pulled in tight lest one should stray over the edge and be lopped off by a knife from underneath the bed.

I beg Mother to let me have a light, and she grudgingly leaves the door from the lighted stairwell ajar so that a weak glow filters through Sally's room and the bathroom and the length of my room, deepening the shadows in which the knife-wielding giants hunch and wait. Maybe she thinks this dimness will inure me to the dark. She's wrong. For the rest of my life, whenever I stay alone, I'll have to leave a light on, and even so I'll lie stiff and sweaty and sleepless much of the night. When my own children's night fears begin, I'll leave on whatever lights they want. Hell, I'll install floodlights if they ask.

ii

"I can't really *see* Sally," comments a friend who knows us both after reading an early draft of "In Exeter." It occurs to me then that this visual gap occurs because I don't naturally "see" Sally, any more than I "see" myself, during these years. I haven't begun to distinguish between us, to differentiate myself from her. To Mother, and to the rest of the family as well, we form a unit: "the girls." To me, "Nancy" is no more an independent entity than "Sally" is. They are elements in a composite creature, which has begun to differentiate itself from Mother but not to break down into its individual components.

In both our nights and our days, even after starting school, Sally and I are one another's most constant companions. When her repeated earaches and bronchitis lead Dr. Theobald to recommend a tonsillectomy, I get my tonsils taken out as well. One winter, we share all the predictable childhood diseases, drawing out each incubation period to its limit, until Mother, stuck at home with one fretful, feverish child or the other for weeks, no Daddy there to relieve or distract her, must feel like bolting. Luckily, Sally appears immune to mumps, as I am to German measles, and by the beginning of spring we've run the gamut of infections and we're all released from the pesthouse.

Mother makes all three of us pink cotton sundresses printed with cherry-topped cupcakes in inedible hues. Except for the cupcake dresses, however, Sally and I are frequently dressed in identical styles but different colors: pink or blue for Sally with her china-doll features, blond hair, rosy cheeks, and narrow blue eyes; yellow or lavender or mint for me, brown-haired, with grayer eyes and sallower skin. Our appearance is different in other ways, as well. She has a pouting mouth, whereas mine is wide and crammed with large white teeth. Her build is compact and sturdy, mine angular, ungainly, with long neck and hands and feet. Even so, we'll always be taken for sisters. It must have something to do with our speech and gestures.

Being girls, we're given dolls and their paraphernalia. One Christmas we visit Aunt Nora and Uncle Seth, who have only boys. Santa has brought Seth Junior and Matt a set of little plastic building blocks, with windows and doors and roofs and chimneys, and I spend the whole time, feverish with forbidden delight, constructing one house after another. The boys keep snitching pieces for the giant fort they're building, but I don't care about their fort or the plastic cowboys and Indians shooting one another, with whistles and bangs, through its windows. I want a house, a snug house of interlocking bricks, roofed over, sturdy, built with my own hands.

If Mother notices my absorption, it doesn't persuade her to provide me with construction materials, and I'm too embarrassed to ask for boys' toys. I never have Lincoln Logs, Tinker Toys, an Erector Set. Instead, I have Rubber Baby, who has a little hole above her buttocks, as though she has spina bifida, out of which water leaks if I feed her a bottle through her pierced rosebud mouth. Eventually, her head falls off and the tube responsible for this alimentary marvel breaks away. I force her head back on and stop feeding her, so that her body cavity won't fill up and leak at shoulder and hip joints. Later I have a much prettier baby doll named Carol, with a soft cloth body and pliant pink vinyl limbs and head, a real practice-baby.

Just as Sally and I are often dressed to look like sisters, so are our dolls. The first such pair we name Mary (mine with dark hair and a green organdy dress) and Susan (Sally's blond, her dress blue). When these get shabby, one of our aunts, who doesn't have much money for presents, takes them to the doll hospital for Christmas and gives them new wigs and red nail-polish mouths. We also have the Taffy dolls, named for their plaid taffeta dresses. Identical twins, they never have separate names, but we manage to keep them straight, as well as their blue high chairs and houndstooth-checked cardboard wardrobe trunks. Our last pair, dark Cynthia and blond Nancy, are different from the others, slender and graceful, almost like young women, though of course without breasts.

We also have beautiful white dollhouses, made by our Great-Grandfather Virchow the butcher, who died long before we were born. Their plans are different, but the details in both are perfect, the railing on the back porch, the newel post at the foot of the stairs. Mine, with the green roof, was Mother's when she was a little girl, and Sally's, with the red roof, belonged to Aunt Jane. We have wonderful furniture, mostly cast iron and wood, some of which was also theirs: a silver range, a chipped blue toilet with matching pedestal sink and claw-footed tub, and for the mantelpiece, a ceramic clock painted with tiny roses.

For hours I hang my face like a gigantic moon at the open side of my dollhouse, willing the little figures I've positioned inside to come alive and move about without my fingers, willing the lamps to come on, the clock to chime. I've made up stories for them. Now I want to see the stories enacted. It seems to me that if I could observe life from this perspective, in miniature, if I could encompass it, I could comprehend how it really works. "Get up," I whisper to the tiny doll with the bendable arms and legs sitting at the kitchen table. "*Say* something." Her head with its dark, painted-on hair and fixed pink smile stares straight ahead out the kitchen window, her skinny arms lie inert on the tabletop. Life refuses to reveal itself to me.

Sally and I have only one live—and patient, if reluctant—toy, Honeybun, a tabby with a white belly, in the center of which grows one large striped spot. Repeatedly we operate on her to remove this "tiger spot," with a mixture of Dr. West's Tooth Powder and some scented water from an exhausted bottle of Chanel for anesthesia. Honeybun, and her spot, survive. We dress her in doll clothes and bonnets and wheel her through the house in a doll carriage, and she endures this indignity as well.

Except for tricycles, and later bicycles, Sally and I have no outdoor toys, no balls and bats and skis and nets and racquets. We're little girls. Perhaps this early deprivation explains my later hopeless and humiliating lack of athletic prowess, though I'm not sure; Sally turns out strong and well coordinated in spite of it. In retrospect, I'll see that absence of outdoor playing equipment may have benefited rather than deprived us, throwing us almost wholly upon our imaginations, which grow thick and sturdy with exercise.

Even out of doors, almost all our games involve interiors in some way, as though we delimit infinite space and force it to contain and shelter us just as houses do. I love to crawl into a thicket of rhododendron bushes in front of the hospital, whose trunks have twisted to form passageways and low arched rooms. We spend hours in a grove of evergreens between the hospital and our house. Once I climb so high into one of these trees that I get scared and can't start back down. Sally and I spend a long time mapping out plans, involving ropes and baskets, for sustaining my new life in the crotch of a tree before we both get chilly and tired and Sally runs off to fetch Mother, who vetoes the idea of an aerial picnic and talks me down patiently, limb after limb, with only the narrowest edge of exasperation in her voice. I suspect she's guessed that I'm thrilled at the idea of being stuck, and of having to homestead this lofty territory. After all, I'm not afraid of heights, though she is.

iii

At five, I begin—tentatively, unwittingly, irrevocably—to dissolve that unity "the girls," which Sally and I have formed since her birth. She and Mother and I trudge down Prospect Avenue, across High Street, down a dead end to a tidy, low, gray clapboard building. There we split apart, Mother and Sally receding, growing smaller, while I stay the same size, right here, a kindergartner at the Exeter Day School.

The following year, Sally joins the prekindergarten class and Mother, unable to afford tuition for us both, becomes the school secretary to earn it, an arrangement that suits us all, providing Mother adult companionship every day and us, still clinging in the wake of our father's abandonment, the opportunity for reassuring ourselves that she hasn't vanished as well while we're not looking. But even occupying the same small building, in school Sally and I hardly know each other, though we provide plenty of mutual embarrassment. She stands with her class to perform a song in front of a school assembly, so nervous that she clutches the sides of her skirt convulsively until it bunches around her waist, exposing her chubby legs and drooping white cotton underpants. I could just die. But then, the year we occupy adjacent classrooms, she shrinks in chagrin every time she sees me walk by on my way to the bathroom, knowing that all the boys in her class will run to the door because I always hike my skirt up and start to tug at my unders before getting there, a habit I'll persist in even as a grown woman, though I'll try not to do it when company comes.

Later, I'll recognize the dissolution of our unity in the very fact that, from the beginning of school onward, I can catch such glimpses of Sally. She is becoming another child, one with whom

I feel unusually intimate but no longer identical. I can "see" her. At the same time, I begin to "see" myself, as though once Nancy starts to gather into an autonomous being, part of me splits off to take up the role of observer, and later recorder, of Nancy's experiences. This watchfulness will grow excoriatingly keen throughout childhood, adolescence, and young adulthood, modulating only when, perhaps because of my slow fusion into a new unity with my husband, I come gradually to experience myself as continuous with, and therefore less fearful of, the world around me. The fragmentation of self from watching self won't vanish entirely, however. It will turn me into a writer.

Regardless of being wrenched away from the embrace of 17 Prospect Avenue, I soon learn to love school. First, however, I have to know it as a space capable of housing me. From now on, this will be the key for inserting myself into a new situation: not that I meet and get to know the people around me but that I first map out the space I occupy and then lay down habitual patterns for moving through it. Fortunately, even a very small girl can encompass the Exeter Day School: just a handful of classrooms; a long room, with a stage at one end, for indoor games and assemblies; an office; and a basement for storing playground equipment and carrying out large-scale, messy projects like building rickety bookshelves for our mothers and boiling maple sap, gathered from our trees at home, down to amber syrup. After only a few circuits, I'm ready to make myself at home.

Kindergartners have their own separate quarters, in a long room at the front of the building. They have their own bathroom with an enchanting miniature sink and toilet, their own bank of bright cubbies for storing paint smocks and spare underpants (which, to my relief, I never need), their own easels and rest mats, smelling of dust and, more faintly, of pee, where we suck our thumbs and listen to stories. Here I wield a paintbrush with a lot more abandon than talent and squish my fingers through clay and papier-mâché and muddy fingerpaints. Here I sing "The Itsy Bitsy Spider" lustily but so badly that Mother is informed I'm tone-deaf, which will turn out, though not for a long time, to be untrue. Here I paint a plaster plaque of lurid yellow bananas and blue grapes which will hang first in Mother's kitchen and, forty years later, in mine. Here I learn to read. How could I fail to be happy?

* * *

From my very first appearance, as one of Cinderella's ladies-in-waiting, dressed in a long, full gown of coarse yellow and aqua muslin, and throughout my nearly five years here, what I love best are our dramatic productions, a nativity play every Christmas and a mimed musical, performed out of doors, in the spring. I have a good model in Mother, who belongs to a reading theater and also plays Jiminy Cricket in a community production. Imagine having your own mother, her face blackened and feelers sprouting from her head, hopping and whistling up on the stage in front of everybody. I nearly burst with pride.

In the fourth grade, I finally get a starring role of my own, as the Virgin Mary, clutching my well-swaddled baby doll Carol to my breast. "Thank you, kind shepherds," I say as they lay down a hat, one glove, and a toy lamb. And then, "Thank you, noble wisemen." Sally is an Angel of the Heavenly Host. To spread the glory around, you're only supposed to star once, but in the spring my friend Sukey gets cold feet just before *The Wizard of Oz,* so at the last moment I clank into stardom again, my arms and legs encased in number 10 tin cans, a funnel tied upside down on my head, clutching at my cardboarded chest in mimed yearning for my absent heart.

Although, in an interpretive dance class, I've learned to take off my shoes and unfold like a tulip, on the whole improvisation makes me uneasy. A script feels like the perfect format for getting through life without disaster, the way it frees you from wondering where you're supposed to be, what you're supposed to say, gestures and words selected and laid down on the page, inscribed, circumscribed, before your body takes them up and translates them into motion and sound. Lacking a dramatist to construct a design for me, I've begun to compose myself into a series of tableaux vivants: Nancy walking into the corner market to buy a bottle of milk; Nancy pedaling the length of Prospect Avenue on her new cream-colored Western Flyer with the fat tires, first with Mother huffing along behind, then all by herself; Nancy diving into the spice of damp red sawdust heaped in the yard of the mill behind Johnny Thorndike's house; Nancy wrenched by love for freckled Johnny Thorndike himself.

On the playground are two huge wooden boxes, one orange and one green, open on one side. I like to crawl in and curl up, suffused with the tang of the unpainted wood inside, but the teachers want everybody to run around. I like the swings, too, but not the monkey bars and jungle gym, where you're supposed to hang by your knees until your face gets red. At just the thought of turning the world upside down like that, I stop breathing. Sledding is okay, and so are games, Capture the Flag, Kick the Can, Giant Steps, Red Light. I don't care for Hide and Go Seek, the way you have to run exposed across the playground to Home before It chases and tags you, sometimes a really hard whack, but Sardines is fun, crouching safe in a hiding place until the last person finds you.

Best of all are walks. At the far end, the broad playground slopes sharply down into the enormous playing fields—seasonally green, brown, white—of the Phillips Exeter Academy, and when the boys aren't out there with their footballs or lacrosse sticks, we can hike across them. I love these fields especially in the cold soggy weather of March, when snowmelt and rain collect and then freeze in thin broad sheets we can skate across in our black rubber boots, and later when they begin to green and sprout dandelions and patches of tiny four-pointed bluets. My favorite hike takes us over the fields and across a wooden footbridge to a shadowy park carpeted with silky brown needles, where several large cannons loom. I can't imagine what they're doing here, these black iron hulks cold beneath my straddling legs, aimed pointlessly into the brush across the Exeter River, and I love their mystery. The world is full of puzzles like this, not just scary ones like the Water Tower or What Could Happen on the Swayze Parkway.

A prodigious reader, I advance quickly in my studies. I also suffer fools badly, myself in particular, growing furious and despondent if I make the littlest mistake. Reasoning that putting me into a situation where the material will be so challenging that I can't possibly expect to get all the answers right all the time will alleviate my perfectionism, my teachers recommend that I skip the third grade. Later, Mother will rue this decision, ascribing all my future difficulties to my being a year "too young" for whatever is going on in my life at the time. But this is simply the self-blame mothers are heir to. The fact is that she skipped the second grade without catastrophe. And the troubles I'll find myself in probably have to do more with temperament than with age, though I do miss multiplication tables by skipping third grade and have a terrible time learning them later on.

Another possible consequence, more severe, is that I don't readily make friends. In second grade I have a best friend, Susan

Fowler, a freckled girl with bobbed light-brown hair who lives with her surprisingly elderly mother in the next town east, in a large house with a dark cupboard in the stairwell big enough for two little girls to crawl into. The next year Susan hates me, and she gets the other third-graders to join her in chasing me around the playground taunting, "Smitty Spider! Smitty Spider!" Mother explains to me that Susan might feel jealous, but I still can't make sense of this betrayal, any more, no doubt, than Susan can make sense of mine. I run from the pack of them, panting and blubbering, but I haven't anyone to run *to*. The fourth-graders who are now my classmates tolerate but do not welcome me. "Who's your best friend?" grown-ups trying to make conversation frequently ask, as though naturally every girl has one. I just shrug, but my heart shrivels in the first shudders of a fear that will grow obsessive: I'm not a normal girl.

But I might have wound up feeling cut off even if I'd stayed in my "own" grade. The watcher growing in me is aloof. This is a matter not of will but of nature. She is my nonsocial part, introspective, wholly inarticulate until she learns to write, to keep a diary, and later to make poems and stories and essays. Even then, she will communicate in stutters, spitting out fragments of experience without ever getting them whole, or right. She watches sturdy, dark-haired Mary Jameson in her blue corduroy overalls, weeping inconsolably when the school suddenly decrees that henceforth girls will have to wear dresses every day because, she finally blurts out, her mother makes her wear long underwear all winter. She sneers at Bunny Fish, a porcelain doll with blond corkscrew curls who, coddled by anxious parents because rheumatic fever has damaged her heart, sulks and tattles unless she gets her own way. She's stung when Emily van den Bergh, a tall, pale Dutch girl, spells her down with "anxiety."

Janey Griswold, moving from Ohio so that her father can be treasurer of the Academy, provides a kind of rescue, though she's too prickly and I'm too introverted for us to be "best" friends. She doesn't know I'm "supposed" to be in third grade, and I don't care that when she says "roof," she sounds like a dog barking, so we start off even. She's a volatile friend, jealous and quick-witted and sometimes cruel but also inventive and often funny.

I love to walk to the Griswolds' wonderful three-story gray Victorian house on High Street. There are four girls there: Susan, older than us, thickset, with glasses, always bossing us around; Janey, slender, with crisp brown curls and intense blue eyes; Betsy, Sally's age, plump, with the coloring of a china doll; and a littler one we all ignore. Their mother's name is Bonnie, a round woman with dark hair wound in thin braids around her head, who always seems a little blurred around the edges, not much minding what we do, a style startlingly different from Mother's directive vigilance. We even eat candy whenever we like, cutting chunks from a roll of peanut butter fudge ever present in the refrigerator. We listen to children's shows on the radio, and Janey can sing along with all the tunes and jingles. We wander throughout the house, all the way up to the third floor, and pester Susan whenever we can sneak up on her.

In Janey's house I begin to recognize something I've sensed inchoately from being in other people's houses: we are poor. Our shabby furniture has been scrounged from family attics. Mother sews our clothing instead of buying it in stores. Our house is on Prospect *Avenue* at least, not Prospect *Street*, but all the same it's on Prospect Hill. We are also the only family I know without a father, so I assume some connection between fatherlessness and poverty. I'm right, literally as well as metaphorically. The Veteran's Administration pays Mother a monthly check, and Daddy had some life insurance, though not double indemnity, so our income is steady but small.

But of course poverty is relative. Mother's upbringing and education prepared her for different circumstances, and so we live on the margins of those circumstances. In Exeter we attend private rather than public school. Later we'll move to a very wealthy community, and still later I'll go on scholarship to an expensive private women's college. As a consequence, I'll grow up feeling deprived in comparison to my friends, even though I'll never lack anything I really need.

The disadvantage I feel is perhaps more social than economic, and it broadens the gap between my inward and outward lives. Fiercely affectionate toward each house I live in, I'm nonetheless ashamed to bring my friends into it. In this I feel as protective of the house as I do of my reputation. I don't want people laughing or sneering at the space that shelters me. They won't see what makes me love it. They won't know about the Little Crack, or that dusky dance on the porch roof, or the way Mother's body jounces with laughter when she reads, "Help! Help! A horrible heffalump!" They won't understand.

Garm and Pop aren't poor. They live at 89 High Street, a large white house with black shutters within walking distance, where we go whenever Garm invites us. Never without invitation, though. That's the way Garm is: proper and severe, the sort of woman you don't just drop in on. You can tell it to look at her, a tall woman, erect, her body already rail-thin, wasted by diabetes. Her features are sharp, framed by thick waves of hair that turned gray in her thirties. Every week she goes to the hairdresser, who curls it and puts in a rinse to enhance its tone; once the hairdresser gets carried away and Garm comes home with decidedly lavender hair, but usually it's pale and elegant.

I learn very little about her, except that she graduated from Wheelock College before marrying Pop and having four children. A determined woman: "The iron hand in the velvet glove," Mother says of her once, and her voice holds admiration, even affection, but also anger. Though she wangled my father's appointment to Annapolis, Garm opposed his choice to make the navy his career. She opposed his marriage to Mother as well, preferring the young heiress he had dated. Even so, when the marriage was fixed for a May afternoon in San Francisco, she joined Mother and Granna on a train journey across the country for a hasty ceremony before Daddy had to get back aboard his battleship and go on fighting the war. No doubt she wanted to make sure that the deed was suitably done. Propriety is her forte. Once when she was walking down the street with a friend, family legend has it, the elastic in her panties gave out and they dropped around her ankles. Without looking down, without missing a stride or a word in the conversation, she stepped free of them and continued her progress.

When we're with her, she expects her own polished manners to be mirrored by even the youngest of us children. For all her severity, she is never mean. She instructs, and expects, but doesn't punish. I learn to walk upright, my shoulders back and my chin raised. I learn to put my white-gloved hand out promptly at an introduction and to shake hands firmly, "not like a dead fish." I learn to dip my soup away from me and never to lick my ice cream from my spoon but to put the entire bite at once into my mouth, no matter how excruciating the ache between my eyebrows. She upholds a standard of behavior even Granna defers to, so that after Garm's death, if I'm uncouth—sit with my legs spread, say, or yawn without covering my mouth—Granna doesn't chide me directly but refers me to Garm's ghost: "What would your Garmie say if she could see you like that?" Lapsed manners betray loyalty.

With our best manners in place, even Mother's, we go up the front walk, through the door set to the left in the high, narrow face of the house, into the hall with the front stairs running up one side. Through the living room, cool and green, with framed family photographs on one table, past the closet that holds all the tattered volumes of *My Book House,* through the dining room, into the small den with its sunny bay window. Here children may play. At the back is a long kitchen with a screened porch beside it, overlooking a wide lawn and a big Victorian house, the Evening Star Nursing Home, where we Brownie Scouts go at Christmastime to sing carols to old, old people. On the other side of the kitchen is the back hall, with back stairs rising steeply, and the back door opening onto a narrow porch and the driveway.

Upstairs, at the front of the house is the bathroom. Then Garm's room, her dressing table with her silver-backed brushes and her Blue Grass toilet water. Other bedrooms. At the far end of the back hall, another bathroom with an enormously long and skinny bathtub. From the back hall a narrow flight of stairs leads to a partially finished attic. In this large, low, messy room lives Joel, the son of Garm's best friend, now dead. He's a student at the University of New Hampshire, handsome, easygoing, deep-voiced, fond of sleeping late. Sally and I love to be commissioned by Garm to get him out of bed. Up one flight of stairs we thump, then up another, tumbling onto his rumpled bed, squealing, "Garmie says time to get up! Up! Up! Up!" He never once throttles us, or even grumps, though sometimes he sends us away and falls back to sleep, so that we get to go through the whole routine again. It must be from this bed, into which he's crawled with a headache, that he stumbles down to the landing and calls over the railing, "Help! I can't see." An ambulance races him straight up the hill opposite the house to the hospital, and another whisks him to Boston for more expert medical care, where his eyesight returns but never his strength; months of rehabilitative therapy are followed by a lifetime of uncertain steps tapped out with a cane in bitterness, no matter the drugs, no matter the alcohol, always bitterness.

Attached to the back of the house is a large white barn. Perhaps once it housed carriage horses, but now it's a garage. Steep, narrow stairs climb into a loft jumbled, like an attic, with discards. A book called *Fraidy Cat* might have belonged to my father or his siblings. Perhaps one of them, like me, had battled along with googly-eyed Fraidy Cat the terrors of the dark, and perhaps that one, like Fraidy Cat, had better luck than I ever do. I peer, with my delight in the miniature, through the windows of a wooden windmill, perhaps three feet high, painted white with green trim, meant for a weathervane, its wooden sails still in the dead attic air.

Best of all, an organ. Yellowed keys and rows of stops that shift the wheezing tones pumped out by a pair of rapid feet. I can scarcely reach the pedals. Sometimes I persuade Sally to crouch down and knead them with her hands, but she gets bored. She doesn't like the loft as much as I do. So I sit here alone, pumping and panting and pulling at the knobs: STRINGS, BRASS, BELLS. Over and over I pick out the lugubrious melody of "The Lost Chord" from a yellow sheet of music because, Mother says, it was Daddy's favorite hymn.

> Seated one day at the organ,
> I was weary and ill at ease,
> And my fingers wandered idly
> Over the dusty keys. . . .

The light is brownish gold, the color of shallow lake water when you open your eyes under it on a hot day. Dust blackens the tips of my fingers and itches in my throat. The tune lurches and hiccups its way to the space straight above me, which is heaven, where Daddy listens as vigilantly as he watches over me whatever I do. I think he's pleased, though I can never actually tell. I feel sure of his presence but never of his mood.

v

The summer I turn nine, Mother sends me to summer camp. This is a perfectly dreadful idea, though I don't suppose she can be blamed for having it. She and Aunt Jane always went to summer camp. Apparently a great many children do it. At least there are a great many camps to choose from. She settles on a Girl Scout camp called Spruce Pond. Two weeks should be long enough to start with, she decides.

Two weeks is at least thirteen days too long. No, all fourteen. I am so unhappy that, for the first time in my life—not counting getting sucked by the undertow into the milky green surf on the beach at The Port and tumbling over and over until some grown-up's arm yanked me, shuddering with terror and cold, back into air and light—I think I am going to die. Every afternoon during rest hour, I lie on the cot I've been assigned in a stuffy cabin, face toward the wall, yearning for my own bed, safer in spite of giants and knife-wielders than any other in the world, and scribbling pleas for rescue: "I hate it here. *Come and get me!* RIGHT NOW! Please, please, please!!!" But she never comes.

She'll be sorry, it turns out a few weeks later, when she discovers the reason I'm digging frantically into my thick mop of hair. A quick check of Sally's fat braids reveals that the infestation has spread, and we have to stay home from school, holding peppermint patties on our tongues while Mother pours vinegar through our hair and squalling as she tugs a fine-toothed comb along one tress after another. Our Kind of People do not get lice, and she is horrified and humiliated. But no punishment is harsh enough, as far as I'm concerned, for abandoning me to eating Spam and swimming in murky water with bloodsuckers in it for two whole weeks, especially not a punishment involving vinegar rinses of *my* head.

So poignant is my homesickness that when I leave my own daughter for the first time at Camp Whispering Pines, I'll steel myself for the inevitable deluge of rescue notes; but all that comes are brief sketches of tentmates and queer-looking insects and mountain hikes in the rain.

"Were you homesick?" I ask with feigned nonchalance when we retrieve her.

"Not really," she shrugs. She means it, I can tell. Something in her knows that, like a turtle, she is her own home, a knowledge that will eventually settle her alone with a tabby kitten in a house without electricity or running water in a tiny African village. "Remember," says one of the characters in a silly film called *Buckaroo Bonzai*, "no matter where you go, there you are." Anne remembers. One day, I will too, but during my days at Spruce Pond Camp, that time is unimaginably far ahead.

When, at the end of my incarceration, Mother comes to fetch me, she mentions my homesickness to my counselors, who are surprised. A couple of days after my arrival, I got a package from Mother containing a couple of items we'd forgotten to pack. Sitting outside the dining hall under the pine trees, I gazed at the green plastic mug we'd bought together and burst into silent tears; but when a counselor came over to comfort me, I told her that nothing was the matter, I just got a paper cut on my finger while opening the package. Other than this incident, no one ever saw me cry. I did it in the latrine, or while we were walking in single file to the lake, or during swimming while the tea-colored water streamed down my face. So the counselors' surprise is genuine. How could they guess to comfort a child who denies her own sadness?

In this way I discover that the feelings other people might find unacceptable can be hidden in the same place from which I watch myself and others acting out socially acceptable stories, a kind of cache hollowed out behind my surface self: the Virgin Mary, the Tin Woodman, Nancy. From now on I will bury my inner life deeper and deeper beneath the best imitation of a lively and cooperative child I know how to inscribe. It mustn't be a very good likeness, since people seem increasingly to label me moody, hypersensitive, perfectionist: in a word, difficult. But the semblance strikes me as infinitely preferable to the wretched being secluded within. The dissonance between the person I feel myself and the person I think others perceive me to be grows so sharp that, before many more years, I'll think myself crazy.

The next winter, Mother does something far worse than packing me off to Spruce Pond. She moves me away from Exeter entirely. Until this time, it hasn't occurred to me that my location, and the life I lead there, will ever change again. Daddy's death wrenched us halfway around the world, true, but that was an extraordinary event. Mother has promised us she won't do something terrible that could get her arrested and thrown into jail where she won't be able to take care of us. She has said she doesn't plan to die for a long, long time. She hasn't pledged not to marry again, but it's okay if she does. The man can just move into 17 Prospect Avenue with us and everything can go on as before. If we want to retain our own recognizable selves, we mustn't move elsewhere. Our feet must retrace their steps through the house, out the door, to school, back, weaving a pattern of undisrupted order: no change, no death. As long as we stay where we are, we're safe.

Elsewhere

i

"J'M LEAVING HERE," I mutter, strangled on tears. Sally is the shouter in the family; I mutter. "I'm running away." I pull out my small blue cardboard suitcase and start to pack. Sometimes, Sally pulls out her matching red one, like last summer when we didn't come home at Mother's whistle and she put us straight to bed without any supper, only saltines and water.

This time, though, I'm the sole victim of Mother's tyranny. She still makes me wear nitey-nites, though I've begged her and begged her for a pair of real pajamas. So, with her curved nail scissors, I cut the feet out of a pair of baggy faded yellow ones and now she insists that I wear them anyway, all ragged and bunched up around my knees.

"Where will you go?" she asks coolly. Later I will understand that if Mother was ever really guilty of tyranny, it lay in this unfailing emotional control.

"To Garm and Pop," my father's parents. I carry the map of the short walk to their house in my head: down Prospect Avenue to the end, left a block, right another block down the hill, across the street (looking both ways), straight up the drive and through the door of 89 High Street. I could say, "To Granna," Mother's own mother, but that haven, involving a car ride of more than an hour, beckons less strongly. Eventually, we'll move into a house with Granna, and then the possibility of running away to her will vanish altogether.

"What makes you think they'd have you?" Mother asks. "They don't want to have to take care of a little girl. Especially one who's pouting like you. Get the tea kettle." This is the immemorial family response to a pout, rooted perhaps in German folklore: the tea kettle is to hang from the jutting lower lip. And so, persuaded that I am a burden whom my grandparents don't want, whom only Mother herself in fact will reluctantly take on, I empty my suitcase and remain, Mother my keeper, in the prison of my ordinary existence.

Doubtless, Mother is right: my grandparents wouldn't welcome the care of a little girl, even one with her lower lip tucked in properly and curved into a perpetual smile. After all, Garm and Pop raised four children, and Granna, three. One day I will eject three children into the world, with varying degrees of force, and achieve grandmotherly status myself. (Can this be? Can I ever reach the age of my grandparents when I first knew them?) Then I will know that, although I delight in my foster son's little boys, I don't yearn for days filled once again with grubby jeans and bleeding knees and black handprints on the bathroom towels. Like Garm and Pop and Granna, I will have had my turn.

I am a welcome visitor, however, in my grandparents' houses. I'm sure of that. The first child of two first children, I have the benefit of novelty on my side. I feel cherished by both my grandmothers, the short merry one, round as a brown wren, and the elegant white-haired one, like an egret, angular and remote. One of the great blessings of my childhood, I know even while it's going on, is conferred in the time I get to spend with my grandmothers and even my great-grandmothers, whose presence places me firmly within that structure we call "our family," each of us a post, a beam, a panel, a joist, nobody left out, nobody alone.

My own daughter, similarly blessed, will tell me one day that as a young child she loved her Nanny but didn't like her Grandma at all because she didn't seem like a "real grandmother." Nanny, wearing wire-rimmed glasses and flowered housedresses, baked cookies and riveted her full attention on Anne's entertainment, whereas Grandma, busy with her youngest children and then with her job as the town tax collector, took Anne's presence warmly but casually. The difference, I suppose, is analogous to that in the Church calendar between Feast Days and Ordinary Time.

Using these criteria, I don't have "real grandmothers," either. Granna, although she sometimes bakes cookies, has been divorced for years, and she works every day as a bank teller. Garm, although she doesn't have an outside job, goes out all the time for bridge and luncheons, and because she's a diabetic, she doesn't bake cookies at all. They talk to me, and sometimes read to me, but they don't play with me. They're full of family stories, often funny ones. And sometimes the family tells stories on them. Like the time Garm shut her longish thin nose in the refrigerator trying to find out what became of the light after the door was closed. I am destined to become the sort of woman who can shut the door on her nose in order to see whether the light has gone out, though of course I never actually do just that.

ii

The whole time I'm growing up, we never travel much. During holidays, other families fly to Bermuda or take the train down to New York City or drive slowly up the coast to Nova Scotia. But we can't afford such jaunts. Anyway, Mother doesn't seem to have much heart for travel, having voyaged bravely halfway around the world only to return with her husband in a coffin. She's worn out. I don't mind. I don't like to sleep in other people's houses, anyway. I don't know who I am there, as though my real self is squeezed into shape by the walls of my own house but collapses, amorphous and anonymous, as soon as it wanders away. Visits to grandparents are bearable, however, especially if Mother comes too. In their familiar houses I am very nearly the same person I am at home.

Sometimes we drive down to Danvers, Massachusetts, and stay with Granna.

"Are we there yet?" I ask Mother as soon as we're under way.

"Not yet," she says.

"Are we there yet?" I ask again when I feel sure that a very long time has passed.

"No. Stop asking."

"Are we there yet?" Sally asks, bouncing up from the back seat where she has been lying to ease her carsickness.

Mother shakes her head. Trying to distract us, she points

at a truck with a gigantic tank revolving slowly on the back. "Ce-ment mix-er, putt-y, putt-y," she chants, and Sally and I double up, shrieking with laughter, at this witticism.

Then, at last, she says, "We're there," as we pull up in front of the white mansard-roofed duplex on Lindall Hill. The front yard is steep, with retaining walls on either side of a long flight of wooden stairs that once drive a terrible splinter into my duffy, which Mother works out with a long needle sterilized in a match flame. Waving at the top stands Granna, a short woman with round cheeks and soft brown hair as fine as a baby's. When we climb up to her, she scoops each of us up in a big hug.

Granna lives with her mother, Grandma Virchow, who is very old now, gaunt, hard of hearing, with little, round, wire-rimmed glasses and whiskers sprouting from her chin. Grandpa Virchow, who was a butcher, died a long time ago, when Mother was in high school. Everyone still talks about him, though, so he seems real to me. With my own father dead, and Mother's and Granna's as well, the presence of dead fathers is no mystery to me. Live ones seem stranger.

Grandma was plump and jovial when she was younger, I'm told. She and Grandpa immigrated from Germany in the 1890s. They had four boys and then Granna, on whom they heaped all the girl's names they hadn't been able to use yet: Elfrieda Augusta Johanna. Now Grandma can be grumpy. When I lean against the prickly arm of her chair, transfixed by the coarse cream-colored web spinning from the end of her bone hook, she offers to teach me to crochet. But all I can make are tangled lumps, tinged faintly gray by my sweaty fingers. She snatches the mess away from me, and I cry.

"Guten Morgen, Grossmutter," Mother teaches Sally and me to chime when Grandma first appears each morning. She beams at us, showing the red-gummed teeth that spent the night in a jelly jar on the crocheted doily covering the little table beside her bed. She has made glossy purplish blueberry preserves, which we heap onto our toast. Grandma's breakfast is always the same: a biscuit of shredded wheat softened with a splash of water from the boiling tea kettle. I hate shredded wheat, though I love the games printed on the squares of cardboard separating the layers of biscuits, and I can't imagine anything duller than eating the same thing for breakfast every single morning. When I'm grown up, it will turn out, I'll have a glass of juice and a bowl of cereal every morning, often shredded wheat; I may even come to the boiling water part eventually.

The large backyard is filled with Grandma's flowers. Tall lavender phlox, whose individual four-pointed blossoms she teaches us to pull away carefully and suck for the drop of honey at the base. Tangles of roses. In one corner Grandpa, the same one who built our dollhouses, built a summer house. The white paint has flaked down to the silvered splintery wood, and large wasps and bumblebees sail scarily through it. Even so, on hot days Sally and I take our dolls and tea sets out there and set up housekeeping, just like Marcella in the Raggedy Ann and Raggedy Andy stories. I pour water out of a teapot painted with roses and set one tiny cup in front of my dark-haired doll Mary and another in front of Sally's blond Susan, watching myself the whole time, turning myself gesture by gesture into a character in a book.

Now Granna is the plump and jovial one, though she's had sorrows enough. I glean evidence of them slowly, sifting through overheard conversations, asking sudden questions that sometimes surprise shreds of information from adults' tight lips. As a young woman, I learn, she went to Salem Normal School, preparing to be a teacher. But instead she married my grandfather, a handsome young Harvard graduate from a family of some means, owners of a chain of drugstores on the North Shore. Drugstore ownership won't strike me, in later years, as a particular mark of aristocracy, but the family was an old one and apparently gave itself airs, for Grandmother Pedrick sneered almost openly at the immigrants' daughter her only son had chosen.

We visit Grandmother Pedrick sometimes, in her large house full of dark polished furniture and woodwork. She is too crippled by arthritis to leave her bed. After a few minutes of listening to her creaky voice, Sally and I leave Mother sitting at her bedside and tiptoe downstairs, past the grandfather clock on the landing, into the dining room. There we've found a button under the oriental rug. Mother has told us you can push it to call the maid, though there isn't a maid anymore, or anyone to call her, for that matter. We push the button anyway. Then we go back upstairs and begin fidgeting. That gives Mother a good excuse to get us out of there.

We don't like Grandmother Pedrick because she was mean to Granna. And we don't like her son, our grandfather, either. We don't even have a name for him, because he was dead long before we began to call out to the people around us. Mother, his oldest child, tries to speak fairly, but we can tell she despised him; Aunt

Jane, the baby, adored him; Uncle Robert never mentions him in my hearing. Granna herself will tell me only one tale, one night after I'm a grown woman. He was a good provider, so that she had a large home in Marblehead and nurses for the three children born within three years, but was a distant father and a faithless husband, the sort who secretly (but not secretly enough) took his secretary along on a cruise and brought Granna a gorgeous set of amethyst jewelry as a sort of consolation prize. He came to a bad end, Mother will finally allow, shooting himself to death in the throes of passion for a woman who jilted him and ran off to California. I, too, will turn out to be a suicide. Except for this taint, unrecognized until much later in my life, I'll never feel connected to him at all. He's just a blank, like the missing piece in my favorite thousand-piece jigsaw puzzle, of Millet's "The Reapers," which the cat swallowed years ago, so that in the glowing twilit sky the empty space looms incongruously in the shape of a gigantic crow.

Just how painful Granna must have found this marriage is suggested by the fact that she divorced my grandfather in the 1930s, though she faced social opprobrium that women fifty years later can hardly guess at. Her own mother could scarcely speak of it. Sorting Granna's possessions after her death, Mother and Jane will come across a diary kept by Grandma Virchow containing this entry: "Today Frieda got her d——." She couldn't even spell it out. And yet, cheated on, divorced, forced to work for wages, Granna more than holds her head up. She will spend the nearly forty more years of her life weaving an elaborate and elastic emotional web of family and friends. On the night of her death, preparing candied orange peel for her grandsons-in-law, she will make sure to get the glistening fruit and syrup into sterilized glass before asking Mother to call an ambulance; and when Mother returns from the hospital alone, she will find a row of topaz jars, ready for their lids, giving her something to keep her hands busy.

In Danvers, though, Granna seems infinitely far from death. She is still taking care of her own mother, who will die at ninety-two ("of double pneumonia," I will inform people importantly, two being obviously better than one). When we grandchildren are around, she doesn't pay us much attention, the way some grown-ups do, making you feel like all the breath is being sucked out of you. But she lets us make little tarts out of the pie-dough trimmings and even shake cream in a jar till it turns into damp pale butter. And she sings to us. She sets us astride her ankle and bounces us along: "How many miles to Boston town? Four score and ten" or *Hopp! Hopp! Hopp! Pferdchen lauf galopp!*" When we get too heavy, she holds us in her lap or on the couch beside her. "Postman, postman, why are you late again?" she sings; or " 'Tis March and the wind doth blow / And soon we will have more snow"; or "Kerchoo! Kerchoo! sneezed the bullfinch on the bluebell's head. / With the influenza bluebell went to bed"; or my favorite, a plaintive German ballad about a little ring that burst in two when the lover was faithless. I lean back heavily against her, staring through the window at black branches against a gray sky and wondering what "influenza" is. Her body feels different from Mother's, not bony but pliant, like the blue comforter sprigged with flowers that covers her bed. Her sweet, reedy voice kisses the top of my head.

When Sally and I misbehave, she tells us cautionary tales about bad things that will happen to our bodies. We mustn't flip towels at one another, because Grandma Virchow knew a woman who'd had her eye put out that way. We mustn't scratch mosquito bites, because Grandma Virchow knew someone who'd died of blood poisoning from a bite infected by a dirty fingernail. We mustn't raise our arms to strike our mother because after we die they'll grow up out of our graves. Years later, teaching a course in mythology, I will discover that this last threat comes from the Brothers Grimm; for now, I simply assume that Grandma Virchow knew a furious little girl whose pale dead arm had risen, fingers writhing and clutching at a pot of wilted red Memorial Day geraniums. Granna gives us these grisly little pieces of wisdom time and again until we are grown, and before long they lose their force and become, like dead metaphors, simply markers in the syntax of correction. Unless you're awfully careful, bodies get you in trouble.

Granna and Grandma live on the second and third floors of 59 Lindall Street. Sally and I sleep on the third floor, in the bedrooms Mother and Aunt Jane had through high school and college and until they got married. The other half of this floor is an attic where red squirrels frolic noisily. At least, that's what Mother says they are, though one night I hear a lion in there, I know. I want to sleep in with Sally, but Mother insists I sleep in her room and Sally in Aunt Jane's. Lying rigid on my back, my breath frozen at the top of my chest, I watch long black shadows cast by the streetlight through the tall maple outside the window writhe up and down the wall, and I listen for the lion bumping among the old boxes across the hall. I'll never make it to the steep narrow stairs with the door shut fast at the bottom. I'll be eaten up. Sleeping restlessly at last, I reach the stairs and float downward above them, searching disconsolately for the miniature can of Pet milk which in day-life I dropped irretrievably between the banister and the wall. This is the first of a lifetime of nightmares in which my body, weightless and out of control, bobs above the world like a balloon at the end of a fragile tether, frantic to return to gravity's free fall.

In the long, narrow bathroom with its pink walls, I am nervous. I am always nervous in bathrooms, except my own at home, and even there I prefer to have Sally with me. After I'm grown, Mother will recount an incident that might explain my anxiety: she once accidentally flushed one of Sally's diapers down Granna's toilet while I was standing beside it, and the water overflowed. I was perhaps two, and my eyes mustn't have been much higher than the rim, over which the water welled and cascaded onto the floor. I screamed and screamed, Mother says. I get over the screaming, of course, but strange plumbing will frighten me ever after, forcing my husband into a career of first flushes and faucet-twirlings in motels and guest rooms from one end of the country to the other.

Mother tells me another story, from an even earlier time. My father placed me on a potty seat on Granna's toilet and gave me a church key to entertain myself with. When he returned, he found me, head tucked between my legs, peering into the water and clucking: "Honey Miff, how cootchoo, how cootchoo." Nobly, he plunged his hand through the feces to rescue the church key, and no harm was done. But ever after, when I do something not truly reprehensible but decidedly dumb, members of my family chide, "Honey Miff, how cootchoo, how cootchoo." From such bits of private silliness evolves the affectional constellation "family." For most of my life, few people will know that my maiden name is Smith. Fewer still will call me "Honey Miff"; those who call me thereby claim me.

Sally and I sit together in the deep tub and Granna tells us to wash our penivuses. That's what she calls them, and until I'm nearly grown I think that's the "real" name for what seems actually to have no name: the smoothness, the absence, the lack, the penis I haven't got. I've never heard anyone seriously refer to it as "my *mons veneris.*" Sometimes she calls it "possible": "Wash possible," she says. She teaches us to rinse our washcloths in cold water to prevent them from smelling sour. When we're out and dry, she plugs in the curling iron beside the sink and twists corkscrews into our straight, heavy hair—Sally's a pale honey, mine dusty brown—while we hold her hand mirror and primp.

After Grandma gets very old and she and Granna move to the first-floor apartment, I have no bedroom. I sleep in a folded sheet on the living-room couch. There, on Christmas Eve, I lie stiff and breathless, not afraid this time but excited, my whole being focused up through the dark quiet air to the slate roof two floors above, waiting for bell chimes, the tramp of hooves. I hear them, too, but just then I fall asleep, waking the next morning to find I've missed the event of the old elf's visit itself.

I believe in Santa Claus with crystalline conviction—not the feigned, indulgent sort my own world-weary children will one day drag out for George and me as they tumble into the living room on Christmas morning to unpack their stockings—until I'm quite old, eight anyway, maybe even nine. Mother fosters my faith, without any real subterfuge, for when I begin to ask whether there really is a Santa Claus, she responds, "Of course there is. Santa Claus is the spirit of Christmas." Each year the meaning of "spirit" unfolds a little further, and the pudgy white-haired gentleman with his pipe and his pack fades benignly, and I am never bereft.

My belief in the Tooth Fairy and all her companions is just as absolute, and in this Mother engages more actively. One night I tuck under my pillow, together with the latest lost tooth, a letter full of questions about elven life; the next morning, beside the ransom dime, lies a note: "Fairies are about four inches tall; they weave and sew their clothes from cobwebs; they eat the pollen and drink the drops of dew from flowers. . . ." Now, Mother is as plain as bread, she'd have you think (and she gets me to think so for much of my life); her sister and her daughter are the "arty" ones, the poets, not she. But one night she sits at the kitchen table and, disguising her penmanship with care, recasts Mercutio's fancies for a purpose he could never have dreamed.

One day my husband will bemoan his difficulties in teaching a group of adult learners to write: "They have no imagination. They don't understand me when I say, 'Just make something up. . . .'" Of course they don't, I'll tell him, because no one has fostered that faculty in them. From an early age most children are exhorted, "Don't make up stories. Tell me the truth." Children do need some help in sorting out what has "really" happened from what they hope, or more often dread, has happened. But in the relentless stress on "reality" which most adults believe salutary, childhood fantasies shrivel, and their mummified remains excite denial or embarrassment, never good writing and (for me the two become inseparable) good living. What children need are fathers like George, playing Peter's Perfect Pet Store with our small daughter:

GEORGE: Good afternoon. Peter's Perfect Pet Store. May I help you?
ANNE: I'm looking for an aardvark. Have you got any good aardvarks today?
GEORGE: Why yes, we just got a shipment this morning. And they're a bargain: only four thousand eighty-eight dollars each. Would you like me to set one aside for you?

What children need are mothers like mine, at their kitchen tables with their pencils, spokeswomen for the fairies.

What children don't need, I discover during a visit to the Danvers house the summer I turn eight, is a mother for a teacher. My schoolteachers and my mother have decided during the preceding spring that I should move straight from the second grade into the fourth. If I'm going to skip third grade, however, I've got to catch up with my classmates somehow. So the teachers have armed Mother with a stack of workbooks, and every morning I have to complete a set of exercises before I can play. Hours bleed away into the stupid lives of Dick and Jane and baby Sally and Puff and Spot.

After a sullen, spoiled hour or so, Mother dismisses me wearily. I don't, of course, think of *her* spoiled hour. I dive between the covers of a volume of fairy tales that I've been reading over and over. I love them all, "Snow White and Rose Red" and "Puss in Boots" and "Jack and the Beanstalk" and the poor sad "Goose Girl." I quake as the thirteenth fairy curses Sleeping Beauty in her cradle and laugh at the brave little tailor strutting and boasting that he's killed "seven with one blow." "Bluebeard" enthralls me. I stare in horror, reading after reading, into the dark room filled with dead women, and rub vainly at the bloody key, and quaver up the stairwell to the figure at the window, "Sister Anne! Sister Anne! Is anyone coming?"

* * *

Sometimes, then, sister Sally shows up at my side, sweaty and bored and importunate, and I pull myself languidly up out of the book and go outside with her. Because we don't live in Danvers and Mother is afraid we'll get lost, just the way I did on the Swayze Parkway in Exeter, we aren't allowed to wander far. Mother has the same fretful temperament Sally will turn out to have. "Don't get lost," Sally will admonish her little daughters when, on a visit to my house, they set out on a trek around the block. Now, either a child is going to get lost or she isn't going to get lost, but no amount of chiding is likely to sway the outcome. A vagary is, essentially, beyond maternal or any other sort of control.

Snapshots show us, Sally still a pudgy toddler, dressed in matching corduroy overalls, jackets, and crew hats, pedaling our tricycles beside the stone wall in front of 59 Lindall. Later, we're allowed the length of the street, which crosses a narrow hill. The houses are large, set in deep yards shaded by elms and grape arbors and hydrangeas, where sometimes we find kitties to pet. Our own cat, Honeybun, gets lost here on one of our visits, and we mourn her inconsolably. Three months later Granna arrives at our door in Exeter clutching Honeybun her very self—tiger spot on her white tummy and all—and she resumes living with us for several years more. In which of the tall houses with their shady yards she took refuge we never find out, but she returns clean and fragrant and sleek as though from some pleasant dalliance.

In spite of Mother's strictures, twice Sally and I get lost. Once, that is, we know where we are but Mother doesn't. The other time, nobody knows where we are. The house at 59 Lindall sits on a corner, and beyond the cross street the pavement peters out into open fields that will become the grounds of Hunt Memorial Hospital. Most of the open spaces of my childhood will be devoured in one way or another, following some relentless American imperative: Occupy! Occupy! Now there are just a few smaller, poorer houses along that stretch. One hot day as we wander around with the aimlessness of small children in territory they don't daily possess, a sweet-faced young woman invites us into one of these, gives us cold drinks, and chats with us as she irons. Finally Mother's whistling and calling penetrates our sociability and we hail her from the doorway. She comes up, flushed and frowning.

"I'm sorry if they bothered you," she apologizes to the young woman.

"Oh, no. They're no bother. They've been entertaining me. Telling me all about their life."

"Really," Mother says, glancing at us. "Like what? What have they told you?"

"Well, you know. Where you all live, and who you're visiting here, and what they do in school. They even told me how old you are," she laughs. "Twenty-one!"

Mother blushes. "For heaven's sake! I only told them that as a joke."

"Of course." Somehow the woman knew it was a joke, but I certainly didn't. I feel stupid.

"Thanks for your time," Mother says, shooing us out the door before her, and that's the last we see of our new friend. On the way up the street Mother scolds me for telling a perfect stranger the private details of our lives. I scuff my feet. I don't see what she's mad about. I didn't tell any lies, except for the one about her age, but that wasn't my fault. How could I know she was joking? She didn't laugh.

For the first time, I sense the demarcation between "private" and "public." What you can share with some people you must hide from others. But which is which? I know that adults are always hiding things from me, and I hate it: the way they roll their eyes when I come into the room and drop their voices and say, "Little pitchers have big ears." Sometimes when I ask a question, like "What's Kotex for?" they say, "I'll tell you when you're older." The world is full of secrets, of events and rules I don't understand, and not knowing frightens me. I won't hide anything from anybody, I vow, scowling at the ground to keep from crying in shame. Unlike many childhood vows, this one I will, in some ways, be able to keep, even though the scoldings never stop.

Another day, Sally and I get lost in earnest. We've been mistreated by one or more of the women in that high white house, each of whom confers power on the others, and for once we're making good on our threat to run away. We stomp right off Lindall Hill and into the town. This would have been the familiar territory of Mother's adolescence, which I will read about in a few years, during my own adolescence, in a diary she lets me see. She walked to high school through these streets, and wandered through them after school with her friends, especially her boyfriend Darren, whom she might have married, thereby eradicating me from her future and my own tenuous present. They all went skating together in the winter and swimming at West Beach in the summer, they danced on the weekends, they watched countless "swell" movies starring Bing Crosby and Frank Sinatra, the diary will tell me.

But I haven't read the diary yet, and even if I had, I wouldn't have gained much sense of geographical direction, though the unfamiliarity of the streets might seem less menacing. Sally and I wander past streets of houses and on into the business district, clutching hands, increasingly confused and nervous. Being together protects us from panic, however, as though we can never go really, truly, irrevocably astray in the world unless we lose each other. We're even a little titillated to be having the experience we've so often been warned against: Getting Lost.

Fortunately, this excitement doesn't quite wear off before Mother pulls up beside us in the gray hump-backed Chevrolet. We clamber in, eyes down, dreading a scolding that never comes. She just seems glad to have found us and to drive us back up the hill where we belong. In later years, though I seldom dream of the house on Lindall Hill, the streets of Danvers will become a kind of locus of lostness, to which I return without Sally, anxious and uncertain where I am, every now and then in sleep.

iii

It's June. The last day of school is over. Mother fans her face and lifts her curled hair off her neck as she moves through our bedrooms, making sure she's packed everything we need. Pajamas and unders and jerseys and shorts and swimming suits, swimming suits, swimming suits. We're going to The Cottage. For the *whole* summer.

We live at The Cottage in the summer the same as Garm and Pop, and for this reason I hardly mind leaving home at all. For a long time I don't even realize that it belongs to them, not us. Pop had it built around the time we came back from the Tropics. I remember going to see it before it was finished, just a skeleton of pale beams and rafters against a wintry sky.

"Dunfrettin," Pop calls it, even though the name makes Garm wince. He has it carved on a wooden sign to hang out front. In later years, when I turn into a city-dweller and then a desert-city-dweller, Exeter will seem to me quite bucolic enough for a summer retreat. I'd be glad enough of a little house by the river there. But Exeter is "the town," and The Cottage, ten miles due east in North Hampton, is "the beach." In the summer we retreat to the beach.

It really is cooler there. Not on the beach itself, of course, where the sand shimmers and burns our dancing soles as we race toward the waves. But we don't have one of the clapboard cottages perched on grass-anchored sand right above the sea wall, with long wooden steps leading to their doors, though we children often wish we did. The Cottage is tucked back under the pines in an area on the other side of the shore road called The Colony. Here, along curving dirt roads, are a hodgepodge of summer dwellings, some very old, from ramshackle three-story houses to rose-covered cottages to two-room shacks.

Garm would not have a shack, I know, any more than she would let her hair hang straight or go out wearing a cotton housedress. A house is like a garment. It covers your nakedness, of course, but it also lets others know who you take yourself to be. The Cottage, a classic Cape Cod with a shed dormer on the back, tidy and modest, just the way we ought to dress, sits back from the road above a fern-covered retaining wall. It has gray shingles, which weather to silver over the years, white trim, white shutters with red S's. The front yard, under the gloom of several tall pines, is scattered comfortably with metal lawn furniture. Garm sends us out, as soon as we're big enough, to sweep the drifts of red-brown pine needles from the porches so we don't track them in.

In the house Garm and Pop draw together a great tangle of children and grandchildren, and the dreams I have of it ever after will seem tumultuous. "Children should be seen and not heard" is the family rule, but here it relaxes. The interior of the house, though spacious, is oddly inconvenient in some ways for the confusion we create. There's only one bathroom, for instance, and no dining room. The original plan must have been to take our meals on the large screened porch at the back, and we often do, but it's a long walk from the kitchen and unpleasant on the inevitable drizzly days. Soon Pop has a breakfast nook built off one end of the kitchen, an improvement, to be sure, but with its own shortcomings. It seats only eight comfortably, on gray and red plastic benches, sticky on bare legs, along either wall. Those who slide in first are trapped, unless they want to disturb those who come after. We children grow adept at dropping to the floor and scrambling in the sudden twilight across the grown-ups' ankles as soon as we're excused from the table.

The interior is rustic, as though too finished a condition would dampen the vacationers' spirits and carry them back into their ordinary lives. The walls are all rough pine, pungent in the damp air, and at night, light pierces the cracks between the boards and the knots in them. Sound too. I lie in bed and try to fathom the grown-ups' conversation until it blurs, the trill of women's voices and the rumble of men's voices, into oceanic sleep. The floors are covered with woven straw mats, muted green and tan like beach grass. At one end of the living room, which rises two stories, the ceiling pierced by small dormers, a huge fieldstone fireplace provides the only heat.

Since usually a lot of people are there at once, the five bedrooms are full. The two downstairs go to Aunt Nora and Uncle Seth and their boys, a new one every two years: Seth Junior, Matt, Rich, and Howie, all tow-headed and blue-eyed. Thanks to their appearance at regular intervals, Sally and I increase in value over the years. Uncle Seth used to tease Mother and Daddy unmercifully that all they could produce was girls, but that was before his sons began to be born. Even Aunt Sadie, marrying late and producing only one child, had a boy. In the manner of all scarce commodities, Sally and I enjoy something of the status of treasures. Uncle Seth, in particular, makes pets of us.

Upstairs, where the rooms open off a landing overlooking the living room, Garm and Pop have the first bedroom while Sally, Mother, and I share the second. The third is very tiny, scarcely big enough for a cot and a dresser, but it has a window that opens onto the kitchen, which delights us children because it makes us both inside and outside at the same time. "Hello, hello!" we wave down at the grown-ups, who sometimes absently wave back. The live-in babysitters sleep in this room, first our own Janice and then, when she gets too old, Aunt Nora's Toby, who sometimes gets headaches so terrible that she can't take care of us but lies on her cot underneath the window to the kitchen in the half-dark.

There's even a cot in the back hall leading to the screened porch, where a child sometimes gets put if the bedrooms overflow. Most of the time it's a good place to lie on one's stomach and read. The house is full of old books, and I devour them all: the Bobbsey Twins series, the Five Little Peppers series, *The Box Car Children*, *Anne of Green Gables* and its sequels. My favorite is *Flash Gordon in the Caverns of Mongo*, which rouses me to a fever of romantic sexuality. If only Flash were real. If only he would come alive right now, sweep my lifeless form into his arms, race with me through the dim underground tunnels, burst out into light and safety, clutch me to his chest, press my wakening lips to his. Oh Flash, oh Flash. The pages of the book are brownish and musty. Grains of sand grate in the binding and sprinkle the woven bedspread under me. I finish the last page and turn straight again to the first. Oh Flash.

Flash never comes alive. But during the same summer that I devote to *The Caverns of Mongo*, Janice has a boyfriend named Jimmy, a lifeguard who is maybe sixteen, rugged, with curly brown hair. Uncle Seth is a tease, and one night when Jimmy comes to pick Janice up, he instructs Sally to stand on the landing above the living room and call down through the railing, "Oh Janice, I need to you-ri-nate!" Sally isn't even sure what she's saying, since in our family we never do anything but tinkle, but Janice blushes under her tan and scurries up the stairs to escort Sally down to the bathroom. Jimmy stands by the door with his hands shoved into his pockets, shifting from foot to foot as he waits. I'm so embarrassed I don't know whether to giggle or weep.

I never do anything to call Jimmy's attention to me. But at night I lie in my hot, damp, sandy bed and go off to Thinking Land to join Jimmy. Since he's a lifeguard, the only thing I can do is drown. I wade and then paddle out beyond the breakers until I feel the undertow take me. This isn't hard to envision, since I'm a weak and timid swimmer. My head drops into the green water and bobs out again.

"Help!" I sputter. Under. Up. "Help, help, help!" Jimmy races down the beach in his orange trunks and dives into the water. His brown arms close around me and tug me to him. He lays me out on the warm sand and gives me artificial respiration, his hands big and hard on my back. In. Out. In. Out. My breath comes back. He turns me over and pulls me against his heaving chest.

"Thank heaven, you're all right!" he says, pressing his tight lips to mine.

"Oh Jimmy."

Of course, I could never drown. Mother would never let me. She keeps what she calls "an eagle eye" on Sally and me, and so does Janice.

We go down to the beach twice on every fair day. Slathering on a thick layer of 6-12, clear as water but greasy and pungent, against the mosquitoes that cluster under the pines of The Colony, we trudge down Briar Road, through a thicket of sumac where snakes wriggle onto the path, across Route 1A, up to the bathhouse. There, in stuffy dim stalls, we pull on our swimming suits and rush out onto the beach, prancing across the scorching sand to an empty spot for laying out blankets, towels, thermoses, Copper-tone, a rickety canvas umbrella, low canvas chairs. Straight on down to the water, Mother calling, "Don't go in yet, girls! Wait for me!"

The water is usually icy. By the time I'm a teenager, I'll scarcely be able to coax myself in beyond the ankles. Every so often, though, with a stiff onshore wind, water from the Gulf Stream will surge in, almost tepid. I like low tide better than high tide, when the beach is narrow and tall waves hump up and break hard, spewing pebbles and seaweed. The ebbing tide leaves behind puddles that warm in the sun, damp sand for castles, long tapered trails of pebbles where you can sometimes find bits of broken glass, pounded smooth and milky, light green and amber and aqua and, if you're terrifically lucky, red or dark blue. We pull long strands of kelp behind us like rubbery rust-colored tails. We pop seaweed bubbles that spray us with brine.

Over toward Plaice Cove we clamber over smooth rocks collecting periwinkles and tiny blue-green crabs in our buckets. Sometimes, if you hold his shell long and quietly enough, a snail will ooze back out of his tiny house and slide across your palm, bobbing his eye stalks. A crab is harder to catch. You have to turn a rock over, *slurp*, and plunge your hand quickly into the pool underneath before he digs into the sand. Sometimes you get pinched, but not hard. When our fingernails and toenails and lips are blue and we're shuddering too hard to stand upright, we run back up to the grown-ups and bury one another in baking sand until the heat seeps luxuriously straight into our bones.

Sometimes the grown-ups pack a picnic and we stay on the beach for lunch, waiting a whole hot, restless hour afterward before going back into the water, but usually we go back to The Cottage. The walk home is twice as long as the walk down, even though we sometimes take different routes for variety. Our bodies, alternately chilled and baked, droop under the weight of wet towels. Sand grinds in our crotches, between our toes. Once, Janice steps on a snake. Our 6-12 has long since dissolved in the sea, and mosquitoes feed at our shoulders, on the backs of our knees.

Finally, we're there. We line up at the big rock beside the house to have the sand hosed off. The water feels icy trickling down my back, though Mother insists it's perfectly tepid and I'm just being silly. After we're dressed, we rinse out our swimming suits and hang them on the line in the backyard. Low wild blueberry bushes grow here, and we check to see if any new berries have gone from milky green to rose to dusky blue. They are tiny and tart, and we infinitely prefer them to the fat cultivated fruit, mealy and sweet, that tourists can buy at roadside stands. Even on fine days, swimming suits take a long time to dry out here under the pines, and no matter how many suits you have, at some point you get stuck, shivering with dread, having to pull on a damp one, clammy on your buttocks and across your warm belly and chest.

After lunch we all lie down for a rest. Our room, tucked up under the roof with windows at the back, is stifling and dim. Sometimes Sally falls asleep, her thumb in her mouth, her sun-bleached hair darkening with sweat. Sometimes she stays awake and twitches restlessly. "Is it time to get up yet?" she wails every few minutes until Mother sighs, "All right, for the love of Pete, get up!" I don't know who Pete is, that's just something she says. My father's name was Jack. I spend rest time chewing my fingernails and reading.

On a good day, we get to go back to the beach after rest. One overcast afternoon we walk down in our clothes, not intending to swim. But despite the clouds, the air is mild and the water at extreme low tide, absolutely smooth and almost opaque like a greenish pearl, is warm. Mother lets us strip off our sunsuits and wade into the water in our white cotton underpants. I lie on my back, the buoyant, milky water lapping my bare chest, savoring the strangeness of the light, the still air, my mother's surprising permission.

Someone takes a snapshot of Sally and me in the enameled metal shower stall. When we're both in our forties, sitting in a bar with a few friends, Sally fishes the photo out of her wallet, and suddenly there we are again, forever: two glistening little bodies with round tummies and plump penivuses, our giggling faces peering from under huge rubber bathing caps. I can feel again the prickle of water on my shoulders and the grate of sand under my heels, hear again the separate resonances of water on metal sheeting and on the rubber stretched over my head. I thought the photo was long since lost, but Sally will never be the sort who loses anything.

As the family grows, Pop buys a little fishing shack, tall and narrow, covered with red shingles, to use as a guest house. He has it brought in on a truck and set on blocks in the backyard. It makes a good place to play on rainy days. Sally and I beg to be allowed to sleep out there, and Mother settles us in with blankets and flashlights. We feel terrifically grown up. But we're always too scared to make it through the night.

When Garm and Pop are with us, as they usually are, they sleep later than we do, and we have to be quiet until we hear their voices. Then we can open their door and fling ourselves into their room at the head of the stairs. They have a tall ceramic pot painted with flowers, the "thunder jug," with tinkle in it, and we like to pull down our panties and add to the yellow collection. They have three-quarter beds side by side, big enough for little girls to climb into, though the mattresses are stiff and crackly. Maybe they're made of straw. I don't like to climb into Poppa's bed because he rolls over on top of us and roars in his deep voice, "Pig pile! Pig pile!" Sally shrieks and giggles, but I'm terrified of suffocating and I scramble free. Poppa always hangs his trousers from the top drawer of his dresser. One of his middle fingernails is horny and yellowish brown. He slammed in it a window or something. Looking at it makes my stomach roll over. Later, both my little toenails will thicken and toughen like that, though I never slam them in anything, and I will shudder to touch them.

When Garm gets up, she always puts on a flowered cotton dress. These button up the front, but she always holds them backward by the shoulders and steps into them, then twists them around and puts her arms into the sleeves. Everyone has asked her why she dresses this way, but she doesn't explain.

Garm has diabetes. In the refrigerator are little bottles of clear fluid with reddish rubber caps. Every morning she boils a glass syringe and a needle in a white enamel saucepan on the oil stove. Then she sticks the needle through the rubber and sucks some insulin into the syringe. Sometimes she lets us watch these preparations. But never the injection itself. No one has ever seen her give herself a shot, Mother says. At least once I peer through the kitchen door and see her with her skirt pulled up, one leg up on a bench, but her back is to me and I can't see her hands.

Walking is good for her diabetes, the doctors say. So every night, after dinner, we smear on a fresh layer of 6-12 and head off on a ramble along the dirt roads of The Colony and sometimes beyond. "Good evening," we all say to anyone who happens to be out in a yard, and occasionally the grown-ups stop to chat. Once

Garm and Pop even go to a cocktail party in the rose garden of a cottage down the street, dressing up incongruously in their Exeter clothes, but mostly we keep to ourselves. Sally and I occasionally play with the Door girls, Nancy and Betsy, from the next cottage. And one summer I make friends with a girl who lives in a tall old summer house down on Raspberry Lane. She has reddish blue lips and fingernails, as though she had always just come out of the ocean after staying in too long, but in fact she's never allowed into the ocean at all. A "blue baby," Mother calls her. Something the matter with her heart. When I'm with her, I feel nervous and a little excited, wondering whether she'll die right while I'm there. She doesn't, but the friendship falters under the strain.

On the porch after our walk we sometimes play Hearts in the fading light. On the wall is a thermometer with the Coppertone girl on it, the one whose little dog has pulled her swimming suit away from her plump white bottom. I'm embarrassed to look at it. The wicked slit-eyed black queen shows up in my hand and I lose my breath, compose my face, wait for an opening to pass her along. When it comes, I go limp. I like to win.

Later the grown-ups listen to the Red Sox game on the radio or play bridge, often both at once. Sally and I spy on them through our half-open door or, if we're sleeping downstairs, through cracks in the walls. They drink beer and smoke cigarettes. Their talk is full of homers and flies and no trumps and doubles and slams, grand and baby. We haven't any idea what they mean so the words thrill us.

Sunburn. Every summer begins with it. Maybe that's why, at The Cottage, I feel myself all surface, a vast stretch of skin stroked by damp air, scratchy fabrics, trickles or gushes of water. Mother slathers us with Coppertone and scrutinizes our bare shoulders and yanks our jerseys over our heads at the first pink tinge, but we get sunburned anyway. Sand in the sheets. Brush, brush, brush, but some always lurks behind. Sand in our sunburns, on our damp backs and behind our thighs where they press the sheets. Mother goes out for a night of fun in the amusement park at Hampton Beach and comes home with Noxzema, wakes us, restless and feverish, rubs the pungent cold white goo all over us. It doesn't kill the pain, but we feel important being waked in the night as though we were an emergency. Later the pain and flush vanish and our skins darken, Sally's rose-brown, mine gold-brown. At the end of the summer her tan fades prettily. I turn yellow.

Though the rooms are usually bursting with family, I am often lonely at The Cottage. Of course, I am often lonely wherever I am. But here I feel worse because Sally and Seth Junior, a year apart in age, usually exclude me, jeering, from their games. One morning I sit in a canvas chair out front under the trees, pretending to read but actually sniffling and planning how to run away from this cruel place after a particularly painful attack.

"Do you want to come with us?" Mother's voice sounds unusually tender, and I am at once embarrassed and grateful to realize that she feels sorry for me.

"Where are you going?"

"To Durham to see Joel's new baby."

"Oh, yes!" I leap up. My book flies in one direction, my misery in another. "Yes, please."

Joel has just got out of the hospital in Boston after his stroke. While he was there, he and a woman called Penny, whom I don't know, got married. That was in the fall. Now Joel and Penny have a new baby.

Joel is staying at The Cottage and Penny lives with her parents in another town. This arrangement seems queer to me. I always thought married people lived in a house of their own, but Joel and Penny aren't ready, Mother explains. Later I will think how young they were, barely into their twenties, I suppose. I will try to imagine entering married life with a new baby and a young husband still partially paralyzed, but I won't do a very good job. *You never know what you can do,* my own experiences will teach me, *until you have to do it.*

Joel comes out of the house with Garm and swings his legs slowly down the steps. Garm gets behind the wheel, Joel beside her; Mother and I climb into the back.

"Do you want to drive?" Garm asks him when we're in sight of Penny's house. She helps him move over and gets in the passenger's side, and he rounds the corner into the driveway. Penny runs out, exclaiming at the sight of Joel at the controls, almost crying.

The house is small, a little run-down, and filled with baby things. I'm most impressed by a cuff you can plug in for heating a bottle. No, I'm most impressed by the baby. I've hardly ever seen one before, and Buddy seems awfully tiny and frail to me, though everyone keeps exclaiming, "What a big boy!" I try to sit close to him as he gets passed from one person to another.

We don't stay very long. Joel says good-bye to his wife and his little son and gets back in the car. They will live together eventually for many years in California's more merciful climate, where Joel becomes a technical assembler and later, finishing college by correspondence, works at Port Hueneme. They'll have three more sons and two daughters; the last three I'll never see. Joel's Valium addiction will finally drive them apart, and Penny will stop sending Christmas cards, and so I'll never learn how their story turns out.

After Pop sells his Chevrolet business, he and Garm keep The Cottage for summers, but they rent the house in Exeter, keeping only a couple of rooms at the back for a pied à terre, and spend winters in Florida. The year Sally and I are nine and eleven, they invite us to spend Christmas down there with them. Since Mother just got remarried, the idea is to give the newlyweds some time to themselves, I figure. I feel very nervous. After our exceptionally peripatetic early childhood, Sally and I have hardly been anywhere, except for one trip with Mother to Washington, D.C., of which I remember nothing except that I found a five-leaf clover. Even an overnight stay at a friend's house disorients me. How can I find my way and retain my identity in a place I've never seen before? At least Sally's coming, too. Together, surely we can't lose ourselves.

Two weeks go by in a jumble of unfamiliar images: The flight from Logan to Fort Lauderdale, whiled away with games on a miniature checkerboard. Dinner at Howard Johnson's on the way home from the airport, something queer and crunchy called hush puppies served with the fried clams, tasting strongly of onions and oldish grease. Garm and Pop's house, stucco painted chocolate, strawberry, and vanilla like those blocks of harlequin ice cream sliced for parties. Coconut palms, whose slender smooth trunks and glossy-husked fruit I haven't seen since my father was alive. A pair of beloved black corduroy bermuda shorts, my first, which Garm lets me select and buy, though their boyishness troubles her ever after. A freakish cold snap. Tropical birds screeching in an aviary. An endless New Year's Eve party with some "young people my age" Garm has found for me, where I sit in my taffeta dress from Mother's wedding, listening to their odd drawling speech, and no one asks me to dance.

One incident stands whole and clear. A picnic on the beach. Watch out for the Portuguese man-o'-wars, everyone tells us, so Sally and I dance around practically on tiptoe, as far as we can keep from the water's edge. It's too cold for swimming anyway. A large group of Garm and Pop's friends has gathered. One of the men kisses me square on the mouth, and my whole body shrivels inward to form a tight, sick, dark core. All at once, the chattering group around me recedes until I can't hear their voices at all. Even Sally has disappeared. I am alone at the white edge of endless waters through which translucent bubbles trail venomous streamers. One sting, and you're dead.

Over the years I will explain my response to myself: Mother had just remarried, entering a union I knew, though not explicitly, to be sexual; young for my grade, I hadn't yet started menstruating, but some of my friends already had; I was curious and nervous and still in the dark about sex; in a manner typical for my age, I misread an old man's affectionate gesture. These explanations will all be, in their own way, true. None of them will erase this revulsive shrinking from an old man's mouth on a chilly Florida beach the December I'm eleven. After that I avoid the man. I don't laugh at his jokes. I don't answer his questions. He likes me, I can tell, but I—always greedy for approval, affection—I can't respond at all. Garm thinks I'm rude. I can feel her embarrassment. I can't tell her what's wrong. I will never tell anyone, except possibly one day my husband. I will bear that kiss on my lips, and my shame in my flesh, alone, ever after.

Still, whatever its dislocations and dangers, the vacation isn't wholly a loss. Garm and Pop cherish us, and grieving at parting from them, Sally and I make a subdued flight home. Images that seemed startling, exotic, when we encountered them glow now with the familiarity of memories. Sun. Bright birds. Bougainvillea. The gray clouds above Logan bear down with the weight of cold metal. The wet wind pries under our coat collars and up our sleeves. For the first time in my life I have an inkling that the world holds other places (especially warmer places) to be, and I yearn to be there. You can leave home without either running away or getting lost. Entering new space, you can open yourself and let it enter you, pour in, mingle, incorporate itself into the new person you are once you've been there. I'll still hate leaving home. I'll always believe myself in danger of dissolution. But gradually I'll learn to light out anyway for the delayed satisfaction of having gone.

* * *

Garm dies. That's the end of life at The Cottage for me, though it's the only one of my childhood homes that remains in the family and I continue to go there occasionally. Aunt Sadie and Uncle Leonard will winterize it and live there for several years, and later Aunt Nora and Uncle Seth will retire there, building a big garage with a cupola that sports a rooster weather vane and converting the funny little bedroom overlooking the kitchen into a laundry/bath. "Come for a visit," they say. "Come anytime." But after Garm's death, it becomes someone else's house, not my own.

The last summer I stay there with Garm, the summer I turn fifteen, I have no idea that she will be dead long before the next one, though she has some idea herself. Although I no longer spend whole summers at The Cottage, that summer she has me with her more than usual, because Pop has gone off on one of the business trips I have by this time figured out are binges, and we talk more. She loves all her grandchildren, but for me she holds a separate warmth, not just because I'm the first but because I'm the one who reminds her of my father. During the summer she even speaks about her death more than once, but I only laugh and tease her, unable to imagine losing her. She has developed heart trouble, though, and the evening walks have had to end. If I go to the beach, I go alone or with the Door girls. I accompany her on trips to the doctor and stay awake with her when she has a bad night.

Ignoring these signs, I say good-bye to her at the end of the summer, but not "good-bye." I don't even know that word. I was too young when my father died, and anyway he never gave anyone the chance to use it. Garm's death teaches it to me. On November 22, 1958, back in Florida for the winter, she slips off in a diabetic coma. When I hear that she's dead, I'm stabbed by remorse: she's always loved my letters, and I haven't written her one for weeks. Now I've lost the chance. I can't atone. But I'll spend the rest of my life shooting off "last letters" to my loved ones to ward off fresh sin.

The funeral takes place in the big cream-colored Congregational church in Exeter. Mother keeps Sally and me out of school. The day is bitterly cold, and under my coat I wear a short-sleeved navy blue dress in a fabric too thin for the season, but it's the darkest garment I own. I've never been to a funeral before. To my horror, Garm lies in an open casket banked with flowers at the front of the church, and after the service someone leads me forward to look at her, lying on her back in a dress I know well, her thick bluish hair as always perfectly waved, her features sharp in her lined, emaciated face. I would prefer to remember her some other way.

The next morning, in an icy rain, we drive up to The Port, weave slowly through the empty town, and commit her body to the plot of ground next to my father. "We have lost but she has gained," Auntie B tells me with a hug. "She is with your daddy now." This is not a funereal formality but a statement of genuine solace. Ever since Daddy died, he has occupied a place for me, elsewhere to be sure, but intact. Now Garm has gone elsewhere too, to the same location: up there, mother and son reunited, leaving me behind, down here, alone. Then, and thereafter, a part of me will want only to wander out to join them.

"236"

i

MOTHER AND GRANNA are building a house. Actually, several men in denim overalls and plaid flannel shirts and heavy boots, with hammers and tape measures hung on their sagging belts, are building it. But this is what Mother and Granna say: "We're building a house in Enon." Now that Grandma Virchow and Daddy are both dead, the two women are alone. Mother, of course, has Sally and me, but we don't make her any less alone in this sense. The company of children is not necessarily bad, we gather, but neither is it sufficient. Something in us is lacking. Ideally, this lack is banished by a man, we know—a Pop for a Garm, an Uncle Kip for an Aunt Jane—but Mother and Granna have lost their men. So they've decided to build a house together.

The half-acre they buy is about two and a half miles from the village out on Larch Row. "Row," we'll always have to repeat, "not Road. R-O-W. 236 Larch Row." And there are some larches, with their sad sweeping branches, farther in toward the village, though none right where we live. Only a magnificent silver birch beside what will be the garage and driveway. The road, which winds and dips out of town, climbs steeply and then curves past a rubbly cliff in front of our property, which sits slightly below it. At the back, the land keeps descending gently to a brook, then rises again to woods on one side and, on the other, a ridge with a handful of houses. We can see our neighbors, but only from a distance.

We drive down from Exeter periodically to visit the house-in-process. First a muddy gouge in the ground with piles of brown dirt humped up here and there. Then a deep concrete-walled cube with little window frames sticking up aboveground. A red brick chimney. An airy frame of fragrant boards. Walls. Six-over-six windows. Shingles, painted gray, and white trim and Nantucket-blue shutters. A little covered front porch with trellises on either side.

At this point we can move in. The tan plasterboard walls wear buttons and belts of white Spackle and a sickly yellowish wash of primer. The floors have been varnished, though they're still tacky and we have to keep to pathways of brown paper laid from room to room. Mother and Granna will finish the rest of the interior themselves. They paint miles of white trim. On boards laid across sawhorses they lay out wallpaper and slap it with big brushes dripping with rheumy pungent paste and fold it and raise it against wall after wall: beige paper, textured like grasscloth, in the living room and dinette; Pennsylvania Dutch, white with red figures, in the kitchen; pink tea roses on gray in the back bedroom; huge gladioli sprays in the front bedroom; foolish turquoise fish wearing life rings in the bathroom. They have chosen these designs from heavy square books. I would have chosen differently, but I'm not building a house. Upstairs are two more large bedrooms, one for Mother and the other for Sally and me, and a half bath. But Granna and Mother have run out of steam, and these walls remain bare for several years.

Having tracked these steps closely, I understand now where a house comes from. It is not an excrescence of the ground, like a toadstool or a tree. It is not, like a cave, the purposeless outcome of some absolutely different process which is later discovered and adapted for human use. It is an intentional object, constructed out of need but even more out of desire. If Mother and Granna can build a house, so can I. I too can enclose space and make it beautiful (if I leave out the little red hearts and the foolish fish). From now on, I have a passion for floor plans, for paint chips, for swatches of paper and fabric. They are the stuff of dreams.

For now, however, I have to live in Mother and Granna's house. I'm only a little girl. And just as I have to sit on the rose-carved horsehair sofa covered in dusky pink velveteen, whether

I find it comfortable or not, I have to live according to the rules they prescribe, which form a ghostly structure of permissions and restraints: doors and windows, sometimes open, sometimes shut, and solid walls through which no one can pass. Because the eight years I live here, from nine to seventeen, are the ones during which learning the layout of this ghost-house is most critical, I have a more complicated relationship with 236 than with any other dwelling. I am at once terrified of and seduced by the outside world, and so 236 functions alternately as a cherished refuge, whose rules like its walls protect me from the unknown, and a despised prison where I chafe and suffocate.

ii

Only when alone can I feel at ease, even though I sometimes long for company of a sort I have yet to find except, occasionally, with Sally: the sort that doesn't make you wonder if what you've just said or done is making people snigger inside. Alone, I inhabit a world shaped by magical belief, and the stories I tell myself about myself flow clear and continuous, without the obliterating static conversation creates. For months I take my beautiful, slender, dark-haired doll Cynthia into bed every night and lie flat on my back staring into the dark while I *will* her to come alive, to breathe and rouse beside me and become a perfect tiny secret companion who will dissolve my loneliness. I work so hard that I stop breathing myself and my whole frame stiffens, the two of us lying side by side rigid as dolls, but when my breath shudders back and I roll over to touch her, she is still cold, the bristles on her eyelids flat against her cheeks, and I believe myself at fault. If I wished hard enough, if I believed in my own power of wishing, she would live, I just know she would.

I wish to see the fairies, too, with no greater success. They live in the broad round holes, about six inches deep, sunk mysteriously into the field dotted with cedars next to our house. I lie belly down on the long, straw-colored grass, rigid again, breathless again, peering over the edge to catch them out. The holes are lined with dead grass and pebbles and dark moss, a miniature of the winter landscape around me, and the fairies live in the caves pocking their sides. Sometimes I almost catch sight of one flitting from behind a hummock of moss into cliff-shadow, but I'm never looking in quite the right place. The cold leaks upward through my woolen jacket and pants, through the flesh of my chest and pelvis and thighs, deep into my bones. The little light from the iron sky dwindles. They are waiting, I know. They are waiting for me to clamber up and stumble across the stubbly field toward the yellow square in the back door where Mother is baking meatloaf and thick-skinned potatoes for dinner.

Farther down the hill behind our house lies a jumble of granite chunks blasted free when the road was put in. Freckled black and brown and gray, glittering here and there with mica, they still bear tracks and holes for dynamite. One with an angled cleft makes a perfect easy chair, except after rain, when I have to scrunch uneasily to one side to keep my bottom dry. Another, broad and flat, makes an ideal operating table for the endless medical emergencies I enact. Sometimes Sally comes down to the Rocks with me, but even then we act out individual scenarios, or settle in separate locations with separate books, rather than playing together. We no longer slide readily in and out of each other's fantasies, and anyway the silence of the brushy scree imposes solitude.

At the first snowmelt, the brook at the bottom of the hill, so small that during a dry summer it vanishes altogether, turns briefly into a freshet. Then I pull on my tall black rubber boots to explore its length from the point where it emerges from under Grapevine Road to its disappearance in the boggy woods. Long golden grasses, frozen all winter but greening now, stream in its current. Otherwise it doesn't hold much life yet. But I love the amber depths of it, and the silvery surface, and its chill tug against my ankles and calves. Year after year, I miscalculate its depth, or slip on the silky weeds, and icy water spills over my boot-tops. Shuddering, I squelch up the long slope toward the back door, behind which Mother is heating Campbell's Vegetable Beef Soup and waiting to tell me that I'll surely catch my death of cold.

Early on, I figure out that Mother doesn't like my solitary forays. "What do you *do* out there all alone?" she asks. With this question, tension begins to grow between the sociable woman, member of Wheaton Club and College Club and church choir and PTA, who plays bridge and bowls and later golfs and serves for a while as the town tax collector, and the introverted girl trapped between her desire to emulate her mother and her greed for silence and solitude.

"Think," I say vaguely. How could I possibly detail the febrile dramas, fraught with the romance my life, like hers, lacks, which I formulate and act out among the Rocks? Or, by contrast, the empty raptness of my gaze into cold weedy water? She'd laugh. Or worse, puff a little air through her lips and turn her face aside, the way she does when she's exasperated. The furrow in her forehead suggests she isn't quite exasperated, but she's not satisfied, either. I get the feeling she doesn't believe me. Either that, or she believes that thinking is another means of catching one's death.

A summer night, hot, still. I am wearing only a full, short-sleeved nylon robe, gray printed with blue and pink ballerinas. Sally and I slip out into the dark and cross the field behind our house to the opposite hill. We can see the hulk of the house, the light through the shaded windows. How did we get past Mother wearing our nightclothes? What are we doing here? I can't tell. Out here in the summer dark, faintly luminous, the moon perhaps backlighting the clouded sky, I feel cut off from the rational world, dumb, all bones and skin and fine down.

An impetuosity, familiar but inexplicable, grasps me. I unbutton my robe and soar, leap after long leap, down the damp grassy hillside, nearly free of gravity, the air stroking collarbone, breast, belly, buttocks, knees, spread toes. My skin prickles at the strange sensation, nakedness outdoors, at night, for no reason. For just the duration of the descent, I feel as though I might sail free of myself entirely.

Most of the time it's winter. When it snows, Sally and I huddle over the radio shushing each other as the list of no-school announcements unfurls. No school in Enon! Hurray! We pull on our woolen snow pants and our hooded woolen jackets, our mittens and scarves and boots, and race outside to build snow men and sweep our arms and legs into snow angels and dig tunnels into the drifts. We have a Flexible Flyer, too, and if the snow isn't too powdery we careen down the long slope behind our house over and over until our clothes are soaked and crusty. Sometimes Mother drives us uptown to the golf course, where some kids have toboggans we can share, and flying saucers.

There's a skating rink uptown as well, by the tennis courts behind the Enon Tea House, and when there's no snow for sliding we go there. I have a good pair of skates, white leather, but no matter how tightly I lace them, my ankles wobble. The blades seem to raise me to a terrific height, from which I peer down in alarm at the ice, black with white powdery scars. I push off tentatively, teetering, rigid with fear of falling. I don't usually fall, but neither do I let go and really skate. My friends swoop and twirl around me. Some of them have real skating costumes, bright bulky sweaters and short circle skirts above flesh-colored tights. In wet winters the swampy areas in the woods around our house flood and freeze, and Sally and I go skating there. Sally skates as comfortably as she dances, striking out, shoulders forward and knees flexed, without any images, as far as I can tell, of falling over backwards and smashing her head into the ice. She doesn't ridicule my timidity, though, and sometimes without a crowd of flying bodies around I almost have a good time.

I never like being cold. The best part of being outside is going back inside, stripping off stiff clothes, fingers and toes aching and prickling, cheeks stinging, hot chocolate sliding past cracked lips, shudders subsiding into sleepiness. The house folds up around me: a place where I can't fall, can't catch my death of anything.

iii

Mother goes to work a few months after we move to Enon, this time as a secretary at Building Blocks School for Exceptional Children. I think that this is a queer name for them, as queer as I will one day find the label "differently abled" when it is applied to my now crooked, limping body, but Mother says that in its literal sense "exceptional" describes them. And it's true that I've never known anyone like them. On days when I don't have school, Mother takes me along to Building Blocks. At first I pull back from the children, from their flailing limbs and husky voices and snotty faces and clinging fingers, from the smell of urine that never seems to come off even though I help to change their damp overalls and bathe them. After a while, though, they stop being exceptional children and become just Marilyn, Sue Ellen, Janet, Dean . . .: the people who live at Building Blocks.

During the summer Mother regularly takes me to Building Blocks to play with Sarah, the daughter of Marian, one of the women who teaches at the school. Sarah is in my grade, though she goes to a different school. Ordinarily, I dislike spending the night away from 236. Owing to an accident at school, however, Building Blocks takes on the protective qualities of home: I fly off the seesaw and land on my head, getting a mild concussion, and since Mother is away from her office on an errand, Marian fetches me and puts me to bed in Sarah's room. Thereafter, I feel adopted, and during summer vacation I beg to stay the night so frequently that before long I've essentially taken up residency, just another exceptional child.

I hate the food there, which runs toward peanut butter and honey sandwiches and orange Jell-O, but Sarah's company makes up for it. An energetic girl with thick brown hair and narrow green eyes, she's a year older than I and a lot more sophisticated. She already has a boyfriend, the brother of one of the Building Blocks residents, who goes to Tabor Academy. She introduces me to teen music, having bought a 78 rpm record of "Sh-Boom," which we play over and over on her little Victrola—"Sh-*boom*, sh-*boom*, ya-da-da-da-da-da-da-da-da-da-da, sh-*boom*, sh-*boom*, ya-da-da-da-da-da-da-da-da-da"—singing along fervently. At home Mother would be screaming at me to turn that wretched wailing off, but this house is so big that when we're up in Sarah's room, the grown-ups can't even hear us. Anyway, there are fewer prohibitions here.

The house is really a converted mansion, set in the middle of wide wooded grounds, with twenty-four rooms and twelve bathrooms. Sarah and I try out a lot of different bathrooms, but our favorite is the one with blue plaster walls on which pout, in bas-relief, red-painted plaster lips. We lie covering ourselves with soap bubbles under the pounding shower until our lungs are choked with steam and our hands and feet turn sickly pale and puckered and rubbery, and even then we don't get out until Marian, weary of pounding on the door and shouting, stomps in and cuts the water off.

One night, drowsy from our long bath, Sarah and I pull on our cotton pajamas and lie on her twin beds talking aimlessly. We're nearly asleep with the lights still on when we hear footsteps stomping up one flight of stairs, then another, and the shouts of Swift and Suzanne, the two other women who teach at the school. Swift is a scrawny woman with dyed black hair, very rich, Mother says, divorced with three children. Suzanne, handsome and pale, has children, too, and a husband, Chaney. Everyone lives here at Building Blocks.

Through the closed door we can't hear their words, but their fury comes straight through. In my family, Sally and I stage shouting matches regularly, but among the grown-ups emotion is so modulated that it vanishes in wisps on the breeze of polite conversation. Hearing the screeches of two women my mother's age freezes me.

Sarah remains calm, though, even matter-of-fact. Swift has fallen in love with Suzanne, she explains, and is trying to get her away from Chaney. Nothing I've been told, nothing I've read, nothing my own body has experienced has revealed to me that a woman can fall in love with another woman, but Sarah assures me that it happens, that it's happening to two women I know, and she has always told me the truth.

"What will happen?" I ask. I have no doubt that those cries up and down the stairways portend catastrophe, but I'm not sure what kind.

"Well, if Swift gets her way, Suzanne will leave Chaney and go away with her."

"What will happen to Building Blocks?"

"I don't know. I suppose it will have to be closed." She sounds kind of resigned, the way she does when she talks about her parents' divorce, as though she thinks difficulties occur inevitably, in the normal course of human affairs, and do not necessarily diminish or disappear no matter what she does. This is a vision I will struggle against literally almost to the death for over a quarter of a century before its plainness and accuracy persuade me to take it for my own and get on with my life.

This is the summer of Hurricane Carol, which Sarah and I also ride out together. We are very excited, but the grown-ups, who apparently went through a terrible hurricane way back in the thirties, seem frightened, especially after a thick tree tumbles across one corner of the house, narrowly missing the plate glass that walls one whole end of the living room and of the master bedroom, used now as a dormitory, above it.

Because the electricity has been knocked out, the pump doesn't work and we have no running water. Everyone needs running water, but exceptional children more than most, so we have to move them all to a borrowed house for several days. Now Sarah and I become useful in a way I, at least, have never experienced before. The children are used to us, and we're good with them. True, sometimes we can't resist teasing Sue Ellen until, lacking language, she grunts and quivers menacingly. "Don't tease Sue Ellen," the grown-ups say. She's sixteen and half again as big as we are, and she has a history of random violent attacks, so we really are putting ourselves in danger. But we do it only a few times. Now, with the disruption of the hurricane, staff and children alike are in disarray, and we join the rest of the staff in soothing and settling the children. "Sh-*boom*, sh-*boom*," we sing, popping Jell-O into their mouths each time they laugh.

With hurricane season, school opens again, and Sarah and I are separated, though I talk with her every night, hunched over the telephone in one corner of the kitchen, my legs wrapped around the rungs of a chair, nibbling on strand after strand of uncooked spaghetti. Since we go to different schools, I never have to worry whether she's the "right" friend the way I do at school, where everybody, me included, wants to be best friends with Patty Fitzsimmons. And Sarah doesn't make fun of me for being smart or clumsy or for wearing funny clothes. She doesn't even seem to notice. I guess after all that time at Building Blocks, she figures everyone in the world is an exceptional child of some sort.

Before long I lose even the telephone contact. Swift has finally prevailed, and she and Suzanne take their children and move away. Marian can't keep the school going by herself. Anyway, she and Chaney have decided to get married and make a new life. Sarah moves with them to High Street in Exeter, not far from Garm and Pop's house, and our visits are pretty much restricted to school vacations. And yet she never moves away from my life entirely. I've long since lost touch with Patty, but from Sarah I get a letter every Christmas. She is as right a friend as my solitary nature will ever permit me.

iv

All of a sudden, right after the Building Blocks summer, Mother gets married. During nearly seven years of widowhood she's had plenty of dates. The only suitor she seriously considered, however, turned out not to like children. He had a great deal of money, with which he planned to send us off to boarding school as early as possible. Mother may not find our company sufficient, but she seems fond enough of it. She decided to keep us around awhile longer, and so the rich man got sent off himself, back to his big house in Cincinnati.

This suitor has no way of knowing whether he likes children or not, never having known any, but he seems willing to try. In later years I will marvel at the generosity of spirit this willingness suggests: a modest banker, unmarried at forty-one, the sole support of his parents since he was sixteen, how did he dare to leave his now-widowed mother to take on not merely a wife but her two petulant prepubescent girls as well? When I'm even older than he was on his wedding day, I'll suspect that he never knew what hit him. He and Mother were introduced by mutual friends over a game of bridge at the end of August. On her birthday, September 24, she removed the miniature Naval Academy ring my father had given her and slipped on a diamond solitaire. On October 23 they married.

I'm terribly excited about the wedding because I get to wear nylon stockings for the first time. Sally still has to wear white ankle socks. I have a white elastic garter belt with a bluebird embroidered on the front. All day the garter belt slides downward over my skinny hips and my stocking seams twist up the insides of my thighs, and finally I tear a hole in one knee so that the next day I'll have to go back to white ankle socks for Sunday School, but at least I've worn stockings under my turquoise taffeta dress and crunchy crinoline, swishing silkily with every step.

Granna gets so flustered at being the mother of the bride again that she climbs into her dress before removing the hanger and stands shouting, hunchbacked, till we work the wire free of her plump shoulders.

We go to the church. Mother is wearing a blue knit suit, the yoke appliquéd with sequins and seed pearls, and a small beige hat trimmed with pearls and a little veil. I am already as tall as she is. Aunt Jane is her matron of honor. They stand up at the front, under the pulpit, the groom and his brother beside them. I'm not sure what they're saying. They sort of whisper.

Then we all surge out of the church into the cold autumn afternoon and come home again for little sandwiches and wedding cake. "Wrap a piece in a napkin and tuck it under your pillow," someone tells me, "and you'll dream of your future husband," but the trick doesn't work. My future husband remains undreamed of for seven more years.

Before the newlyweds go off to Split Rock Lodge in the Poconos of Pennsylvania, Sally and I approach them. "What shall we call you?" we ask the man we've known for two months as Mr. Cutter.

"Oh." His eyes widen. "I don't know. Would 'Daddy' be all right?"

So Daddy it is. Of course, our own father was Daddy, too, but that doesn't seem to be a problem. We're not likely to get the two of them mixed up.

After they've gone, I am wracked by unexpected grief so intense I vomit on the floor. Poor Granna cleans up and puts me to bed and feeds me sips of ginger ale, but I yearn for Mother, though of course I say nothing, then or ever. This is the relation to speech adopted by my family. You may prattle (indeed, should prattle in order to fill silences that might otherwise turn awkward or productive) all you like, but you must not express emotionally troublesome thoughts: fear of losing your mother's full affection, say, or uneasiness at being forced to live with a stranger, especially a man, even a nice man. By the time of Mother's marriage, I know well which utterances are permissible and which are not. I have no trouble with the joy I feel at seeing Mother happy in a way new to me, or with my excitement at having a normal family like my friends. I swallow the impermissible feelings bravely, like milk of magnesia, before they quite erupt into my mind. What spews forth is vomit, not forbidden words.

This new grief, this unutterable grief, this sense that the known world has once more shifted and shattered, that nothing will ever be the same, or as good, again, will live in my gut like a silent parasite through more years than I can, at the age of·eleven, imagine. Change, once difficult, threatening catastrophe, is now intolerable: catastrophe itself.

When Mother and Daddy come home from their honeymoon, we leave Granna to decide what to do with the house at 236 Larch Row while we move into the second floor of an old white colonial with green shutters in the center of town. Enon is picture-postcard pretty, the sturdy steepled white clapboard First Church Congregational at one end of a little village green, across Main Street the white clapboard town hall, next to it the steep-roofed Claflin-Richards house with its dark clapboards and tiny diamond-paned windows, the only structure remaining from the town's seventeenth-century settlement. Main Street is lined with eighteenth- and nineteenth-century houses, set back under maples and elms. Outside of town are vast estates, with gatehouses and stables of hunters and polo ponies, but no one I know ever goes there.

Within walking distance of school, church, town hall and library, post office, and the homes of all my friends, able to join activities thought up on the spur of the moment without depending on Mother for transportation, for the brief time we live here I feel part of the social world in a way I never will again. It's as though, through a slight shift in literal space, my metaphorical position has become central, not marginal. I've even got two parents. For once I'm not on the outside looking in. In this way, my sense of catastrophe is ameliorated temporarily. I associate this respite with living in town, and ever after I'll dislike the thought of rural life.

I am waiting for my period. I know I'm going to get it, because Mother told me just before I went to summer camp the summer I turned ten, following up her presentation with the gift of a paperback called *The Stork Didn't Bring You*. In this I'm luckier than my friend Sal, the tall, rangy, redheaded girl who used to go to North Shore Country Day School but has joined us public school kids for junior high. Though we're in the same grade, she's two years older and has it already. But her mother never told her, just handed her a pad and a belt wordlessly when Sal whispered that she'd hurt herself, terribly, down there. When Mother told me, she enjoined me strictly not to tell anyone else, especially my sister. Telling was a job for mothers. But in Sal's case I make an exception, and between me and the Kotex movie at school she gets enough information to cheer up a bit, though she still throws up every month.

As for me, I'm impatient. I'm at least a year younger than the other girls in my grade, and I don't want to be left behind. I, too, want to shriek and dive when some boy grabs my clutch purse and threatens to peek inside. Soft brown hair has started growing in my armpits and on my penivus. Mother gives me a heavy old razor and Granna buys me a jar of Yodora to rub under my arms. My breasts are beginning to grow, too. At first I was scared, because the left one started to swell and hurt after Sally jabbed it with her elbow trying to beat me through the front door and I thought she'd given me cancer. But Mother said to wait a little, and sure enough the other one started to swell too, though it never does get as big.

Mother buys me some white cotton-knit bras to replace my undershirts, so now boys can grab snappily at the backs of my blouses, too. I hate these bras, though. Not so much because they're uncomfortable, riding up and down my chest with nothing to hold them in place, as because they're ugly. One night Granna brings me a pink satin bra that hooks in front, which somehow manages to create a little cleavage, and then I'm fulfilled, even if my bras aren't. Trapped in a convention designed for some other woman's bodily reality, I'll go on harnessing myself into one and yanking it down from its stranglehold on my throat until I'm nearly thirty.

Happily, my period starts fairly early, just before I turn twelve. I'm prepared. My blue box of Kotex and my white elastic belt with the metal clasps on each end are stowed in my bedroom closet. Then, of course, I'm nowhere near my bedroom closet when it starts. I'm spending a few days with Aunt Jane and Uncle Kip. I peer anxiously at a brownish spot on the crotch of my underpants. Oh no. It can't be. But the next time I go to the bathroom, a couple more spots have appeared. And a couple more the time after that. I can't ignore them. They're not going away. Composing myself, I tell Jane I'll have to borrow a belt and some Kotex. I'm too embarrassed to tell her it's the first time, and apparently my composure is convincing, because she's surprised when Mother tells her later.

It's not much of a period. Just some rusty streaks on a pad for a couple of days. No matter. I've got it.

Not too long afterward, as soon as I come home from summer camp, Mother sits me down on the living-room couch. She is wearing a white skirt with big pink, red, and navy polka dots. Her manner is subdued, serious. She tells me that she and Daddy are going to have a baby. They hope it will be a boy, but if it isn't, they'll try again.

A baby!

Apparently she's read that an older child is sometimes upset and embarrassed by a mother's pregnancy, and her manner is tentative. But I haven't read the same book. I think the idea of our having a baby is thrilling, and I don't care what my friends think, though it turns out that they think it's thrilling too, and this pregnancy becomes a kind of shared eighth-grade project. Mother makes herself some skirts with holes cut out of the front and some wide tunics and goes around for months looking something like a toadstool. Then, sure enough, she goes off to the hospital and produces a fat, ruddy baby with wandering blue eyes and pale hair like a blown dandelion.

Though he's got a proper name, we call him Chip. My

Chip-a-dee. I love him more than I've ever loved anything else. My dolls. My fathers. My sister. Even Mother. I am beside myself with love.

With a baby, our apartment on Main Street, already cramped, becomes impossible. Granna hasn't yet sold 236. So Mother and Daddy arrange to add on two bedrooms and a half-bath for themselves and the baby. Granna will put in a little kitchen and move into the two large rooms upstairs. She papers the living room/kitchen in a small, neutral geometric print and the bedroom in deep green splashed with yellow and white daisies, and settles in snugly, with her own little stove and refrigerator and table and television, though as a rule she eats dinner with us.

This arrangement, throwing three generations of women together with a man we still hardly know and an infant, creates an emotional chaos, ill controlled but unacknowledged, of course. At the center, stone-silent, sits Daddy, about whom everyone complains, especially Granna, who is none too fond of men. He bears our verbal batterings almost wholly without recrimination. Once, awash in a flood of adolescent whining, he tells me to shut up. A few years later, when while learning to drive I turn a corner too sharply and the car lurches up over the curb, he clutches the dashboard and shouts, "Jesus Christ!" Two outbursts in all our years together. The price of this restraint, however, is an emotional absence as a result of which I'll have trouble recognizing that my words and actions have genuine power to wound.

More often than not, I treat Daddy as a colossal inconvenience. Or I act as though he simply weren't there. Eventually, for instance, he has to ask Mother to suggest that I put on a robe over my bra and panties when I wander around the house. Growing up among women, I've seldom given underwear a thought unless I was out in public. Now, with Daddy around, I'm always sort of out in public, apparently, and I have to learn a modesty I don't feel. Perhaps, as psycholanalytic theory would probably have it, I'm being seductive, but during later reflection, I'll suspect a truth I like less: that in attempting, through ignoring, to efface him, I never even perceive him as an authentic object of seduction. The others in the household, like me although in different ways, seem bent on turning him into a cipher.

We women whirl and collide in the storm surrounding this blank eye. Sally and I, three grades apart and in separate schools now, spend little time together except after dinner, when we are required to wash the dishes, and our childhood arguments turn rancorous. Once, she wallops me over the head with a cast-iron frying pan. She and I both fight with Mother in our different styles. She erupts, shouting and stomping and slamming doors, to emerge shortly as sunny as the landscape after a summer squall. I vanish in floods of weeping, and once I've closed the door behind me, I can't get out again. Sometimes hours go by. I just do not know how to reenter the social world, and no one from that world is about to come rescue me. Mother has always been very strict about that: no emotional rescue. Each episode cuts me further adrift.

We all fight with Granna. When they're angry, Mother and Granna stop speaking to each other and use me as a go-between. "Tell your grandmother . . . ," says Mother, and I trot up the stairs. "Well, tell your mother . . . ," Granna replies, and down I trot again. Eventually all this trotting strikes me as not just tiresome but silly, and I get up the nerve to quit the job. Granna complains about us. She calls me lazy and selfish. But I'm not lazy and selfish. I'm thirteen. And fourteen. And fifteen. My diary is full of entries like this: "No school. I'd have had a quieter day in school, for I fed & dressed Chip, put thru' 2 loads of wash, burned rubbish, washed dishes, folded laundry, fed Chip again, ironed, & even managed [to write] a letter. . . ." But when Mother is ill or away, "she has the strain of being supervisor," I note. Working five days a week at a job she never much likes, she must find this noisy and disorderly household an added tax on her patience.

The trouble is that we never confront these tensions. No one comes out and forbids us to talk about our anger or explains what might happen if we did speak, but I have a clear premonition of disaster though no idea what form it might take: desertion? divorce? death? I can't even get as far as naming it. I just feel in my bones that it lurks behind our submerged furies. In order to ward it off, we have our several outbursts, get over them as best we can, and resume our routines as though nothing had happened. On the whole, this process works and we all remain functional, I suppose because we persist in loving one another despite our dif-ferences. But the wounds fester. At least mine do. I can't speak for anyone else because they've never told me. I wind up with emo-tional abscesses sealed away under scar tissue which will one day poison the lives of those in the new household I establish: the consequence of refusing permission to speak.

In school, I'm usually afraid. Home, in spite of its occasionally ominous atmosphere, is still home. The people within its walls go on loving me, no matter how bad they say I am. They just do. And I go on loving them. This is what I'm coming to think of as the essence of family: the stubbornness of love. But when I leave home, I can count on nothing.

Right from the start, school in Enon is nothing like the Exeter Day School. On the first day, in the middle of the school year, Sally and I enter the old square two-story structure of cream-colored clapboard, to which the yellow school bus has delivered us, through the boys' door, to the screeching hilarity of the whole rest of the student body, who are not accustomed to welcoming strangers into their midst. This is the first of a tangle of unfamiliar rules, most of them tacit, which we transgress. We learn them as quickly as we can, but the knowledge provides no protection. After all, there may be one more, unspoken, to trip us again. And after that, another. And another. Unlike the Day School, this school is mined with rules.

After the first day, we enter appropriately and hang back until the rest of the girls have clattered up the stairs. Quickly, surreptitiously, we exchange a kiss and then race, breathless, to our separate classrooms before the shrill bell catches us out. For weeks, even at the risk of more jeers if we should be spotted, we comfort each another with these stolen kisses. But they can't protect us from the loneliness and humiliation that, although they diminish over time, may rise again in a suffocating rush as long as we remain out here in the world.

I hunch over my scarred desk with the hinged lid under which lies a morass of textbooks and library books and gnawed yellow pencils and crumpled spelling tests, prefiguring every desk I will ever possess, and ram the metal nib into my wooden pen holder. In the nib is a little square hole. "Be careful how you dip your pen," Mrs. Reever tells us. "A little fairy lives inside, and if you cover her window, she'll get mad and push the ink out and make a blot on your paper." She gives us ruled sheets and writes the practice letters on the blackboard. My teacher at the Day School, educated in England, taught us italic writing, which is no good here. Here we use the Palmer method, all slants and curlicues.

I dip my pen into my sooty inkwell and start a rococo capital F. The fairy gets mad. Phhht! What was under the blot didn't look like an F anyway. Greenish black splotches bloom on my clenched fingers. My vision blurs.

I am so unhappy here that I might burst out sobbing at any moment. But I never do. I couldn't stand the stares and snickers. I go on hunching over my appointed tasks. In sewing, we have to fringe and cross-stitch placemats and napkins; mine are light blue with black and white stitching. Long after all the other girls have gone on to blouses, I am still picking out ragged stitches and putting them in again, the needle sticky with sweat, the cloth crumpled, grayish. In cooking, my white sauce lumps. I might do better at building a bookcase, which the boys get to do, though I doubt it. I am better at academic subjects, like reading and spelling and later Latin, but even those provide little ease or satisfaction. Getting an A on a test is less an accomplishment than a deferral of failure.

The teachers foster our fear. Miss Buker, the principal, scanning the lunchroom with the squinty left eye behind her rimless glasses and silencing us by rapping on the door frame with a fork, the tines bent and splayed, some say from being whacked on bad children's heads. Fat old Mrs. Murray, who ridicules Joey for jumping rope with the girls at recess by calling him "Josephine" for a whole afternoon. Miss Bullis, with her turned-up nose and sagging cheeks that pull her lower lids down from her pale eyes into the baleful expression of a bloodhound without its sweetness, yanking Itchy Summit's hair because he can't remember all of "Breathes there the man with soul so dead . . ."—or any of it, for that matter.

Years later, as we reminisce, my friend Phil will drop his customary gentle manner startlingly: "Miss Bullis was a mean, bitter old bag who taught us nothing but terror!" So Phil felt frightened, too. . . . And what about Natalie Abbey, who sat in front of me and made me turn my paper at an angle so that she could copy my answers? I never understood that. She was smart. She didn't need to cheat. But maybe she did it because she was scared of failing, just the way I was. I never dreamed the others were like me.

I remonstrate with Phil reflexively in the voice my mother habitually used to counter my own complaints about my teachers, but in fact Mother's voice is wrong and Phil's is right. Miss Bullis—and she wasn't alone—used her teacherly authority as a means of forcing compliance and docility. At some point, then or later, Phil, for whom as a male these qualities had less social value, repudiated her attempts to smother restlessness and curiosity in order to shape us into good citizens. My failure to critique her view of the world—a world in which all right-minded people can put the subject and verb of a sentence on a divided line and depend adjectives, adverbs, and prepositional phrases from them—was part of my larger failure to question my own relation to such a world. Virtually all my citizenship grades, the report cards glued among corsage ribbons and Valentines in my scrapbook tell me, were "highly commendable."

Recess provides scant surcease from anxiety. When I first get to Enon, we all troop out, girls through their door and boys through theirs, and cross the street to the field beside the little white American Legion Hall where we have religion classes once a week (all except Robby Brennan, who's Catholic) and Girl Scout meetings. We form two lines, and I tense myself for someone to call, "Red Rover, Red Rover, let Nancy come over," but they almost never do.

The next year we abandon Red Rover, and play becomes segregated by sex. We girls take up hopscotch and jump rope. I have terrible trouble learning to time my jump into the swinging arc, so I usually trip the first time the rope comes around and am called out before I'm ever truly in. I spend a lot of time swinging the rope and chanting the rhymes for others. One, Two, *Three* O'Leary, My First *Name* Is Mary. . . . And at the end, Salt, Vinegar, Mustard, *Pepper*, the rope slapping the asphalt double-time until the jumper finally lags a fraction of a beat and the rope sags in tangles around her ankles. Gradually I catch the necessary rhythm and get my full turn at bounding until I'm breathless, though I never get the hang of Double Dutch.

Boys, forbidden to jump rope, play marbles, which is all right for girls to do, too, and for a while we all sport drawstring bags dangling from our sashes, which thump and click against our thighs. I love the marbles, especially the translucent colored ones, saffron and aquamarine, and the clear ones with a swirl of opaque color, but not the milky mottled ones. I don't enjoy risking their loss, though, so I usually squat beside the circle scratched in the playground dirt and watch the boys flick theirs around.

After we start junior high, when instead of playing organized games at recess we hang out aimlessly, I can stop fretting about my lack of physical prowess. But I go on worrying about popularity, which eludes me. At first I have a best friend, Mary Wilder, a freckled girl with short brown hair who lives in an old farmhouse near the railroad tracks with her old father, a fat good-humored balding man with a fringe of gray hair and wire-rimmed glasses who sometimes drives the school bus. Her mother is dead. My father is dead, too, but for a long time no one knows that, even Mary. I'm too embarrassed to admit it, so when any of my class-mates ask about him, I say he's in the navy. That suffices to explain why they never see him, apparently. Maybe their parents finally explain about him, because after a while no one asks anymore.

Somehow I know, however, that Mary isn't the "right" sort of best friend, the one I want whom everyone else wants too: Patty Fitzsimmons, a little plump girl with short, shiny brown hair and brown eyes. She lives with her mother, father, and older brother in a handsome brown house where she has her own bedroom with a double bed and a glass cabinet displaying a dozen untouched Madame Alexander dolls. As soon as he turns sixteen, her brother gets a pink and gray Mercury convertible. In the school lunchroom we girls elbow one another out of the way to push up to her and beg, "Can I sit beside you today?" Her nature is so genuinely sweet that, far from handing out her favors like a queen, she earnestly tries to keep track of our turns and grant them even-handedly, so from time to time I get one. Not Mary, though, who doesn't even ask.

Later, in my diary, I will claim Patty as my best friend, but of course she never really is. I'm only wishing. The power she radiates delimits a magical space occupied by some girls and not others. I have no idea how to qualify for admission, and I never will, into this or any other charmed territory. As a result, my position always strikes me as provisional and marginal. Still, slowly I feel myself drawn into Patty's circle, at least tolerated there, and ignoring twinges of remorse, I leave Mary outside.

Late June. School is almost over. Some of us girls are clean-ing the library, which is our old fifth-grade room lined now with dusty shelves of the books our teachers think we ought to want to read. I've read just about all of them. Not a passionate embrace in the bunch, except of Irish setters and black horses swift as the wind. The tall windows have been thrown up to let in the hot, bright afternoon. Leaning out to shake my dustrag, I'm seized by the impulse to clamber over the sill and stand on the ledge below.

"What's she doing?" a voice squeals behind me.

"Look at Nancy, she's crawling out the window."

"Nancy, what are you doing out there?"

"Come in! Come back in! You'll fall!"

I'm not afraid of heights, and I don't feel like falling at all. I don't believe I can fly anymore, and I'm not tempted to let go. I balance there on the ledge, one hand hooked onto the window frame, and look down and out, at the bright grass two stories below, the asphalt drive, the cars in the parking lot, the dusty light streaking through thick leaves. I feel feathery and remote, as though the girls behind me have receded into a dark and distant world from which I might free myself for good, never worrying again about who likes me and who doesn't.

Their shrieks, floating out the window, have attracted the attention of some of the boys walking by, who look up, pointing, with shouts of laughter. I am wearing Mother's full white skirt with the red, pink, and navy polka dots, and it crosses my mind that they can probably look up it and see my white cotton underpants.

The trouble with pulling some weird stunt like this, something you know no one else would ever do, something you wouldn't have thought you'd ever do yourself, is figuring out how to stop doing it. I feel frozen by embarrassment. But I can't keep standing here showing off my underpants. I scramble back over the sill, and after a few more squeals, everyone stops talking about what Nancy did and acts as though it never happened. It did happen, though. They may never think about it again, but it will stay tucked in some fold of their memories, keeping them at a slight wary distance. They're inside, dusting and singing "Party Doll" and fixing one another's ponytails, and I stay stuck out on that ledge forever.

vi

More and more, real life takes place away from home, outside of school, in that dim region, crossed by electric flashes of attention, between boys and girls. One Saturday evening a month, the PTA sponsors a square dance. We girls all put on felt circle skirts with piles of crinolines underneath and sissy blouses with bright bows at the neck. My skirt, blue with silver metal studs, doesn't have a poodle on it, alas, and I never own more than two crinolines at a time, one of white nylon and the other of pink net. Even with such disadvantages, however, complicated by the attentions of Elwood Mulvey, who barely comes up to my belly button, I usually have a good time.

On Wednesday evenings we go to a new dancing school. The old one, on Saturday afternoons at the Community Center, was awful. The teacher, Miss James, so old she'd taught Mother and Aunt Jane though her hair was still bright brown, wore taffeta and tulle waltz-length gowns and clicked a pair of castanets to signal each new dance. Then the boys leaped and slid across the floor, aimed at the girl of their choice, who was never me. Patty and her best friend Hutch wore matching sweater dresses, one mint green, the other blue, and nylon stockings with black flats. I wore black patent Mary Janes with white ankle socks and one of the castoffs from the children of wealthier friends Granna is gifted at scrounging—a rose-beige silky fabric printed with tiny ivory flowers, the gathered waist tied at the back with a bow. Years later I'll think of the dress fondly, knowing it the most distinctive one there, but just now distinction is not my goal. At the new school, Mrs. Warner never admits more boys than girls. In her class, even I get a boy to dance with. She teaches us to tango, cha-cha, and lindy, not just to waltz and foxtrot. I can't dribble a basketball or connect a puck with a hockey stick, and if I turn a somersault I faint with fear. Dancing turns out to be the only physical activity I'm ever good at.

Getting partners outside of dancing class remains a problem, though. People have started pairing off. On a hayride one icy October night, I sit up beside the laconic elderly driver, hunched and shuddering, while the others bury themselves two by two in the hay. For a while I go back and make out with fat Petey Stanley, but by this time I've read *Ramona* and *Ivanhoe* and *Wuthering Heights,* I know what it means to melt with pure true passion, and kissing Petey only makes me feel cheap and sad. At a party in Joany Parson's basement rumpus room we play spin-the-bottle, and Roddy Ames demonstrates to me that it's all right to open your eyes while you kiss, but I am so miserable because no one there I want to kiss wants to kiss me that I rush upstairs to call my parents for a ride home.

This wretched single state has a couple of consequences. One is that I take to writing bad poetry. Writing isn't a new venture, of course, though I've stuck mainly to prose. After my friend Sal returned from a summer in the Tetons, having fallen in love with a Jackson Hole dude rancher named Peter, she commissioned me to write a steamy novel. I don't think either Sal or I knew just what she and Peter were up to in their shared sleeping bag under a starry Western sky—*The Stork Didn't Bring You* was short on concrete detail—but our hearts raced all the same.

Actually, I've been writing some bad poetry all along as well, but now it gets worse. For the rest of my life, I'll have to come to terms as best I can with the knowledge that I've written stuff like this:

> Well, here it is—
> My heart on a string.
> Take it—keep it safe.
> It has given me so much pain.
>
> If you want it
> It is yours to hold.
> With you it is happy.
> If you have it, it can never hurt
>   me again.
>
> I love you. The gift
> Of my heart proves it.
> Please love me—care a little, and
> For you I'll do the same.
>
> We have just met. Our
> Lips have not touched, but
> You're very wonderful—
> I love you, and you are to blame.

Ever after, most of my poems, even some quite good ones, will be called up by the relentless yearning after some man who doesn't want me. Misery my Muse.

The other consequence, more disastrous to me if not to the literary world, is that I fall in love with my science teacher, a handsome, arrogant twenty-four-year-old navy veteran. "Philip W. Natale, Jr.," I scribble over all my papers and book covers. I go into a hectic trance at the sight of his cropped blond hair, the white moons of his fingernails, his smoky gray-green eyes flecked with gold. I think this is what dying feels like. Desperate for his attention, I buzz and dart around his desk, respond to his questions with a newly mordant flippancy, erupt in fits of weeping at the slightest correction. Inexperienced and not awfully bright, he has no idea how to handle this scrawny thirteen-year-old Fury except by punishment; but no insults, no failing grades, no number of hours in detention can quell my desire. "He's mean to me," I record matter-of-factly in my diary, "and I adore him." A dangerous paradigm, this feverish and fruitless ardor that will enable me to write poetry only if I feel like death.

April 11, 1957. A gray afternoon, windy and raw. I've missed the bus again and will have to walk the two and a half miles home. My friend Buddy McKenzie, who lives about halfway, will walk with me as far as his house, but first he wants to help some little boys fly model airplanes. I hang around at the edge of the playing field in front of the Buker School.

Kelly Kane and James Hopper come by on their bicycles and stop to talk. Lately I've been noticing James a lot: a tall, slim boy with even white teeth, a turned-up nose, dark eyes, dark hair spilling over his forehead. He's only in the eighth grade, but that's all right. There are only ten ninth-grade boys to twenty girls, and most of them are creeps, so the girls have been crossing class boundaries.

Perched on the front wheel of James's bicycle, I chatter and laugh and toss my head in a burst of self-confidence. Suddenly from behind me I hear an ominous crunch and whirl around to see Rupert Lillie's old humpbacked black Chevrolet rolling over the books I left at the edge of the drive. No one ever uses this drive. But here's pale, skinny Rupert, my art teacher, with grayish skin, grayish hair, a bobbing Adam's apple above his grayish shirt, peering cautiously as always through his windshield as his tires bump—front: *bump!* back: *bump!*

"My books!" I shriek. "Why don't you watch where you're going? You've squashed my books!" His grayish eyes peer at me through rimless glasses. He's awfully deaf, but too proud (or, more likely, too poor) to get a hearing aid, a fact that doesn't cause real trouble except when he fills in as organist at church, since his uncertain fingers are apt to slide one key over and produce whole phrases, even whole verses, of cacophony. As a rule, his deafness simply means that he's seldom entirely certain what's going on. My wails penetrate, though.

"You shouldn't have left your books on the pavement," he says in his mild, rusty voice.

I'm shivering with irritation and embarrassment, but James seems delighted by the incident. All along, he's seemed on the verge of leaving, but now I settle back on his front wheel, and when Buddy's ready to leave, James walks along, balancing my books and his bike.

The next day six different people whisper to me that James Hopper likes me, but I don't dare believe them. That would be like wishing for your own hi-fi with all the most popular forty-fives— "Blueberry Hill" and "Peggy Sue" and "Love Letters in the Sand"—for Christmas. You know you won't get them, so you don't even let yourself think about them. Otherwise, you'd die of disappointment.

7:10 P.M. The telephone is for me. "Hi," says James. "You didn't believe I liked you, did you?"

"No."

"Well, I do."

This is how simple it is to get into heaven.

I live in heaven for about ten weeks. During that time James and I are nearly inseparable. He lives about as far out of town as I do, but in the opposite direction, so ours is a peripatetic courtship. We ramble through the weeks of forsythia, and then of apple blossoms, and then of lilacs. We talk as though we'd spent all our thirteen years under vows of silence, now miraculously lifted. We hold hands. At dances we dance the "forbidden" way, with our arms around each other. We go off into the woods and kiss. You can kiss for a long time, I discover, if you don't hold your breath. We lie in the new grass of a field, making whistles of blades stretched between our thumbs. We kiss some more.

Suddenly my stock goes up, a phenomenon that may serve as a kind of adolescent validation of Lévi-Strauss's theory that women are commodities whose value depends on their scarcity. Belonging to the handsomest and richest boy in the school certainly seems to confer desirability. Shedd Abbey, whose love I'd have died for a year ago, is suddenly dying for mine. While Adam Wade and I are studying science, he kisses me unexpectedly and asks me to go steady. I feel giddy, giddy, giddy. Still, somehow I know to scribble in my diary, "Better enjoy it—it won't last long!" I am not cut out for the role of what Granna refers to as the Belly of the Ball.

* * *

"236"

All the world may love a lover, but that doesn't include parents. Our parents go nuts. They're never sure where we are. Instead of shunting predictably between home and school, we keep wandering off. We show up at our houses an hour late. They take away our telephone privileges. Mother forbids me to use my bicycle for two weeks and instructs me to "meditate on my sins." Embedded in this cliché is the germ of the matter: they don't know what we're doing.

We're kissing.

I make one of those vows children make repeatedly in the face of parental injustice and break nearly as often under the pressures of parental responsibility: when I have children, I won't sniff suspiciously around their love lives. As it turns out, I'll make good on this one, so good as to embarrass myself silly. Coming home one afternoon, I see an unfamiliar bicycle in front of our house. Matthew's been failing courses, so he's supposed to come home alone after school to study.

"What's going on here?" I demand as I open the door. Stepping inside, I see two pale bodies disentangling themselves on the living-room couch. "Oh," I say. "I see." I flee for the kitchen, slowly pour myself a glass of seltzer water, dial my daughter's telephone number, start to chat aimlessly.

"Mom," she interrupts, "I'm studying for a biochemistry test. Did you want something in particular?"

"No. Not exactly. I'm just trying to give Matthew and Poppy enough time to put on their clothes."

"*What?*" She starts to giggle. I start to giggle. Some years later, when they've gotten over the shock, Matthew and Poppy will giggle, too. They probably thought the worst thing in the world had happened, getting caught having sex by your mother, but the catching, I assure them, is just as bad. Maybe parental suspicion is just a duplicitous form of self-protection.

Graduation from junior high. I wear a white organdy shirtwaist—who knows whose originally—and a Mamie Eisenhower carnation. The June night is hot and filled with mosquitoes. Mother has forbidden me to cry, but I do anyway, sobbing into my sodden lace handkerchief until Davy Russo gallantly offers me his more substantial one. One day he will be a funeral director.

Patty holds the graduation party in her spacious, shadowy backyard. James and I dance for a while and then wander deeper into the shadows, where he holds me upright against his thin boy's body and mops my tears and kisses me until I have to go home.

Except for a handful of phone calls and casual dates a year later, which serve only to reopen my love like a wound, we're never together again. And I will not be happy again in just this way. You can only ever have one love untainted and untutored by loss.

Sorties

i

IN SPITE OF my first, literally lousy, experience, Mother continues to send me to summer camp. She might be motivated, at least in part, by the longing for two weeks or a month free from my prickly presence. More likely, though, she simply believes in the wholesomeness of outdoor living. One summer, during the height of the polio scare, no one believes in this and most camps close down. I spend my time belly down on the living-room rug in front of the radio, listening limply to *Stella Dallas* and *The Romance of Helen Trent*. Other summers, after a week of frantic shopping and ironing and sewing in name tags, I pack my duffel bag and head for the wilderness.

She shifts me to Camp Runels, where she and Aunt Jane and Aunt Lucy used to go. In fact, that's how Aunt Lucy became Aunt Lucy, some years after Mother and Jane introduced her to their handsome if somewhat feckless brother, maybe on Visiting Day, making a match that will always serve me as the model of a durable and affectionate marriage. I don't want to go to camp, and I'm certainly not sanguine about getting a husband if I do, but since I've plainly got to go, Runels seems as good a choice as any.

I'm never particularly happy there, but at least I don't suffer devastating homesickness again, only a constant, mild, uneasy ache, sort of like a month of coming down with the flu. I don't mind sleeping in screened cabins, and I get along well enough with the other girls, though I never make friends with them. I detest the latrines, especially when it's my turn to scrub them with milky disinfectant and a wire brush. And twice a day, whatever the weather, we have to pull on thin rubber caps and, two by two, buddy style, splash into the brown lake. Raised on the ocean, I hate the flat taste of the water, hate the silt squishing between my toes, hate the way I sink, leaden, when I try to swim. To the despair of the waterfront counselors, I never really get beyond the stage of panicky thrashing, and I never, ever learn to dive. At the mere thought of putting my head below my feet, I swoon.

Camp's not all beastly, though. I like arts and crafts, where we learn macramé and wood-burning. And I love nature studies, which sends us off on solitary scavenges through the woods, searching for galls and sweet fern and bundles of needles from red and white pines. I learn to build a tidy log-cabin campfire and light it with one match. I adore roasted marshmallows, sagging precariously from the end of a green stick, caught in burnt fingers, the liquid white center bursting through the golden crust, so sweet it makes me shudder. We sing all the time.

At Runels I experience my first ecstasy. I don't know what else to call it. All the campers have gathered for a Sunday-night campfire in a ravine that, with logs rammed into the steep sides for benches, forms a natural amphitheater. I am sitting quite high up, far from the campfire, which flickers and crackles and shoots resinous sparks spiraling into the dusk. A mist winds off the lake, blurring the trees around us, our own contours, even somehow our high voices as they spiral upward with the sparks. Suddenly the scene seems so beautiful that I nearly stop breathing. I sit absolutely still. I feel as though I am bursting my skin, floating out on the thick blue-gray air. I feel as though I am the scene. Not in it. Not looking at it. It, itself.

I've taken this sort of fit before, I think, but never self-consciously. I'll go on taking them. Slowly circling the house at 236, instead of running straight in, one bitterly cold night when the full moon crackles on the snowy fields. Sitting alone on a beach on Berkeley Harbor at sunset. Hanging clothes at The Farm on a summer morning chilled and clarified by a rush of Canadian air. Gazing from the library steps down the length of the Wheaton campus, across the Dimple, past the rosy brick buildings, through long bars of late light one glittering October afternoon.

These moments give me no end of trouble. In part because, despite the pleasure they bring, they also hurt. Not figuratively.

Broken breath, bursting skull and skin. And also because they isolate me, who am lonely enough already. When I try to articulate my feelings, no one seems to recognize them. People who are kind smile opaquely. People who aren't look at me quickly and then quickly away. Later this won't matter. "Stop the car!" I'll shout when, on the drive home from Nogales, I spot the full moon like a persimmon rising behind the Santa Ritas. George doesn't smile or stare. He simply stops the car. He and the children and I all jump out and watch the moon until it breaks free of Mount Hopkins and soars, paling, into the infinite Arizona sky.

But later isn't now.

Adults, especially the ones in authority like teachers and camp counselors, begin to call me hypersensitive, a label I receive with a mixture of satisfaction and chagrin. I like the idea of sensitivity but not its social consequences. What I don't do is scrutinize the word in its literality: "the responsiveness of an organ or organism to external stimuli." Whenever I imagine my body, I feel bundles of wires stretched tightly from the top of my head down through my chest and belly, out along my arms and fingers, from my hips to the soles of my feet, alternately plucked and rubbed by damp fingers until they resonate and screech. This is how I respond to the world around me, to sights and sounds and scents that are apparently often quite faint: as though I were a stringed instrument, my son's bass viol, perhaps, sometimes in tune but just as often not, played by a flustered and sweaty pupil.

Stripped of its emotional freight, then, "hypersensitive" describes me pretty well. The world reaches me through my senses, especially my sense of smell, with unusual keenness. On a crowded bus with broken air-conditioning in the middle of summer, this condition can render life pretty miserable. But there's nothing intrinsically "wrong" with it, no moral violation, no reason for the shame that has shaped me. In some societies, perhaps in some families in our society, hypersensitivity might be tolerated or even encouraged. I happen to grow up among people who, feeling nervous in its presence, condemn it and discourage me from expressing my responses aloud.

Because I find hypersensitivity hard to acknowledge and talk about, it takes me till I'm past forty to figure out that people whose senses are less sharp are neither stupid nor cruel. They're just different. When George fails to wake in alarm at the smell of smoke drifting on summer air through the bedroom windows, he's not trying to make me crazy by pretending that he doesn't smell smoke, too. In the world of his senses, there simply isn't anything burning. (In this instance, my sensory world is "truer" than his, as the gutted house down the street later proves.) Once I understand that our difference lies on a physiological, not a moral, plane and grasp the absolute plurality of sensory worlds, I find human existence both more charming and more astonishing, though no less difficult, than I'd ever dreamed.

In high school I switch to a sailing camp on Martha's Vineyard, and here Mother's faith in the delights of summer camp is justified, though not in ways she would approve if she could fathom them. Here my senses are as heightened, and my nerves as taut, as they will ever be.

For one thing, the place is staggeringly beautiful. Oh, not the physical plant, I suppose: a large frame rec hall with a primitive kitchen and a screened eating porch; a small frame infirmary; five clusters of olive-drab four-woman tents on pine platforms, each cluster with its own frame washhouse, real flush toilets, and running water in the sinks and showers, though only cold. The whole is set, though, on a bluff overlooking a broad lagoon between Vineyard Haven and Oak Bluffs. At the foot of the bluff is a small sandy beach holding canoes and Cape Cod dinghies; off the beach are moored a dock and six small skiffs, old eighteen-foot wooden-hulled Menemshas later replaced by sixteen-foot Ospreys with fiberglass hulls.

The fact that we're on an island (though admittedly, even in the 1950s, a crowded one) lends life there a castaway quality, remote from the affairs of the mainland and of my quite unsatisfactorily pedestrian existence at home. We've entered a space out of time, an idyll of salt air pungent with pine needles and wood smoke in which girlish voices interweave cacophony and melody into a poetry that pricks and pierces: "Baby owlet, purple owlet, singing as dawn shines above. . . ."

We fill our days with swimming and sailing, and in the first summer we also bicycle more than ten miles a day. I'm still a poor swimmer. I can barely finish the hundred yards required to qualify for sailing. But I'm glad to be back in saltwater, even when it's crowded with tiny, translucent pink jellyfish. I turn out to be a poor sailor, too, unable to sense the position of the boat in the wind, just as later I won't be able to sense where the car is on the road. I watch the Sunday races and the Edgartown Regattas enthusiastically, but only once am I selected to crew in one. Although I'm an experienced and competent cyclist, I have no stamina. I struggle along at the end of the line, gasping and sometimes weeping with fatigue.

I endure all these activities for the sake of love. The first summer I fall in love with Kitty, our unit leader, a sturdy, fair, freckled woman with lively blue eyes. The second summer I fall in love with Josie, another unit leader, darker and quieter, with short wavy hair and glasses. The third summer I try and try, and finally work up a pale affection for a counselor named Renee, but whether because the "right" person isn't there or because, turning sixteen and in love now with a boy named Caleb, I've changed, the magic of those earlier passions eludes me.

"Crushes," I've been taught to call them, these adorations of older people, both men and women, to which I'm prone. The way Mother uses the word makes clear the childishness—and therefore the triviality—of the attachment, and so I try never to speak of them. But though they may be childish, they also prepare a route out of childhood, the yearning toward the depth and complexity of adult bonds. Thus, they're anything but trivial. Indeed, in terms of the obsessive energy I pour into them, they are one of the great forces of my growing.

I never connect my passion for Kitty and later for Josie with the relationship between Swift and Suzanne at Building Blocks. I may know the word *lesbian* by this time, but I never apply it to my own feelings. In view of my essential ignorance about that relationship, which seemed to me, to the extent I thought about it at all, merely violent and disruptive, I suppose this is just as well. At this point, *lesbian* could only be a "bad" word to me.

And in fact, my affections, passionate though they are, lack the fullness I will later associate with lesbian attachments, because they are bodiless. Mother and Granna and Sally and I have always been casual about dressing and undressing in one another's presence, and other women's bodies excite me no more than theirs do. I don't want to touch Kitty's breasts, to put my mouth on Josie's. I don't not want to, either. I just never think of it. Nothing about them triggers the catch of breath I used to feel at the sight of James's bony wrists below his shirtsleeves. If I am ever aroused sexually by either Kitty or Josie, the sensations remain purely somatic, never seeping through into consciousness. It's too late for that, or too soon.

Instead, my passions for these women induce a kind of craziness. They send me dreams so vivid that I thrash inside my sleeping bag and cry out, drawing Kitty to my bedside to wake and comfort me. They make me sullen and reclusive, so that I withdraw from group activities to a sheltered spot on the bluff, where I hunch, ecstatic, composing a poem, until Josie comes, distracted and cross, to fetch me. They induce fits of giddy good humor followed by tantrums and then self-loathing: "If you only could understand how I despise Nancy Smith," I write, "how horrid and loud and rude she is. . . ." By the end of the month, I am worn out, and no doubt Kitty and then Josie are, too.

These sojourns are followed by what I call "campsickness," days of disorientation as I attempt to sever the lifeline I've been thrown by Kitty, by Josie, even by Renee, and to reenter the eleven-month-a-year ordinary world. I characterize myself as depressed, and years later I will recognize my diagnosis as clinically correct: a sense of vagueness and unreality, thoughts circling frantically, the longing to flee back into the lost magical realm, terror of going insane, desire for death.

I do not report any of these feelings of sadness and dislocation to anyone at home, and because no one ever mentions the possibility that I might be feeling them, I assume that they're abnormal and therefore, by definition, bad. This is the 1950s, remember, in a small, affluent town not far from Salem, Massachusetts, where everyone worth knowing shows up every Sunday morning at the Congregational church, the direct legacy of the Puritan fathers. A child here is supposed to be cheerful, robust, sociable, polite, and obedient to elders. She should always look as though she's having a terrific time. She should always *be* having a terrific time. No long faces here.

Even if I did reveal my symptoms to Mother, what could she do about them? Pack me off to Danvers State Hospital, that butt of jokes and occasionally, if an inmate escapes, source of uneasiness and fear? Hardly. This is the woman who will one day refuse to be seen with my son in public for fear of what her friends will think. Granted, he looks a fright, the sides of his head shaved, the remaining hair shellacked into a ten-inch red-and-yellow Mohawk, his body festooned with chains and padlocks and razor blades. My attitude is, If you see the two of us walking together down the street, which one looks the fool? It ain't me, babe. Mother, however, believes that the appearance and actions of her children reflect upon her. She gets embarrassed if someone reports that James Hopper and I were holding hands in front of the post office on Main Street, as though everyone must assume that such a sexually promiscuous girl must have a sexually promiscuous mother. What would they think about a crazy daughter?

For this reason, I can't possibly tell her I feel like I'm cracking up, even if I had the language in which to do so. We do not crack up. To be sure, Aunt Jane is seeing a psychoanalyst, but then, Aunt Jane has always had some weird notions—she's a writer, what can you expect?—and anyway she lives in Boston, so nobody here has to know what she's up to. If I had any sense, I'd tell Aunt Jane I'm cracking up, and I do in oblique ways. There's nothing she can do, but her unstinting love, together with her weird notions, reassure.

Actually, there's nothing anybody can do yet. Psychopharmacology is still primitive. The medication I need may have been invented already, but nobody in Enon, Massachusetts, in 1957, is likely to know enough to give it to me. When I finally do dare to look for help, I get my head shrunk. And shrunk. And shrunk. My biochemistry goes unattended for years.

ii

After my first summer at Vineyard Sailing Camp, almost as soon as I walk through the door, Mother catches me alone and sits me down with her on the living-room couch. She looks a little funny, almost embarrassed.

"We're going to have another baby," she says. "I just found out."

"Huh? A baby? I thought you said that if Chip were a boy you wouldn't try again."

"Well." Her voice drags. "We weren't exactly *trying.*"

"Hmmph!" I splutter. I've finally figured out enough about this baby-making business to find her confession hilarious. "Well, I'll tell you one thing."

"What?"

"I'm never going away to summer camp again. Look what happens when I do."

By now she's thirty-eight, with a toddler to chase, and her pregnancy wears her out. But, exactly two weeks before Chip's second birthday, she produces beautiful Barba, with sparse pale hair, round face, tiny button nose, long fingers and toes, who grows into a dancing sprite. When I celebrate her thirtieth birthday with her, I will still sense this elfin liveliness. As she grows prettier and prettier, Sally and I accuse Mother of saving the best till last. My angular figure and Sally's stocky one will soften into Barba's sturdy voluptuousness; for her, heads will turn and gazes linger as they never do for us. If we were closer in age, we might even feel jealous. But who can envy this golden fairy child?

Barba always believes, I think, that I love her less than Chip. But that's not how it is. The difference is that by the time she enters our household, I feel perched on the rim of it, pushing outward, and perhaps she feels from the outset left behind.

I will go on living at 236 for several more years, and visit there for twenty years beyond that, yet in some sense my graduation from junior high at the age of thirteen marks a departure—I almost said, a betrayal. It's not that I lose my ambivalent love for the house and for the homely life it embraces. On the contrary, the more I strain away from its confinements, the more obsessive my love grows until, when required at last by the conventions of American adolescence to separate myself physically, irrevocably, I almost die of grief. Leaving home will not be for me a step out onto the glorious golden road to independence and autonomy. Fuck independence and autonomy. It will be instead rebirth in the worst possible sense, head thrust downward through ruptured membrane, shoulders and chest and buttocks squeezed and shoved out, out of the bone house, nourishment and oxygen whacked off, the first tremulous breath a howl of pain.

The first pangs begin years earlier, however. They are triggered in part by the pragmatic reality that Enon, which has over the years come to form my matrix, is too small to support a high school of its own. Students must be bused to Berkeley, the small city that bounds it to the southeast. I am thus thrown outward. Simultaneously, reactively, I draw myself inward. Physically timid and socially uncertain, I retreat, beneath a surface acceptably if not ideally "normal," into another sort of matrix, dark, anguished, secretive, where I curve around and protect my self as best I can. In other words, I go further into hiding behind Nancy.

My body begins to betray me. The periods I longed for to make me like other girls rapidly become a monthly assault of nausea, diarrhea, hemorrhaging, and the kind of pain that sucks the whole world down into itself and sets itself up in the world's place. "The curse," Mother refers to the process offhandedly, so of course

I do, too. And that's what it is. Month after month I prowl the chill house in the dark, throwing myself from chair to couch to bed, rocking, panting, moaning. In the toilet, clots bloom like scarlet peonies. Life turns into a gruesome scene of soaked pads, soaked underclothes, soaked bedding.

Finally, when I'm fifteen, Mother decrees that I'm old enough, by some mysterious measure, to use Tampax. Easier said than done. Since I'm going to the YMCA pool every week in an attempt (vain, it will turn out) to earn my Junior Lifesaving Certificate, I'm eager. But hopelessly inept. I've never touched myself down there. Oh, I must have when I was very small, but whatever prohibitions, verbal or gestural, Mother put into place proved terrifically powerful. Not only have I never touched myself down there, I've never thought of touching myself down there. I haven't even got a mental map of it. True terra incognita. I must have heard the word *masturbation,* but it doesn't mean anything to me experientially. It's something boys do, I think.

Nor will the fact that my experience could have been otherwise really come home to me until my own daughter decides at her second period to use Tampax and seeks my advice. "Do you think I'll be able to get it in?" she asks.

"Well, can you get your finger up there?"

"Sure."

"Then there's plenty of room." So she must have had her finger up there, I think afterward. She, at least, isn't poking blindly into the unknown.

Mother gives me a junior Tampax and a jar of Vaseline and sends me into the bathroom. She stands outside the closed door coaching. I press the white tube into several points between my legs, but wherever I push I feel pain.

"It hurts," I report through the door. Sweat beads on my upper lip. My breathing feels ragged. Ouch. Not there. What if I tear something down there? What if I ruin myself? "I can't do it," I say through clenched teeth. "I just can't."

"Okay," Mother says after a while. "You can try again another time."

I bury the greasy tube in the wastebasket and exit the bathroom ingloriously.

The next time I try, I jab fortuitously at the right spot and the tube slides upward without pain. "Got it!" I shout through the closed door where Mother has resumed her vigil.

"Good for you!" she shouts back. I feel myself lurch forward a little further into womanhood.

Now I can better control the hemorrhaging, but I'm stuck with the pain. Since current theory holds that, menstruation being a natural process, dysmenorrhea is caused not by physiological problems but by a woman's refusal to accept her own femininity, I'm also stuck with guilt. If I were a true woman, none of this would be happening to me. The doctor defers my guilt into adulthood when, without doing a pelvic examination, he diagnoses a tipped uterus and says that my cramps will diminish after I have a baby. But after two babies, I'll realize he was wrong, and I'll go on flinging myself about the room, rocking and tossing on my bed, clutching heating pads and hot water bottles, gulping painkillers.

I'll stop calling it "the curse," though. Why confer power through a name on something already strong enough to throw you around like a rag doll? It becomes just my period: not half so delicate and elegant a term as Virginia Woolf's *recumbency*, but serviceable. Finally, when I'm in my thirties, a female gynecologist will conclude, "You just have cruddy periods," and after that, victim suddenly redeemed from blame, I settle down with my cruddy periods to wait for menopause.

The summer I turn fourteen, while I'm away at camp, I start having headaches of astounding intensity. "Migraine equivalents," the doctor will term them several years later after taking an electroencephalogram, and I will think, How like me to come up with an ersatz ailment. There's nothing spurious, however, about the pain, which snakes up my spine, spreads across the base of my neck, creeps up and over my skull to thud down behind my eyes. My own pulse attacks me, each beat a throb in my temples and ears. At the slightest shift my stomach lurches. If I stay rigid on my back in a darkened room with a cloth over my eyes, I can usually get up after several hours and begin to grope my way back into my life, but full reentry can take several days. The headaches escalate in frequency and intensity for several years, then level off, and finally begin to diminish as I enter middle age.

These headaches are, perhaps, perfectly natural. Granna suffered crippling headaches as a younger woman. Mother is prone to them, and shortly Sally will develop them, too. But no one, in a society where the norms of wellness are shaped to the ideals of its medical practitioners rather than to the range of human realities, views dis-ease of any sort as natural. And so I don't get taught that my headaches, as well as my cramps, are simply features of who I am. I think, on the contrary, that they're who I am not, a kind of possession or visitation, and that I've got to expel them in order to be me. When they keep coming and keep coming, I feel defeated and ashamed, as though I've failed to try hard enough.

The doctors assist my efforts at expulsion with whatever drugs are at hand. At first I'm given Cafergot, which causes uterine contractions, not a sound choice in the light of my menstrual history. I get Fiorinal instead, then Darvon 65, even on occasion a shot of Demerol in whatever infirmary or emergency room is handy. Years later, when I've read up on the dangers of all these drugs and assumed a new kind of responsibility for my body, I'll switch to ibuprofen and ice packs, and accept the pain as my own.

Worse is to come. The further I get into high school, the sicker I get. At the first drift of tree pollen every spring, my nose and ears block and my itching eyes stick shut with yellow crusts. In the winter, penned in overheated schools and buses and houses, schoolmates and families begin a wild round robin of infection. If there's a flu to be gotten, I'll get it, with attendant diarrhea, earaches, bronchitis. Once I run a fever for so long that my liver starts to give up and my skin and eyeballs turn yellow. When we return to 236 and Granna moves upstairs, I get her old room, and I spend days at a time there, awkwardly propped on pillows, surrounded by books and puzzles and dirty juice glasses, picking out the faces hidden in the pink and white gladioli on the walls, a habit I will retain, so that under the surface of tile floors and papered walls and wooden doors floats forever a whole world of monstrous and sometimes witty leers.

I develop queer symptoms that don't seem related to infection, though they might sometimes be triggered by allergies. I'm queasy, and my throat aches so that I can hardly swallow. My hands tremble. I have an intermittent piercing pain in my abdomen. I start feeling faint in the middle of church services and assemblies. Worst of all is the fatigue. I drag myself along day after day as though my bones were condensing and transforming, through some improbable alchemy, from porous calcium to solid granite. These I regard as "unreal" symptoms, impermissible to bother others about, just another wearisome outbreak of Nancy's "dramatics"; and so they are complicated by a sense of alienation, both from others and from my own body, which serves as an instrument not of pleasure but of torture.

In this I am no more than the heir of the great Western philosophical and theological traditions that split mind or soul or spirit from body and then glorify the one while they degrade the other; but I don't know that, any more than I feel the gravity that keeps me free-falling toward the earth. Puritanism is my medium, transparent as air. And by the time I'm feeling continually ill, I'm old enough to believe that illness belongs to my body, as though "I" were somehow separate from that entity and could even, with the correct attitude and discipline, transcend it, by which I mean ignore it and leave it behind, the way you give the ugly sweater your great-aunt bought you for Christmas to the Salvation Army as soon as you've appeared in it a few times.

Because all my reading and religious training reinforces this construction of human reality, I keep missing signs that point to alternative, more loving ways of experiencing my body. After making out for ten minutes with a boy I don't care for, for instance, I scribble furiously, "How could I so easily destroy all the things I hold so sacred & dear in one sheer animal impulse. . . . I can kiss as hard & long & sweet as others he has kissed. I'm as good as they are at 'parking,' because I can act. I ought to get an Oscar. Ha! Am I funny. I make myself sick. I'm revolting, disgusting." In this horrific eruption of self-loathing, I bury and slide over the one statement that might be of use to me: "I make myself sick." Bodies feel sick; minds separated, by philosophical tricks, from bodies can only adopt sickness as a metaphor. If I could hear my statement literally, then I'd recognize the critical connection between who-I-am-as-a-body and sickness. I would know, in other words, that sickness has become (it doesn't seem to have been from the beginning, but I know too little about my own genes and hormones to be sure) my way of being in the world. I've got that kind of body.

My ignorance will cost me a lot, but not quite my life.

iii

Mother considers sending me to Northfield, but we don't really have enough money for a prep school, and in the end we settle for Berkeley High School, where most Enon students go. I wonder sometimes whether Northfield would have been a happier choice, a tranquil country setting, an all-female student body, an atmosphere decidedly academic. Probably athletic, too. Oh, Lord.

Certainly Berkeley turns out to be an unhappy one. But just now I could probably manage to be miserable anywhere.

This choice forces me away from 236, and from Enon, for longer and longer hours as my commitments multiply. My day begins early, in the dark for much of the year, in order to make time for the walk to the bus, which stops for me not long after seven o'clock. If I miss it, Granna can take me on her way to work, but sometimes then I'm late, and I have a horror of being late. Almost every school day is drawn out by extracurricular activities: *Aegis*, the school literary magazine; dramatic productions; driver's ed; Future Teachers of America and French Club meetings; Girl Scouts, where I am now assistant leader of a fifth-grade troop. After these, I have to take the public bus, which drops me in the center of town, and walk from there cradling my books, which I weigh in one day at fourteen pounds. We girls always carry them in front of our breasts; boys balance them on one hip; no one uses school-bags or backpacks. Evenings are often full, too, with Rainbow Girls, choir rehearsals, swimming lessons, babysitting.

Weekends offer no respite. School activities like rehearsals often carry over to Saturday. Throughout the fall there are weekly football games and school dances, too. On a typical Sunday I might sing in the church choir at both the nine-thirty and eleven o'clock services, rush home to eat dinner and wash the dishes, go off to a planning session for Pilgrim Fellowship, our church youth group, in the afternoon, and attend the PF meeting itself in the evening.

Fatigue, plainly rooted in this frenzied pace, becomes the constant gray undertone of my days, but I never accept its authenticity. I berate myself for it as my shortcoming, my personal failure, a physical frailty setting me apart from others. Neither do I ever recognize my reclusive nature, which renders the relentless social interaction I have to sustain excruciating, and if I did recognize it, my shame would only flare higher. Mother's tacit disapproval of my wandering off alone haunts me, but precisely because it *is* tacit, I lack words for thinking about the problem. I adopt her stance as thoughtlessly as I speak about "the curse." Solitary activities— reading for pleasure, watching television, throwing my legs across the arm of the tapestried easy chair and drifting into dream—are taboo. Not that I don't do them. I do, all too often. But then I feel the way I would if I sneaked the coveted chocolate-covered cherry from the Whitman's Sampler Daddy gives Mother every Valentine's Day.

* * *

REMEMBERING THE BONE HOUSE

The locus of my life becomes the gloomy pentagonal building of gray-painted bricks that looms on a bleak triangle of land by
the railroad tracks at Gloucester Crossing. It has the architectural
wit of a state penitentiary. But the students lack the volatile and
menacing temperament of convicts. Even the most rebellious of
them, the JDs, the boys who wear dungarees and roll packs of
Lucky Strikes in the sleeves of their white T-shirts and comb their
hair into duck's asses, the girls who wear tight black cotton skirts
and turn their shirt collars up in back and chew gum, don't make
much trouble in school. Occasionally boys get into fistfights, usually
out in the parking lot, but I never see a knife pulled. I don't have
to just say no to drugs, because no one offers me any or even
mentions them. For that matter, no one offers me a drink, until
my mother mixes me a weak whiskey and ginger ale shortly before
I leave for college. When I marry a high school teacher, and teach
high school myself for a while, and keep vigil as my own three
children navigate those treacherous waters, my three years at
Berkeley High will seem to have passed in a dream of calm and
light.

At the moment, though, the place feels anything but safe.
Most students have arrived from one of Berkeley's two junior highs
already established in cliques. The few dozen of us from Enon are
scattered, and the tenuous solidarity I began to establish with them
in junior high scatters as well. To make matters worse, Enon is
sneered at—"The Sandbox," Berkeley students call it—its students
considered even more naïve than sophomores as a whole. The
bright, jostling world that bubbles within the school walls is con-
toured and controlled by a smallish group of seniors gifted with
intelligence or athletic prowess or wealth or good looks or, more
often than not, a combination of these qualities: handsome dark-
haired boys in chinos and Shetland crewnecks and the pert page-
boyed girls to whom they give their letter sweaters. During the few
minutes before the first bell rings, they join hands and circumnavi-
gate by twos the five-jointed corridors, round and round, round and
round, laughing, calling out to one another, parading their current
coupleness, which may of course shift literally from one day to the
next.

A fourteen-year-old with a queer bounding gait and an
enormous mouth to whom the chatter around her sounds thrilling
and exotic, like Arabic or Bantu, is bound to be left outside that
magic circle. I huddle in my homeroom, 205, waiting for the bell,
the flurry, silence, the Bible reading and prayer, the Pledge of

Allegiance—the whole tedious ritual renewed, right down to my solitary lunch, Velveeta cheese with mustard one day, peanut butter and Marshmallow Fluff the next, the full range of Mother's creative capacities as she stumbles around in the dark morning after morning. Boys think of me as a "good kid," a "brain," not the body on which you'd drape your letter sweater for a parade.

I never do get a letter sweater, but by my senior year I have moved into the controlling group and even joined morning's ritual circuit, though I never recognize my position. Because I'm active in dramatic productions and edit the school literary magazine, the *Aegis*, virtually every student in the school may know me by sight. Maybe some of them, like that poor fourteen-year-old of two years before, yearn to be in my position. Maybe, but I won't think of that possibility until I'm over forty, and even then I'll be dubious. As far as I'm concerned, I get where I am by accident and the suffrance of BHS's "real" people, like lanky Josh Forman, senior class president, and sturdy Bobby Lemoile, football co-captain and student council president, and dark, vivacious Hannah Klein, my assistant editor. They just let me hang around.

I turn out to be a disappointing, though generally dutiful, student. That is, I do as I'm told, but only at the last minute and with my mind elsewhere. Although I usually make the honor roll, my grades are seldom high enough to satisfy either me or my mother, who tends to blame the problem on the time I spend on boys. She's partly right. The "elsewhere" my mind dwells in is generally the region of my throbbing and often broken heart. But the increasing responsibilities I take on in extracurricular pursuits certainly contribute as well. These are somehow never considered equal to studies, however, so that I might view myself as choosing the *Aegis* editorship in place of straight A's, a mature and permissible choice. Instead, believing that a genuinely good girl could manage both, I simply feel inadequate. And still, of course, tired.

Of all my inadequacies, the one that stings most sharply is my failure to earn a blazer, the trophy awarded to a dozen of my classmates for scholastic excellence. My sister will follow me and get a blazer, thereby demonstrating that I could have had one too if only I'd proved myself worthy. This grief over my shortcomings will sour my contentment time after time. Though I graduate from college with honors, I fail to be invited to join Phi Beta Kappa. Someone else wins the Walt Whitman Award. The National Endowment for the Arts refuses me a fellowship. I never catch up. I'm never quite good enough.

And I might deserve some sympathy if life had really denied me all recognition. But of course it hasn't. I scant the value of the recognition that comes. If I can get it, I seem to reason, it can't be worth all that much. While I'm ruing that charcoal blazer with the orange crest on the pocket, I'm one of only fourteen students in Massachusetts to win the National Council of Teachers of English award for writing, and letters of recruitment start pouring in from colleges all over the country. But I scarcely notice. Not until I teach high school will I understand that this is a competitive and prestigious award. I mean, I'm glad I get it, but it's not enough to reassure me that my capabilities are genuine. Nothing is ever enough. I want *all* the awards. Every one. Greed like this provides no grounds for pity.

When it comes to boys, I really am pitiable, because I have a terrible time getting one. I get through my whole sophomore year without a date. Slight exaggeration. Without a date from school. Sometimes I go alone to the Saturday night dances and stand around in the dark at the edge of the dance floor, pushed here and there by the shifting mob of other nondancers, watching the couples in the center, lit patchily by the revolving faceted ball above, their foreheads together and their arms around each other, swaying in a single spot from the beginning of a tune to the end. "Dre-e-e-eam, dream, dream, dre-eam. . . ." No one asks me to dance. Most Saturday nights I baby-sit instead. Friday nights, too.

Some boy usually invites me to our Pilgrim Fellowship dances, but of course only Enon kids are there. Once I visit my friend Sarah and she fixes me up with a boy from Phillips Exeter. That's what we call a blind date: getting fixed up. Toward the end of the year, I meet a boy from another high school who asks me to his Senior Reception. I like the idea. Granna rummages me a strapless waltz-length dress of lavender net, and Greg gives me a corsage of yellow roses, and my long shining pageboy comes out just right, and I feel almost pretty. But of course nobody from school can see me. And though I squeeze my heart as hard as I can for a drop of love, the fact is that I can't stand Greg.

Junior year a BHS boy finally asks me out, and it turns out that I can't stand him more than I can't stand Greg. Frank is about my height and stocky, with a homely reddish face below a blond crew cut. He speaks with a lisp. He calls me nightly, inviting me out bowling, dancing, to the movies, to the Adventure Car-Hop, where if you shout "Woo-Woo Ginsberg!" into the speaker, the girl will run out with two orders of the day's special for the price of one. Arnie "Woo-Woo" Ginsberg is a Boston DJ, really obnoxious, but free food is free food.

I don't know how to turn Frank down. After all, I can't say I have a date already, which, besides terminal illness (cramps and headaches and hay fever don't count), is the only excuse Mother permits. He tries my Christian charity by attending Pilgrim Fellowship, even though he doesn't go to our church, where I'm obliged to make him welcome. I don't welcome him anywhere else, but no coolness quells his ardor. "Old blunderbuss," I call him privately. And "the leftovers." A few years later, during a pregnancy scare, he will prove himself a warm and supportive friend, and I will learn to feel gratitude. But never love.

If only my clothes were right, maybe things would be different. Probably not. But here at least is a concrete problem rather than amorphous worries about leftovers and loneliness. And the fact is that often my clothes aren't quite right. We live in an affluent town, and many of the students I'm thrown together with at BHS are comfortably off as well. We're not poor, but we always have to "watch our pennies," Mother says. As a result, though I usually get whatever item of clothing I simply "have" to have, it usually comes too late, after the fad has peaked, or is an inexpensive imitation. Thus, the aqua boatneck jersey with the rolled-up ribbed sleeves instead of the requisite three-quarter sleeves, the madras shirtwaist with a button-down collar and straight skirt instead of a bermuda collar and gathered skirt.

Worst of all are my first high heels. Granna brings home two pairs, identical except that one is brown and the other black. She's very proud, having gotten a terrific deal on them. Oh, they're awful. Suede, with round toes and chunky heels not more than an inch high. Worse than flats. Much worse. But I have to wear them, or Granna will think I'm not pleased. This agony, the agony of clumping into Pilgrim Fellowship every Sunday night, of feeling every eye turned down on my Minnie Mouse feet, leads me to my most distinct act of self-assertion since I hacked the feet out of my nitey-nites. While Mother is in the hospital having Barba, I take my hoarded baby-sitting money and go alone by bus into the center of Berkeley, where I buy myself a pair of smooth navy-blue leather shoes with pointed toes and slender two-inch heels. My desire for these shoes is reflected in the hoarding, because as a rule I spend money as soon as I get it. Once I get these treasures of style, I'm scared to wear them, because Mother will ask questions. I've never bought clothes without her. And in fact, when I screw my courage and step out in them, she does ask, "Where did you get those?"

"Iboughtthemwhileyouwereinthehospital," I say in an undertone. She looks a little puzzled, I suppose because I've never made a shopping foray without her before and maybe she didn't even know I could, but she doesn't say anything more. Thereafter my toes get pointier, my heels higher and skinnier, until they achieve a sort of apotheosis in a pair of Neiman-Marcus shoes I get at a terrific bargain in Filene's basement when I'm in college. By the time I'm reduced to a brace shoved into the dreaded "sturdy oxfords" of my childhood, my passion for rightness will have peaked and I'll pretty well have made peace with my footwear.

My hair is all of a piece with my clothes, a focus of constant fussing. Whether long or short, there's too much of it, a thick, straight mop which never does quite whatever any of the other girls' hair is doing. If I wear it short, I can put it in pincurls every night without too much time or discomfort. But much of the time I wear it in a long pageboy, which nightly I wind around metal rollers held in place by metal cases, so that I'm sleeping held half upright by six or more aluminum sausages. Perhaps all my complaints of fatigue can be traced here. We don't have home hair dryers yet, either, so when I wash it, it stays damp for twelve hours or more at a time. In the summer when I'm swimming almost daily, it starts to mildew.

At first when I plead for lipstick, which *everyone* is wearing, Mother will buy me only Tangee, an odd waxy orange substance with a sickly scent, which goes on clear but darkens slightly. Finally I succeed in getting real lipstick, even white. Nail polish, too. When I take to wearing green eye shadow, Mother tells me I look like a jaded actress, but actually I don't. I look like a seventeen-year-old wearing green eye shadow.

Even later, my brother Chip catches sight of me putting on makeup and asks, "Why do you do that? Don't you like your face?" I'm a little startled. I've been doing it for so long now that I don't much think about it. I don't suppose I do like my face. I'm a product of my culture, after all. But I've gotten used to it, and making myself up becomes less of a repair job than a kind of play. All those crayons and paints, my plain face a canvas waiting for design. Without a scrap of artistic talent, I've found a medium that permits me to create. To put on a face to meet the faces that I meet, one of which, please God, will be snared by my fabrication.

A dress that at last I like, second-hand, of course, but in perfect condition, heavy peach-colored wool, long-sleeved and full-skirted. Fake pearl on a chain around my neck. Out come the rollers, clank, clank. Brush crackling through the thicket of my hair. A slick of coral lipstick, a touch of green eye shadow. Dabs of Evening in Paris behind my ears, inside my wrists. I'm out the door, ready once again to fail to take the world by storm.

Lost in Space

---

i

CALEB. Caleb. Caleb. Caleb. Caleb. This is how the inside of my head sounds for the better part of two years. Caleb this. Caleb that. Always Caleb. I repeat the name over and over, stupefied with the love of it.

Caleb is the wrong name, a friend who has known us both from childhood will insist after coming across this pseudonym in one of my other books. When I explain that I wanted a strong two-syllable name from the Old Testament, he assents, but dubiously. He never tells me, though, what name I should have chosen.

Let him be Caleb.

February 14, 1959. I wear my gold-and-white striped blouse and black velvet skirt. Thankless Frank has invited me to the Pilgrim Fellowship dance and brought me a corsage of white carnations as a Valentine's Day present. For his trouble, I fall in love with another man.

Well, not quite a man. A quiet, intelligent, strange sort of boy. Tall and slender, with dark blond hair and startlingly blue eyes fringed with long black lashes. Almost pretty. He talks funny, always affecting an accent, generally German. Where has he come from? I'll never figure out. All of a sudden he materializes in my diary as my partner for a single dance. He could have lived in Enon as long as I have, longer. He could have moved in yesterday. What attracts me to him? Mother will never figure out. Eventually I'll come to think it has something to do with his bones. The bones of his hand encircling mine, his rib cage and the long bones of his thighs burning through his flesh and my flesh and somehow warming my bones. I fall in love first with the feel of his bones. That, and his wit. He's at least as smart and well read as I am. He never calls me a brain. If anything, he probably thinks I'm a little dim.

If he thinks about me at all. Which, at least to begin with, he never seems to. After the dance, the sudden epiphany that I adore this boy I hardly know, my task becomes to insert myself into his field of vision. Since he's a year behind me in school, we have no classes together, so my efforts have to be confined to PF meetings on Sunday nights, where I sneak quick glances but seldom speak, and weekday journeys to and from school on the battered yellow bus. He sits with his friend Aaron, a stocky, redheaded, freckled boy. Last on the bus each morning, I pray for an empty seat near enough so that I can talk with them. The consequence of this tactic is that Aaron falls in love with me, one more link in humanity's Great Chain of Unrequited Love: Aaron's for me, mine for Caleb, Caleb's for . . . who? Not me, anyway. Aaron informs me bluntly that Caleb knows I like him and, as far as he's concerned, I'm wasting my time.

I go on wasting my time anyway.

The Spring Prom is coming up, and I'm in a bind. I want to go with Caleb, of course, but I can't invite him because we go to the same school. Girls can hint all they like, but only boys invite. No one invites me. Even Frank asks another girl. I can, however, invite Jonathan Morris, my minister's son, because he goes to the Academy. In such a case, the girl is permitted to ask the boy. So I do. And then, somehow, I prevail upon Caleb to invite my friend Sukey Talbot and double with us. I'm not sure how I pull this off. Maybe Sukey is Caleb's link in the Chain.

By the night of the Prom I feel like death, my sinuses solid and both my ears infected, but a flood of tears has persuaded Dr. Love to say reluctantly that I can go as long as my dress doesn't leave me half naked. I've got a hand-me-down gown with a deep blue long-sleeved jersey top and a pale blue waltz-length chiffon skirt, which nicely sets off Jonathan's yellow roses. At last I find myself once more in Caleb's arms. I mean, he pretty well has to dance with me at least once, doesn't he, since we're doubling, and he can't do it without putting his arms around me.

"Jonathan's just invited me to Spring Weekend at Exeter," I confide in him.

"And will you go?"

"I suppose I might," I say archly. "If it suits my fancy."

"And where is your fancy?" he asks, the perpetual edge of irony in his tone, his left eyebrow raised mockingly.

"Ah, that's for me to know and you to find out!" For some reason, this response strikes me as so clever and daring that the adrenaline rushes to my stuffed-up head and nearly knocks me out. I will remember it *forever*.

That's the Spring Prom. We're not getting far.

Spring Weekend at Exeter. In my rather constricted, countrified life, this is quite A Big Deal, and it offers me the chance to free myself from my fixation on Caleb as well. I arrange to stay with my friend Sarah, who lives in Exeter now and has in high school with her my friends from the Day School. Mother sews me two new outfits, a blue-and-white plaid sundress with a matching jacket and a silky green floral cocktail dress with a fitted bodice and circle skirt. She gets the zipper in upside down, which makes getting in and out topsy-turvy, but no one can see, and I feel wonderfully glamorous in it.

In spite of the costumes, the weekend itself is a flop. From the moment of his limp greeting on Sarah's telephone, I know that Jonathan isn't enthusiastic about the whole idea. I don't know why he's asked me. Perhaps his Academy friends pressured him to join them. Or he may have felt obligated to repay me for inviting him to my Spring Prom. As we watch a lacrosse game in silence, stroll glumly, a foot apart, from the playing fields through golden spring air to tea, later pose like dancing-school partners on the polished gym floor, I wait for some little spark or flutter, some touch of the hand or brush of the lips, but in vain. He bores me.

Worse, inadvertently he humiliates me by insisting on meeting me places rather than calling for me at Sarah's house, as Sarah's impeccably mannered boyfriend does. I try to make excuses for him to Sarah's mother, but the fact is that I have to traipse unaccompanied through the streets of Exeter in fancy dress. I doubt that Jonathan means to be rude. Shuttling between well-bred family and boarding school, he's somehow failed to pick up yet the nicety of the squire. All the same, my heart cramps me breathless with mortification.

He does at least know enough to walk me home through the dark after the dance. Under the light on Sarah's back porch I wait tremulously, torn between wanting the kiss I ought to want and yearning for the long, hard, silent day to close.

"Thank you for the wonderful time," I breathe as automatically as my etiquette-conscious mother could have asked.

"Sure," says Jonathan from a foot away. He's good-enough looking, with red hair and pale skin. I could accept the kiss. He moves back toward the steps. "You're welcome." Into the shadows. "Good night."

"Good night," I call.

I'm sure he's as relieved as I at this parting. I go home the next day and tell everyone the weekend was fabulous, of course. What else can you say to your mother about a date with the minister's son? But the sad fact is that I took my heart to Exeter and brought it back, intact and still obsessed.

I wonder if it is a sin to want something as much as I want Caleb to fall in love with me.

I persist. I invite him to the annual Choir Dinner, an acceptable gesture since I'm a choir member and he isn't, and we dance on the porch of the Boston Yacht Club, his cheek against mine, his hand in my hair. On the school bus, our glances begin to tangle. We spend the afternoon together at the PF Picnic and then the evening together at Sukey Talbot's party. He calls me on the telephone once. I think perhaps he likes me. He calls again. I sit with him at the Enon Junior High graduation, and he gives me a rose. He invites me to a party for Aaron, who is moving to Maryland. We dance together almost as one person, one of his hands cupping my cheek and neck, the other holding me close, and talk with our lips so close they almost brush. On the eve of my departure for a month at camp and his for a three-week camping trip with his family, we have become a couple. My dream come true.

ii

I doubt we can last out the separation. If only he doesn't meet anyone completely devastating, if only I've impressed him deeply enough to last, then perhaps I'm safe. But I know I'm never safe. Still, he writes me funny letters full of tentative affection from places I've never even thought of, places at the far ends of the earth, like Arizona. It doesn't occur to me that his tentativeness reflects not uncertainty of his feelings but uncertainty of me. He doesn't trust me. With good reason, it will turn out. At the end of the month, we return to Enon and to one another.

"Teen Angel, can you see me? Teen Angel, can you hear me?" The wavering words are nearly drowned out by the drone of men's voices, the waitress's treble call to the cook, the clatter of white crockery, the sizzle of two new strips of bacon on the blackened grill. We know them by heart anyway. Someone always sticks a dime into the selection box on his table, maybe the same person, maybe a different one every day, knowing which buttons to push without having to flip through the pages. "Teen Angel, can you...?"

Caleb and I sit on one side of the booth, Caleb by the clouded window, our friend Ben facing us. Winter mornings the wait from the time the bus drops us off till the school doors are unlocked is bitter, especially for me, my legs bare above my knee socks up under my pleated flannel skirt. My gray woolen coat, my woolen scarf wrapped around my throat with both ends hanging down the back, my stadium boots and striped mittens aren't enough. I despise the cold. So we've taken to coming to the steamy Miss Berkeley Diner, redolent of dampish wool and hot grease, tears of condensation streaking the windows, where workmen stop on their way to their jobs, hunched in the booths and on the chrome stools along the counter in their dungarees and black watch caps and old jackets lined with red plaid flannel.

"Running Bear loved little White Dove, with a love big as the sky. . . ." The same songs, morning after morning. We hum along as we sip coffee. I've given up sugar, in belated deference to my rotting teeth, but I still take cream, and against the white mug the coffee gleams pale and slick. Caleb and I smoke Parliaments. The one time in our adult lives we talk together, this will be the only thing Caleb accuses me of: that I started him smoking. Sometimes we talk, but a lot of the time we don't. Just listen to the juke box and smoke our forbidden cigarettes and thaw out. ". . . and his love will never die."

I will never stop loving Caleb, I think. And I don't.

* * *

Getting off the bus in the center of town to walk to the dentist, I run into Caleb, wearing a maroon shirt figured in small blue and green diamonds, a dark green crewneck, chinos, a trench coat—so handsome that my breath snags and I can only lift my hand in greeting. Fresh from the shower, he smells warmly of soap and shaving lotion, and I want to drop my armload of books and throw myself into his embrace.

But I can't. So help me, the trees in this town have eyes. And tongues. At dinner one night Granna tells Mother that Aunt Lucy told her that Mrs. Boyd saw us kissing at the choir carol sing. This is the way news travels here. This report doesn't even happen to be true; it's something born of a wayward malice I'll never understand. We did stand very close on the church steps, holding hands, while snow sifted downward, glittering in the church lights, and voices sifted upward through the flakes, but we never kissed until we said good-bye in the car. "Those two are the talk of the town," says Aunt Lucy, according to Granna. The talk of the town. Trees with tongues.

Whether because we're the talk of the town or for some other reason, Mother never takes to Caleb. She doesn't exactly tell me this. It falls, along with more and more of my scrambled interior life, into that vast emotional domain about which we're not permitted to speak. But I feel it when she says he looks, with his gaunt face and perpetually uplifted left eyebrow, as though he needs a psychiatrist, or suggests that I date other boys. She thinks there's something, I'm not sure what, wrong with him. I can't give him up, though. Maybe that means there's something wrong with me.

We can get married in six years, we figure. Six years is such a long time. The equivalent of more than a third of our lives to date.

iii

We should have slept together, I'll come to believe years later.

We can't sleep together, for the same reasons we can't kiss on the church steps if we feel like it. Such an act is socially unthinkable. Occasionally in the corridors at school I hear the whispered rumor that so-and-so Does It, but it's never anyone I

REMEMBERING THE BONE HOUSE

know. And once, sophomore year, a girl in my class, not anyone I know, gets pregnant, but as soon as her belly begins to press against the forgiving chemises in style this year, she vanishes without a trace. It never occurs to me that people I know might be Doing It, just not getting caught and not talking about it. The whole matter is simply out of the question.

I am trying to be a Good Girl, even if people think I'm difficult sometimes: first child in my family, my father's daughter, bright, a high achiever. I may ask questions, but they're never the right ones. Here's the sort of questions I ask: "What will the future hold for me? Will 1960 hold death for me? Will I graduate from high school? Will I like Wheaton? What will I do next summer? Will Caleb and I go too far? Will Caleb and I still be together?" Never mind the decidedly queer emphasis this sequence throws on death. By this time I'm praying to die almost as regularly as I brush my teeth. The more complicated my life has become as I've left childhood, the more urgently I desire to escape it. I could, of course, run away and join the circus, not literally perhaps, but I could alter, even simplify, my life. I don't know that, however. I don't yet know that I'm the author of my own life. That power seems to belong chiefly to Mother, subsidiary rights going to Helena Corbett, my guidance counselor, who won't approve my schedule until I drop Latin and elect trigonometry. And even if I did know it, I cannot conceive any alternative to life exactly as I live it except death. "Our Father who art in heaven," I pray, "let me be there, too."

What's even more important than my emphasis on death is this passivity: none of my questions challenge, even faintly, the received structure of my life. Just as I live at 236, the house that Mother and Granna built, I occupy a framework of expectations: that I'll attend school and church unless I'm ill; that my grades will be high enough to get me into a good women's college; that I'll have the "right" sort of friends and stay out of "trouble"; that before I go to the football game, I'll finish vacuuming and dusting the living room, including the pastel porcelain figurines of the Chinese immortals. I do as I'm told. The only exception I can think of is my refusal to read *Henry Esmond* in Miss Harriman's senior English class. I know I will fail all the quizzes and the final test, but I hate the book so much that I choose not to read it anyway.

If I was going to make just one rebellious choice, I wish I'd chosen to sleep with Caleb instead.

* * *

My mother won't let us have sex. His mother won't let us have sex. Our minister won't let us have sex. The television won't let us have sex, unless we're married and can think of some way to do it in twin beds separated by a table with a lamp on it. Nobody, of course, *tells* us we're not to have sex. Nobody, that is, comes right out and says the words. That's where the power of the prohibition lies, I think: in its absolute muffledness. Even Caleb and I can't talk about it. No one has taught us the words. We talk about ethics, about love, about drawing the line, about marriage, about waiting till we're married. But we don't say what we're waiting for. We don't say *sex*.

As a result, we are at once tossed together and riven apart. We are swept like a couple of castaways onto an island of desire from which we can't escape. It is always night there, always dark, even though we sometimes make out in the daytime: hide in the woods behind my house, roll on dry pine needles slithering over rank black humus. Almost the smells of sex, sharp ones and earthy ones, if I only knew. Still, we're always in the dark, hour upon hour, eyes shut tight, mouths grinding together, hands groping up and down backs, around necks, along clenched arms. We never explore each other with our eyes. Eventually he sometimes strokes my breasts. We don't touch each other between our legs. In fact, I feel almost nothing down there, or in my breasts, or anywhere except inside my head, which feels swollen and explosive. I'm making love without my body.

We do actually try it once, out there in the woods, but it's no go. It's early spring, still cool, so we're wearing quite a few clothes, which we don't take off. I lie on my back, staring past last year's dry, rustly leaves clinging to oak branches, up into a pale gray sky, almost iridescent, like the inside of a mussel shell. Caleb fumbles under my skirt, working my underpants down my legs a way. I hear the sound of a zipper and then feel his weight on top of me, squirming. His head looms between me and the brown oak leaves, flushed, eyes locked on mine. Something is supposed to be happening which isn't and, prohibited gaze or touch, I haven't the foggiest idea how to make it happen, or even that I *can* make it happen. In novels and films, no one seems to be looking at what they're doing. No one seems to be *working*. Seized by chagrin, I clamp my thighs and toss my head from side to side, the model of protesting virtue: "No! No!" Caleb rolls off and lies beside me, breathing hard but not speaking. I want to die of disappointment.

What Caleb feels I never know. We have no way to talk

about that the way we can talk about ethics, et cetera. And this is what separates us, no matter how hard we clutch and writhe. We're not, after all, on a desert island but on two desert islands: His and Hers. This dark incommunicable core of our relationship poisons all other attempts at communication. We spend much of our lives clawing each other apart.

One day, sitting at our dining-room table after dinner, my daughter will tell me about the first time she had sex, at about this age, with her high school boyfriend.

"Where were you?" I ask, thinking glumly about Greg's battered blue Mustang and the condoms littering the gravel out at the end of Swan Road.

"Oh, right here," she says. "We'd all watched a movie on the VCR. Then you and Dad went to bed in your room, and Greg and I went to bed in my room." I feel warmed by relief, visualizing her small safe room with the lace curtains over the wide windows and the sagging third-hand double bed and the bulletin board covered with ribbons won at cat shows. "And it was terrible," she goes on. "It was so bad that we didn't do it again for *months.*" We both burst out laughing.

But they did do it again. Gradually their bodies became friends. And even though they've been apart for years now, taking other lovers or practicing celibacy, their friendship has persisted. I wish Caleb and I had become such friends.

I write Caleb passionate poems.

Because the sun shines over melting snow
And drenches ice in pools of liquid gold,
The tulip petals, tightly clutched, unfold,
And, swaying lightly in the breeze, they throw
Warm shadows over grass too cold to grow,
Rejoicing in their freedom from the cold
And barren prison of the earth. Now bold
And laughing, golden as the sun they blow.
Because when in the darkness of my world
You touched my icy heart with warm spring sun
And then brought forth this flower bright, above
My frozen life I stand, petals uncurled,
The bonds of ice now burst, new life begun.
And now, because you love me, I am love.

He laughs when I give this sonnet to him, offhanded, plainly missing my whole point, which is that he is my life. All the same, he is the only person who takes my intention to become a writer perfectly seriously. Much more seriously than I do. "Only one question," he'll say in a letter when I'm threatening to drop out of college to marry another man. "Do you still want to write? And, if so, how do you expect to be any good with an incomplete education?" No one else ever raises this question. Writing, Caleb believes, may be my life.

I don't stop loving Caleb, and yet I am perpetually unfaithful to him, with one boy after another, although none of the relationships has much significance except for the one with a college student from Sierra Leone I meet during my second year at a week-long Pilgrim Fellowship Officers' Conference in Deering, New Hampshire. This is an idyllic setting for a summer romance, a cluster of white buildings among green hills, hours of training seminars broken by periods like Morning Watch for private reflection, as well as worship services and lively social gatherings. And Ayo is a perfect partner: smart, handsome, humorous, affectionate. Except, of course, that he's black. But during this brief tranquil spell, even that doesn't trouble me much, though I'm startled at the first sight of his long fingers on mine. I fall head over heels, and after I get home I start haunting the dim interior of the rickety yellow post office uptown, twirling the twin dials of Box 192, yanking out the packet of envelopes, riffling through, breathless, sweaty, hoping for one in an angular italic hand. In fact, he does write, and we correspond off and on for several months, though we never see each other again.

My other two great infatuations, both entirely unreciprocated, involve boys at BHS, not half so exotic as a black African, yet each is foreign enough from my point of view to intrigue me, Josh Glass a Jew and Peter Hansen a German with a thick, lisping accent. Neither is handsome, though they both have extraordinary eyes, greenish, Josh's lashes golden and curly, Peter's straight and black.

To understand their allure, you have to remember that I come from a middle-class family with four Mayflower ancestors in a small, largely middle-class town, not yet a suburb of Boston. Thoroughly WASP. Virtually everyone belongs to the First Church in Enon, Congregational, where when a new minister places a plain wooden cross on the maroon velvet hanging behind

the pulpit, part of the congregation threatens to withdraw in protest against idolatry. There are a few Catholic families. We know
who they are. In fact, Caleb's mother is a Catholic, but she doesn't
practice and her children are as Congregationalist as we are, so it's
okay. A handful of Baptists, too, mostly associated with the local
sectarian college. And some Episcopalians among the upper crust,
the "hot potato" crowd my family calls them, in reference to their
exaggerated drawling speech. The first Jew doesn't move in until
I'm in college.

Such a milieu makes Berkeley, with its large Italian and
Jewish populations, and smaller Polish and French ones, seem to
seethe with ethnic variety. In fact, I never see a black, or a Latino,
or an Asian. Certainly not an American Indian. According to
books, such people live in the United States, but nothing in my
experience backs up this allegation. Until I move to the Southwest,
and stand at the bottom of Chaco Canyon among the spirits of a
people who flourished, then vanished, a millennium ago, I'll believe
that this country was settled, or at least civilized, by the English.

I think I'm in love with Ayo, then with Josh, later with
Peter, but they're not for me people to be loved so much as they're
ciphers: of difference, of desire. Arousingly other. Against them
Caleb, as familiar to me now—the smell of him, the press of his
bony shoulder under my cheek, his dumb relentless accent—as a
member of my own family, is powerless.

"I would tell you I love you four hundred times," Caleb
says, "if it would make any difference."

I'm good at falling in love. I just don't know how to endure
the homely tedium of the postlapsarian state. Years later, watching
a film called *My Dinner with Andre,* I'll be struck by one of Andre's
slightest comments. It's easy to have affairs, he tells his friend
Wally, because you learn through repetition just what is expected:
the flowers, the phone calls, the wine. What's hard is to be married,
to go on with a relationship indefinitely, because you're always
going forward into the unknown. By the time I see this film, I can
distinguish between the here-we-go-again loop-the-loop thrill of
climbing on the roller coaster with yet another stranger and the
genuine adventure of traveling one way forever, straight on out till
morning, with the same old companion: a little more wrinkled, not
so skinny, wearing glasses now, but still telling the same jokes and
still laughing at the same ones you're telling. When I'm with

Caleb, though, I haven't learned this kind of courage. I have to keep doing what I know how to do.

iv

My irrevocable infidelity is one over which Caleb and I have no control. I go to college, leaving him behind.

Leaving everything behind.

I have chosen, I believe, a small private liberal arts college for women. Actually, I haven't chosen it at all. I never visit another campus. I never apply to another school. When a friend a year ahead of me goes to Radcliffe, I feel a stirring of curiosity, but Mother says Radcliffe women are so smart that they scare men away and never get married. I'm horrified. My only reason for going to college is to fill up the time, in a safe place, between now and marriage. My writerly ambitions aren't exactly moonshine, but neither do I believe I have the power to realize them, so marriage is my intended end. I'm pretty sure I can pull that off. Meantime, it's either go to college or sling around buttered toast and fried eggs at the Miss Berkeley Diner.

The fact is that, although I can't bear the thought of the Miss Berkeley Diner, I'm nearly as terrified of going to college. But Mother and Aunt Jane both went to Wheaton, and they survived and got married, so it becomes the only possible place for me. I mean it. I absolutely cannot conceive of going anywhere Mother hasn't been before me, marking a safe trail over treacherous ground. If I had my way, she'd also come with me.

Whatever growing away from her I've done in these years while she was absorbed in raising two little children and I in entangling my life with that of a boy she can never quite bring herself to like, our bonds remain, stubborn, sticky as the chaotic nocturnal webs of black widow spiders that will one day seal my windows and festoon the undersides of the sparse plants around my desert home. She is, after all, the woman my father fell in love with, and my attachment to her is as fierce as only the child of one dead parent, perhaps, can have. Even at her most conventional, she has a kind of quirky charm. She's the sort of woman who, when feeling overwhelmed, doesn't whine but bursts out, sighing: "The world is too much with us. Late and soon,/Getting and spending, we lay waste our powers. . . ." Who, after Chip receives an ant farm for his birthday, takes up a vigil beside the glass panels, eats her breakfast there, eats her lunch, would bring the structure to the dinner table too, if we'd let her, snatching up a magnifying glass the better to scrutinize some fresh formicine bustle.

We are often together and usually taken for sisters. Because I'm too timid to take my driving test, she shuttles me everywhere in her old tan Chevrolet station wagon. She buys us a pair of season tickets to local concerts of classical music. We drive up to the North Shore Shopping Center, the first mall we've ever seen, where we roam through acres of stores and finish our errands with lunch at Filene's, always topped off by a "brownie with ice cream polkas," little scoops of vanilla and chocolate, my favorite treat. Sometimes she's still up when I get in from a date and we sit watching some old movie on TV. If she's gone to bed, she lies awake until she hears me.

"How'd you make out?" she calls out of the dark, softly so as not to wake the rest of the house.

"Mother," I say, tiptoeing into her chilly room, perching on the bed, "how many times do I have to tell you not to say 'make out'? It doesn't mean what you think it does." But she always forgets, so I fix her by leering, "Just fine, thanks."

My first step toward separation is inauspicious. To earn money for college in the fall, I take a summer job as a mother's helper for a family in Berkeley. Though I'm only a few miles from 236, and I'm given one day a week to return there, I'm violently homesick. I can't make the shift from one household to the other. Especially since my position in the new household is uncomfortably ambiguous. The woman who hires me never figures out what she wants of me. I don't think she ever figures out what she wants, period, as her spacious, scrupulously empty living room indicates: she's never been able to find just the right furniture, she explains. If Mother and I had any sense, traversing that barren space on the night of my interview should have given us the creeps. But neither of us has any experience with people like Bernice, who is without question the craziest person I've met to date.

She says I'll be a member of the family, responsible for helping her with the house and her three children. Okay, I know how to do that. It's what I've been doing all along. And our own mother's helpers, Janice and Toby, before me. But then she does unsettling things like stopping by the country club on our way home from the supermarket and leaving me outside, because non-

Jews aren't allowed at Kernwood. Like making a big deal out of buying me ham the nights the children are having liver, even though the whole family eats BLTs frequently and enthusiastically. Actually, I'm not all that crazy about ham, though it beats liver. In later years, when more of my friends are Jewish, I'll have some sense of the aggrieved and aggressive anger these small acts mask, but just now anti-Semitism isn't even a word to me, and Bernice simply seems rude.

Finicky, too, to a degree I've never experienced. She wants the floors mopped every day, but only with the sponge mop; Sue, the cleaning woman, comes once a week to do them properly, on her hands and knees. One day, after I've finished, I come across Bernice doing them all over again, so I know I've fallen short. I'm always falling short. Because germs grow in damp towels, each child must have a separate towel and no towel can be used more than once. The laundry piles up. She wants everything ironed, even the kids' T-shirts, even her husband's underwear. The ironing piles up. I forget to sweep down the back stairs. Dirt piles up. As soon as I find places for all the toys, Pammi, the four-year-old, has one of her temper tantrums and flings them everywhere, just as Bernice returns from an afternoon of tennis. "What did you do while I was gone?" she asks. Toys pile up. In addition to temper tantrums, Pammi suffers from chronic constipation, so Bernice lets her evacuate her bowels whenever she feels the urge, like while I'm bathing her one night, so I have to go bobbing for turds. Shit piles up. I'm in a tizzy like the Sorcerer's Apprentice, tearing around from towels to T-shirts to toys to turds, up to my ankles, up to my knees, up to my chin.

"You're costing me forty-five dollars a week," Bernice says, "and you're not living up to all you agreed to." She's paying me twenty-five. I must be eating twenty dollars worth of food. Maybe so. I've started gobbling cream cheese and jelly sandwiches, Oreos. I've put on ten pounds. I know I can't give her more for her money. Two weeks early, I quit.

If I were a little older, I might recognize that of the two of us, she is the more unhappy. But I have no way of knowing that. She has everything a woman could want. A degree from Vassar. A husband working in an established real-estate business. A large Victorian house in an exclusive area, with a slow-cooking element in her countertop range and a thousand dollars' worth of white wicker on the screened porch. Thick blue monogrammed towels. Georg Jensen sterling flatware and Lenox china. She plays tennis every day. She buys her clothes at Saks Fifth Avenue. Her parents bring her a whole set of Orrefors glasses from Stockholm. I don't feel sorry for her one bit. Not yet.

When I leave for Wheaton a month later, then, I've already learned how treacherous leaving home can be. Even without this lesson, however, I think I'd have made a botch of it. For in spite of my sporadic tuggings against Mother's rein, my increasing secretiveness about Caleb, my impatience with housekeeping chores, my quarrels with Mother and Granna and Sally, the fact is that I'm a passionate homebody. The thought of parting from 236 and all it holds doesn't make me sad. It makes me desperate. As though I really might die. "To leave," I write in my diary, "to say with finality, good-bye, old life that I have always known, good-bye house, town, family, love—oh, this is pain & panic & bewilderment far wilder than I have ever known." I feel wrenched out of a woven whole, a fragment hurled over a vertiginous brink into black space.

Mother and Daddy drive me sixty miles through autumnal rain to Metcalf Hall, where my roommate and her family are waiting. She's a tall, cool, long-legged blond with black-rimmed glasses, wearing a monogrammed pink cotton shirtwaist. Serene, I think. She has a proper name, and a nickname formed from it, but her family has always called her Puff, and so do I. Though we'll live together for four years, I'll never quite figure out how to get her to love me.

We have a queer little ground-floor room outside the fire doors off the parlor, once a guest room, apparently, but pressed into dormitory service now that enrollment is expanding. Barely room for two beds, two desks, two dressers. Pink walls. One tall skinny window. But, treasure of treasures, a private bathroom, toilet, sink, and tub, though if we want to shower we have to pad through the parlor and all the way down the corridor. When we get it fixed up, with cocoa-brown bedspreads and chintz throw pillows and the easy chair from Mother's college room, recovered in rose tapestry, and milk-glass lamps, it will seem nearly pretty.

Here Mother and Daddy leave me.

I am scared out of my wits. Literally. If at any time in my life I'll be truly crazy, I'm crazy now. Not later. Not even when I get locked up in a mental hospital. Right now, during these first few months of college. I'm more delirious with homesickness than

I might be with typhoid fever. I yearn for Mother. For Caleb. Even more strongly for the places of my containment: 236, Enon, even the grim corridors of BHS and the clangor of the Miss Berkeley Diner. I feel as though I can be who I am, who I recognize myself to be, within them: a whirling chaos that can coalesce only if confined by familiar space. Here I'm in splinters.

I spend hours in the smoker, a bleak basement room, sitting at a battered, ink-stained wooden table writing sad letters, sucking on Parliaments, staring. Whenever I'm alone, I cry. I get a crippling headache at least once a week, which lasts up to four days. Though I hardly ever study, I never get to bed before midnight, and sometimes I don't go to bed at all. My mind, like my face, grayed by codeine and sleeplessness, I reel from one class to the next, bewildered, behind in all my assignments, certain of failure.

The craziest edge to my misery moderates over time, but I'll never learn to be happy here. I'll major in English literature largely because it requires the least effort. I like to read better than I like to cut up earthworms, say, or meditate on the consequences of the Industrial Revolution. I'll attend classes with moderate regularity and do my assignments because these actions are easier on me than guilt. I'll squeak onto the dean's list every semester. Outside class I'll do what I have to: run projectors and wash glassware in the chemistry lab to earn money, put on a skirt for dinner every night, change my bed on the day the laundry service brings clean sheets. Except for playing the Old Woman in *The Good Woman of Setzuan* and publishing a few poems in the literary magazine, I'll never take up any extracurricular activity. I'll even refuse an invitation to join the English honorary society, not knowing what it is and fearing it might demand time.

One of my campus jobs is to guide prospective students on a tour of the pretty Georgian campus. Standing in the gym one gray February afternoon, in the middle of the talk I've long practiced to sound spontaneous and enthusiastic, I inform a high school senior and her mother brightly that, before it was incorporated as a college, the school was called Wheaton Female Cemetery. "Seminary, of course," I sputter, "I mean Seminary," but my truth is out.

Afterward, whenever I read novels or memoirs celebrating collegiate life, I'll feel puzzled and a little wistful. Whatever was supposed to happen to me here, I'll think, didn't.

Above all, college is hardly the mad, gay social whirl novels have made it out to be. If weekdays are bad—the panicky hours spent trying to find my stinky yellow rat's urogenital tract in bio lab or to insert an *r* into my Yankee speech, not just any *r* but a Parisian *r*, at that—weekends are worse. The dorm corridors fill with chattering girls carrying suitcases, signing out, calling good-byes, and then empty and echo. On Saturday night, Saga Food Service feeds tough but tasty steak to those of us who are left. We huddle at a few tables in the paneled gloom of Emerson Dining Hall, chewing contemplatively at our booby prize.

I do date a couple of boys, one of whom provides me with a really useful piece of information. He's a senior at Boston College, which gives Mother conniptions: a Catholic boy. "For God's sake, Mother, I've just gone out with him a couple of times. I'm not going to marry him." I'm not even all that crazy about him, but although I've taken a solemn vow—"much as I like someone I will not suffer the intellectual [!] insult of so much as a long kiss without love"—when he stops the car on the way back from a show, I don't protest. Actually, I'm kind of horny.

And Jesus, this Catholic boy really knows what he's doing. In the middle of a long, long kiss, he lifts my idle right hand and places it smack on his erection. At least, I assume that's what it is. I've never really felt one before. Something silky and hard brushed the insides of my thighs when Caleb tried fruitlessly to make me his, but I never came close to touching it. Now, I almost jump, snatching my burnt hand back, but I don't want to give my Protestant-girl ignorance away. The feel of it, at once pliant and incredibly hard, has a snake's power to fascinate and horrify. I move my palm back and forth, and Mike moans and puts his tongue into my mouth and tilts his hips upward. He really likes this stuff. And I like his liking it, the confused sense of control and largess doing it to him confers.

Soon afterward, we both get involved with other people, so we never go out together again. No matter. From now on, every man I'm with has a genuine cock, whether I touch it or not. It's there, inserted into my imagination.

When I go home for Thanksgiving, I find no place for me. A bed, yes. Silverware and a plate. But no place. Awash in nostalgia,

I feel sure I had one before I went to college, though in fact I can't say what it was, and I mourn its loss.

"Can't you stay forever?" Chip asks, sitting on my bed with his back against the gladioli-splashed wallpaper and his legs stuck straight out beside my suitcase. He's four now, sturdy and sober, his blond crew cut fuzzy like a baby chick as soon as it's dry. I burst out crying, and two sympathetic tears well in his wide blue eyes and splash down onto his cheeks.

"No," I tell him, "I can't stay here forever." Ever again.

Terrified, spinning outward into a void, I do what I know how to do: I fall in love. With another girl's boyfriend. Bird-dogging, this is called. "Hey, bird dog, get away from my quail. . . ." Worse yet, he falls in love with me. Or so he claims. He calls me one night on the pay phone down the corridor. "Oh Nancy," he blurts, "I love you, I love you!" I stand in the yellowish light inside the dusty box, one hand clutching the receiver and the other on the smudged wall, my breath whooshing out as though I've just jumped overboard.

"Oh Asa, I love you, too!" Do I? Maybe. Maybe not. But I'm wholly enthralled by this urbane charmer, the eldest son of an African businessman, wealthy, widely traveled, not handsome but blazingly sexy. A sophomore at Harvard, he zips between our campuses in his red Alfa Romeo convertible, and between times he telephones, sometimes more than once a day, and writes me passionate letters, though he continues to date Amanda. For some reason, this arrangement doesn't stink to me of duplicity. As the current vernacular has it, I'm snowed.

The situation gives everyone fits. The other girls in the dorm stop speaking to me. When I walk into the smoker, the parlor, the bathroom, silence thuds around me. Mother finds out by reading my diary and Asa's letters during Christmas vacation, leading me to my best-kept vow: never to look at my children's private papers. If, as a consequence, I'll overlook some trauma, fail to meet some need, I'll have to accept that responsibility. The alternative, the violation of interior space, is worse. They may not know it, but I do. To enter another's walled garden—and this is just how I think of private writings, as a place I can retreat to alone—without invitation tells the gardener that she has no ultimate refuge. Her life is only provisionally her own. You may swagger in at any time to claim it in the name of some higher purpose: generally, if you're skilled in these tactics, her own good. In my case, Mother threatens to take me out of Wheaton and send me back to high school, on the grounds that skipping the third grade has left me too immature to deal with my problems.

Amanda swallows a bottle of aspirin one night. Shortly before finding out about this, I go into my private bathroom, take out a razor blade, and draw it slowly and rather lightly across the inside of my left wrist, which opens like a little mouth. Just then Amanda bursts into the room, looking for Puff. I lean half into the room, holding my oozing wrist over the tub, until she leaves, but when I'm free to cut some more, I find I've lost the urge. Though the cut is deep, I've missed any major arteries or veins, and before long it's stopped bleeding enough to be bandaged.

The bandage is noticeable, of course, and occasions a new outcry, including a lengthy grilling by the dorm head and her assistant. I insist implacably, however, that I snagged my wrist getting a pair of scissors out of a drawer, just as I once blamed my homesick tears at Spruce Pond Camp on a paper cut. What can anyone do to me? I'll find out later in the year, when I'm notified that my scholarship hasn't been renewed. By then, ironically, I'll be pretty much the apathetic but untroublesome student I remain till graduation. And the woman who takes it away, whose name is (honest to God) Leota C. Colpitts, will have the nerve to tell me, at graduation, how glad she is I decided to stay at Wheaton.

At the moment wrist meets razor blade, I'm as stupid about racial strife as I am about anti-Semitism, and as far as I'm concerned, our love for each other is all that counts. To his credit, Asa is never this stupid. After growing up in a socially prominent and politically powerful family, he arrived in the United States as a teenager to discover that he couldn't even get a hamburger without incident, and he's angrier than I can possibly understand. "I realise that I am in a strange society," he writes to me, "in which my kind has absolutely no right to fall in love with your kind."

Is that why he did it? I'll wonder one day: to violate that stricture, to get back at "my kind"? Of course, I'll never find out. By the time I know the questions, the opportunity for the asking will have been extinguished for years. I'll have no idea what became of Asa, effectively extinguished along with that opportunity. It's certainly easier to believe that he never loved me but simply used me to lash out at the "white supremacy" he so despised, the fact, as he put it, that "your society has the means of deciding whether or not *my* society exists." But whenever I reread his letters, I sense that the truth is probably no easier in this matter than I've found it in any other. They are undeniably, at heart, the letters of a man in love.

During the few weeks when we are closest, Asa and I spend one good day together. The rest of the times are feverish and fragmentary. On this cold January day, he drives me across the state to his prep school, Williston Academy, to meet his younger brother. We have dinner at the Northampton Inn, down the street from the campus where my daughter will begin her long voyage away from home, which will eventually carry her all the way to Africa. We are arguing amiably about whether I should have gotten the D+ in biology I seem to have earned for the semester or whether, with more effort, I could have passed.

"You're a fine one to lecture," I say. "Look at your own grades. You're not so lily-white yourself!"

His breath hisses hard into his throat and then explodes outward in an enormous laugh. When I listen to what I've just said, both hands fly up to my mouth, but he's laughing so hard I can't help but join him.

"No!" he sputters, grabbing my hands. "Not so lily-white at all!"

In the evening we drive back to Wheaton and make love in his tiny car. I'm terrifically hot, more aroused and aggressive than I've ever been before, but his caresses are restrained, almost chaste. In this treacherous society he'd be a fool to act otherwise, he is already a bit of a fool to be alone here in the bitter January dark with me, both of us shivering a little, his mouth opening under mine, his hand stroking my arm through my woolen coat, but I don't think of that.

Is that what he's thinking when he breaks our relationship off? He does it because he loves me, he says, and wants to protect me from the unhappiness social injustice will inevitably bring. "There comes a time when one must sacrifice what one wants for a greater cause," he writes. I can't think of a greater cause than me, but his, he says, is the "ascendancy" of his people. I'm light-years away from the loftiness of this rhetoric, whether authentic or specious, and anyway he's still seeing Amanda. He's either a saint or a slime, but effectively they're the same. I am desolate.

vi

I am plucked from this vortex sucking me deeper and deeper toward its black heart by the skinny arms of my White Knight. Actually, his arrival is delayed a week by a blizzard, and I spend the evening of our appointed meeting charging distractedly beside my friend Kristina through the streets around campus, empty now of traffic, heaped with heavy, stinging snow. The next Saturday, however, brings only a chilly drizzle, perfectly navigable even by a little gray Renault Dauphine that will, over the next couple of years, prove a triumph of lemonhood.

This is one of those quirky folds in the tissue of human events which, if I were writing a novel, I'd have to smooth away. A blind date. Too convenient. One of Puff's steady boyfriends, who goes to Brown, has had his Corvair stolen, and in order to persuade one of his friends to drive him to Wheaton, Dan has promised to fix him up. I know nothing about him except that his name is George and he's about five-eight, quiet, and intelligent. If I were writing a novel, I would not name the White Knight George. I don't want to go. I can hardly lug my heart out to class and back, dragging it along the snowy paths, let alone to a basketball game and a party. But I've got nothing better to do.

I wear a green woolen shirtwaist borrowed from the girl across the hall. Edgy and glum, I follow Puff into the parlor and immediately take out a cigarette. This George, thin and dark-haired, glances up through thick black lashes, fumbles for a match, and strikes it, but he's shaking so hard it goes right out. He tries again and gets it. If I were writing a novel, would I make him shake? He speaks very little, but my nervousness runs to cascades of language, so really he needs only a nod here and there. At one point, when I lean forward to ask him a question, my knee brushes his and he recoils as though burnt. I don't just then remember the Catholic boy's penis. The evening proceeds otherwise pleasantly and without menace.

Afterward, George tells Dan, who tells Puff, who tells me: "She has an amazing personality." I feel as though I've got six heads or purple hair. One day, when my son really does have purple hair, this will seem a less troubling image.

* * *

If George were left to his own devices, this would be the end of the tale. He has never, I'll learn later, dared ask a girl out a second time. In our case, of course, it's arguable whether he even asked her out the first time. Anyway, I take care of the matter. Finding that he likes folk music, I blurt, "Oh, Josh White is coming next weekend. Come up to hear him." And he drives through the rain and does.

Apparently, George can ask a girl out a third time. Since he's never gotten this far before, he probably didn't even know it till now. We drive through the rain to a hockey game this time, and then to a party. When he lights my cigarette, the match staying lit, I touch his hand, and as I take my hand away, he reaches out for it. No recoil. We stand drinking bourbon and water and holding hands like little kids at the beach.

After our fourth date, when we drive through the rain to Newport and walk the cliffs above the sea, I can't think of anything but him. Not Asa, although he's changed his mind and persists, perplexingly, in courting me off and on for months. Not biology, creative writing, French, European history, Greek philosophy, or basic motor skills, either. Only George, George, George. We've now been together thirty-nine and a half hours. I collect a mound of change and go to the stuffy phone booth.

"Oh George," I blurt. "I love you."

"I love you. I love you. I love you," he says.

This feels almost from the first moment like a much different love, an intimacy I've strained for but never quite reached before, as though some pieces of myself, inadvertently left out in my making, had been discovered and restored. The "always" feeling, I call it. The movement from home into home. I will not, in fact, always feel in love with George. I will not even always like him. Such feelings ebb and flow in a relationship as sustained and intimate as ours. But for the rest of my life, whenever he lopes unexpectedly into my field of vision, my heart will lurch and knock about the cage of my ribs until I'm giddy.

Imagine: someone who can make your heart leap up and lark around forever.

The Farm

i

I HAVE LEFT OFF living among lilies. At least for now. Perhaps forever. At the age of forty-five, deteriorating physically almost by the day, I have to confront the fact that I may no longer be able to do even those things I most want to do. "You can do whatever you put your mind to" is a watchword of rugged Americanism, and the incapacity to carry out an action is thus seen as a failure of will. In truth, however, you can't necessarily do whatever you put your body to. Some bodies, like mine, damaged by unfathomable processes of degeneration, just don't work. And there are no minds without bodies. None. The failure is not of will but literally, not metaphorically, of nerve. My central nervous system is now so wrecked that I could probably no longer cross the lawn at The Farm in one direction, to sit out under the apple tree, or in the other direction, to dip in the pool. I might not even be able to drag my feet across the humps and hollows worn by nearly three hundred years of footsteps into the wide warped floorboards of the house. I'm afraid to go back and find out.

I arrived for one of my last sojourns at The Farm on a chill sunny day quite early in June 1979, just after Aunt Jane and Uncle Kip had moved up for the summer, while the lemon lilies and iris were still in bloom, before all the asparagus had gone to fern. After settling my considerable baggage in the downstairs front bedroom, which would be mine now that I could no longer climb the stairs to the one above it, I wandered back to the kitchen. It was new to me, the ample wooden cabinets and yellow Formica counters and stainless-steel sinks and especially the wide bay window above the table. I stood staring through the newly ample panes at the sweep of garden, lavender flags and yellow trumpets against a tangle of green, the whole blurred in the long spreading shafts of late light.

"What are you looking at?" Jane asked behind me.

"Just the garden," I answered. "I was feeling the pleasure of being exactly where I want to be."

"I'm glad," she said. "I'm glad you're here."

Everyone should have one place where, when she's in it, she's exactly where she wants to be. And if she can no longer return to it, well, at least she'll have been there. That's something.

ii

Because I usually spend a few days of spring vacation with Jane and Kip, I happen to be with them the day they find The Farm. May 3, 1958. A gray Saturday, a steady cold drizzle streaking the windows of Kip's Nash Rambler station wagon. He and Jane sit in the front seat. I share the back seat with Lars, who's three. In a car bed in the way back, Jon alternately frets and wails. At nearly six months, Jon is well out of the danger posed by being born two months premature, though his features retain a fetal cast, huge brown eyes dominating a long, thin face, far into childhood. He lacks the placidity of the rosy plump babies at home, Chip and Barba, however, and today's itinerary would try even their cheerful temperaments, all this winding along the back roads of southern New Hampshire, stopping to look at one derelict house after another, places with gray asphalt shingles, cracked and crusty linoleum floors, heaps of old tires in the backyard. Lurching along with the windows up against the rain has made me queasy, and whatever joy the prospect of house hunting might have held has long since washed away by the time we drive up beside a dark house in Brentwood, the last of the day, Jane and Kip have promised, its brown siding stained almost black by the soaking rain.

Jonny has finally fallen asleep, and we leave him in the car. I gulp wet air, sweet and grassy, and look up at the house. It's larger than any of the others we've seen, and older, a two-story square front section with a one-story kitchen attached to the back, and a shed attached behind that, and a separate barn behind the whole. All its lines slope as though it were some giant elderly animal settled into the tall grass to drowse. On the west side and at the back tower old maples, as well as a couple of gnarled pear trees and an apple, beyond which the land drops steeply to a swampy bottom and then the rolling fields of the neighboring farm. Not much to the east except a sagging chicken house, an apple tree, a broad, flat alfalfa field surrounded by piney woods.

We go inside. The house has been vacant a long time, the windows boarded up, and the air is dank with damp plaster and old wood. In the gathering spring dusk, we grope our way through the eight rooms of the main part, the two attics, the kitchen and back kitchen and shed, scuffling sometimes ankle deep through detritus—dead bugs and dry leaves and God knows what else. Jane and Kip exclaim about everything. The fireplaces. The wainscoting and wide floorboards. The sagging ceilings, said to hide the original beams. The twisting, steep back stairwell.

I am appalled. I don't know the first thing about architecture of any sort, not even this sturdy colonial architecture that must have housed my own forebears. My ideas about dream houses run to built-in wall ovens and pine-paneled rumpus rooms in the cellar, like many of my friends have. This place hasn't even got a real cellar, only a cobwebbed hole scooped out beside the ledge most of the house sits on. At least a toilet, for God's sake. Here there's no running water. A creaking pump in the kitchen sink. A two-holer in the shed. I can't voice my horror, of course. I'm too uncertain of my own standards. Even in my diary, where I practice adult sentiments, I record neutrally, "A lovely spot—it will take loads of time & money to make the house suitable, but it looks worth it." But privately, I think it's a frightful wreck.

"It's perfect," Jane and Kip say. "We'll take it."

And it is, in fact, perfect. I simply have to learn that perfection, in houses as in persons, is a process, not a state, vision knit slowly into reality through stroke after stroke of straw broom, sandpaper, paintbrush, washrag. Certainly this is a house very much in process. Reassuringly, indoor plumbing arrives early on, although Kip's refusal to spend the money for a deep well creates a chronic water shortage. "Flush only when necessary," admonishes a card above the toilet. Down come the ceilings, and sure enough, hand-hewn beams stretch above. Down comes the wall between the living room and dining room, freeing the sawtooth profile of a fireplace of worn, rosy brick.

The siding on the east wall starts falling away and has to be replaced, as does the rest of the siding eventually, as well as all the windows. The main chimneys have to be rebuilt. By this time the bats have lost their ingress to the attic and can no longer drop, through the slightest navigational error, into Granna's room instead of out under the northeast eave, and so we can throw away the warped squash racquet, known as the Bat Bat, with which we swat strays senseless and scoop them into coffee cans to be carried out to the garden. True, we can no longer watch them drop one by one from the house corner and swoop out across the dusky fields, but they don't migrate far—only to the maples, from which they carry on their flittery rituals.

Slowly the house, whose old bones seemed to me on that May afternoon destined to slump and topple into a sort of elephants' graveyard at the edge of the narrow dirt road, squares its shoulders again. The grounds grow tame, though never too tidy, with wide lawns and flower beds and vegetable gardens and even a swimming pool. Only the barn goes on decaying, its weathered boards listing more crazily by the year. One day, we're sure, it will groan mightily and collapse in a heap of splinters, probably under a load of wet new snow when no one is near enough to hear it.

Hardscrabble Farm, it was called traditionally, and the name sticks. But the chilled and meager life of the Averills who named it, and who are buried now in the old cemetery over on the Gordon Road, has given way to summer after summer of peace and ease.

iii

I come to live at Hardscrabble Farm by happenstance. A scholarship student at an expensive private women's college, I desperately need a summer job. I apply to inns on Nantucket and Martha's Vineyard, to summer camps all over New England, but no one will have me. To help out, Jane offers to take me on as a mother's helper until I can find something better. Nothing, it quickly becomes apparent, could possibly be better.

Jane is not my mother. I mention this self-evident fact because it may be the single most important distinction in my development. Every girl should have a mother, I think, not the sort of predatory monster sketched out and whined about in pop-psych books designed to cop a chunk of the bestseller trade, but an ordinary mother like mine, flawed but serviceable, who will hang your kindergarten plaque in her kitchen and teach you to sew an invisible hem in your skirts and stay up watching a late movie with you both because she likes you and because she likes the movie. She may, like mine, take some of her responsibilities too seriously, especially in matters (not entirely unrelated) of politeness and sex, and in this way cause you both a good bit of unnecessary teeth gnashing and sleeplessness. But unless, unlike mine, she's some kind of a nut, you'll learn to interpret the clamp of emotional hands on your spirit as one of love's shape-shifting signs and to pry her fingers free without breaking them or the heart they clutch.

At the same time, every girl should have a not-mother, a woman who has, in every sense, no stake in you. If you're a bad child, no one will blame her. And she has a much narrower interpretation of badness than your mother, anyway. Almost nothing you do seems to strike her as bad. A lot more of what you do strikes her as funny. Like when you build a "cat house," you solemnly tell her, for sleek, striped Minnie. Or when you lather yourself lavishly with the expensive soap from S.S. Pierce shaped exactly like a lemon, with a lemon's maddening pungency. She's under no obligation to warn you that certain words "aren't nice" or to exhort you to thrift. She's under no obligation at all. That's what a girl needs: a woman who's free to love her without fretting whether she's going to grow up to be all right.

I have Jane.

For two weeks each summer, as our household expands to incorporate Mother, Chip, and Barba, the conjunction of a mother and a not-mother perplexes and pains me. The sisters have evolved an ambivalent relationship, at once intimate and suspicious, which charges the atmosphere uneasily, the way it feels not before or during a thunderstorm but when you're not yet sure whether a thunderstorm will boil up later in the day. They could ease the tension immeasurably, of course, by acknowledging the moments when they're giving each other fits, as though giving another person fits and getting fits in return were the perfectly normal, and generally short-lived, activity I will one day discover it to be. This measure is absolutely out of the question. No, more. *Out of the question* suggests an action contemplated and then discarded. This is unthinkable. In our family, hostile thoughts toward one another are proscribed, which means, of course, that the hostile thoughts, inevitable between intimates no matter how affectionate, have to be sealed off like abscesses, sensitivity to pressure and intermittent fever their only traces. And, in my case, loss of appetite.

"I hate Sally!" I remember shouting when we were children bickering. "I hate her! I hate her!"

"You don't really hate her," Mother would respond in her coolest, most reasonable tone. "You really love her. She's your *sister.*"

But in brief bursts I really did hate her, though most of the time I loved her without difficulty, and without measure. Those brief bursts, though—toward Sally, toward Mother herself, toward anyone I also loved—those brief bursts almost did me in. I swallowed them and swallowed them until they filled me up and I stopped eating and got put into a mental hospital. That sojourn in a mental hospital came about for complicated reasons, not merely abscesses of anger. But my lack of any acceptable means for recognizing, airing, and then abandoning hostile feelings was certainly a critical factor.

The relationship between Mother and Jane seems a little different from Sally's and mine, though—more tainted by the past. Three years apart, separated by their placid brother Robert, they share humorous memories, like the time Granna took one into the bathroom for a spanking with the hairbrush and the brush snapped in her hand before she could bring it to bear on the intended bottom; the other, crouched outside, gasped in horror as her mother exited bearing the brush in two pieces and vowed to be good foreverandeverandever. Or the time, right before dancing school, Jane prevailed upon Mother to cut off her despised braids and Mother obliged without unplaiting them first, leaving six distinct levels for Granna to try to even out and frizz with the curling iron before whisking the girls off to Miss James with her taffeta dresses and clicking castanets.

But they also share sources of bitterness Sally and I lack. Their parents' divorce fell at very different times in their lives, leaving Mother on one side of the rift with her wounded, neurasthenic mother and Jane on the other with her dashing and wayward father, believing herself like him, misunderstood, the black sheep. You can see their different ways of being in their childhood photos: Mother blond and blue-eyed, pretty, smiling; Jane slighter, darker, always glowering at the camera. Mother claims to have felt painfully shy, but the images that float on film are serene, unself-conscious yet self-possessed: the bearing I associate with the first child, who is, even if for only seventeen months, the sole occupant of her parents' house. A few years later, Mother had a high school boyfriend with whom Jane fell in love, hopelessly, of course, being still a skinny little girl in handsome Darren's eyes, a good kid though maybe a bit of a pest, and this experience must have increased her sense of being on the outside, dispossessed. Now that they're adults, Granna has chosen to live with Mother. She visits Jane frequently. Just about as frequently as Jane can stand, I sus-pect. All the same, this arrangement throws the familial alignment out of balance.

During my Farm summers, these patterns are still pro-nounced, though later their traces will fade and the pattern of friendship between the two women will overlay them palimpsesti-cally. Jane's clinging to the image of herself as "the runt of the litter," I note in a letter, "assures her of a kind of independence from her family that the other children can't have." For Mother's part, she sails serenely in her big-sister bubble, outspoken, opin-ionated, oblivious (whether willfully or otherwise I never figure out) to the distress her pronouncements stir up. I cringe inwardly at each offhand remark I know Jane will dislike or misconstrue until I've shrunk into a wretched ball of tension. These are the two women I love the most, in absolutely different but equally intense ways, in all the world; and I haven't yet learned that the trick when two beloveds disagree is not to shrink but to stretch until they both fit into the world you're weaving. Admittedly, such a process makes for some lumps and bumps in the weft, but what counts in home-spun is not its fineness but its durability. I do at least figure out that, except in indirect ways the subtleties of which I'll need twenty more years to understand, the situation has nothing to do with me, and I stop feeling mixed up in it, though I sure as hell feel mixed up about it.

iv

In hiring me, Jane is helping herself out, too. She can't find time for her writing when she has to chase after two little boys. My task is to do the chasing while she makes the poems. Our days quickly take on a slow, ample, summery rhythm. She writes in the mornings. The boys and I can do whatever we like as long as we're quiet. After lunch we all rest. Then, if the weather is fine, we amble a mile down the dirt road toward the Potters' house and go swimming where the river bends under the bridge. This is the Exeter River, which swells and tumbles impressively in the spring, but by this time it's shallow and tepid, the color of iced tea. Even on rainy days, we often put on our slickers and walk, sometimes all the way through the Gordon Road to Lindy's for milk or a loaf of bread.

From one end of the summer to the other, except for rare trips to Boston, I never wear shoes. My feet grow leather soles of their own, thick yellowish calluses, and the toes spread comfortably. Before long, I can walk down the pebbly dirt road, over the stubble of the alfalfa field, as easily as through the soft brown garden loam. I spend the first month of every fall mincing in agony like one of Cinderella's stepsisters.

Back at home, Jane always cooks dinner. Always. She can't stand other people messing around in her kitchen, unless it's Mother chopping cabbage for cole slaw, which she does, Jane assures her, "better than anyone else in the whole world." If you want to get someone else to do a job you don't like, Jane's is a surefire formula. When I have a kitchen of my own, I will use it to get Mother to make the gravy every Thanksgiving. From all the practice, she really does chop cabbage and make gravy better than anyone else in the whole world. I learn to cook here in Jane's kitchen, not through practice, because she won't let me have any, but through observation, and I will never prepare a meal without feeling Jane's presence beneath my skin as I stir and sniff and splash and pinch and sprinkle.

Since Jane is every bit as messy a cook as I will turn out to be, after dinner the kitchen bears its resemblance to the Augean stables. My task is thus not inconsiderable: I clean it up. Then I sing to the boys or read them a story before tucking them in. Before long Jane and I are nodding over our books and tuck ourselves in, too.

Although as a rule I hate housework, here I take erratic fits of domesticity, born of a compulsion to feel this house under my palms, to scour and polish and perfect it somehow: the only way to communicate love to a house. I dissolve Oakite in a big bucket of hot water and scrub all the kitchen and bathroom woodwork. I put pans of steaming water into the aged refrigerator and pry delicately at the polar ice cap it has formed since last week. Jane murdered the previous even more aged refrigerator, and very nearly herself, by jabbing a knife into its Freon-filled guts, so my delicacy is born of terror. I wash the humped and splintery kitchen floorboards on my hands and knees, apply a layer of pungent amber wax, and waltz a borrowed electric polisher back and forth until the surface glows. Making the floor sing, I call it. My fingernails grow an accretion of green oxidized-copper gudge and tar and white paint and paste wax.

For my eighteenth birthday, Jane bakes me a chocolate cake. The oven is old and quirky, and whether for this reason or because Jane has left some vital ingredient out, the cake doesn't rise at all. Not at all. Pried free of the pan, it slouches over the edge of a plate like a dark brown tam-o'-shanter. Plainly we can't eat it. But we're reluctant to throw it out, a whole cake like that, not even a bite taken out. We put it on top of the refrigerator to deal with later. When we discover it there after three weeks, it looks like a furry green tam-o'-shanter.

We are making me a room of my own. That's how I get paint under my fingernails. I am to have the upstairs northwest room, across the hall from Granna's with its green-painted floor and yellow woodwork and yellow wallpaper garlanded with tiny pink and green flowers. My woodwork is white, the wallpaper patterned like a quilt with red and blue flowers on a white ground. I have a heavy dark dresser and a sleigh bed and in one corner a white iron crib in case of visiting babies. Most important, I have my own work table and chair beneath the two front windows, painted light blue and spread with my typewriter and books and pads of paper, where I am to write poems, Jane says. This is just the kind of mother's helper I need to be, one whose duties include writing poems. Later, after I'm married and Sally takes over as mother's helper, this will be her room, and still later it will belong to Jane's closest friend, Ellen Norton. But for now, except when an occasional visiting baby stays the night, it belongs to me.

On Wednesday nights and weekends, our tranquil existence lurches into a different mode. Wednesday nights Kip comes up from his job in Boston, tired and hot and cross, and if everything isn't just right, his crossness spills over and splashes us, corrosive. As each Wednesday wears on, Jane and I scurry faster and faster, making sure both the ice cap in the refrigerator and the zucchinis on the vine are of less than epic proportions. After he buys a freezer, we master a new ritual: picking, washing, chopping, blanching, plunging into ice water, scooping into plastic bags then sealed with twisties and shoved into white boxes labeled with waxy black crayon. Green beans and yellow beans and purple beans. Broccoli. Kohlrabi. In August when the vegetables burgeon riotously, Jane threatens to smuggle loads into the woods and abandon them like Hänsel and Gretel, but she never does. We freeze every sprig and stalk we don't serve fresh.

Usually once Kip sheds his city clothes, climbs into his grubby cutoffs, and ambles barefoot into his garden for weeding and watering, the danger of an outburst is past. Still, we all walk on emotional tiptoe. I've had so little experience living with men, really only a half dozen or so years with my stepfather, whose emotional style is wholly different, contained, even cool, that this man's anger seems as dangerous as a brushfire. I'm too young to imagine its roots, the dissonance he must feel between our easy hours here and his own harried pace over Boston's baking pavements, his impermissible desire to live at home among women, the way Jane and I do, almost as irresponsibly as children as far as he's concerned. We're not children, of course, but sometimes his anger scorches away our adulthood and leaves us as shamefaced as though we were.

The ceiling in the front hall falls down.

On weekends we run a kind of slapdash hotel, where I learn hospitality. I haven't really had occasion to acquire this habit before. The house at 236 holds seven of us, together with our Irish setter Pegeen and a series of cats: striped Honeybun and polka-dotted Muffy Puffy and black Sing-a-Ling who vanishes, perhaps in the grip of a hawk, and Sandy the pale, placid marmalade. We're hard pressed to squeeze in a single overnight guest. Nor do Mother and Daddy give parties very often. I suspect they don't care to introduce any more confusion into the house than dwells there permanently.

Confusion doesn't seem to bother Jane and Kip. In addition to their large and intimate families, they have a wide and motley acquaintanceship, drawn in large measure from Boston's Chorus Pro Musica, in which Kip sings, and the writers Jane knows; and a weekend without houseguests is rare. Sometimes we are fourteen or more at table: the wonderful long trestle table one houseguest put together out of pine boards he found out in the barn, built entirely with pegs, no nails or glue, which Jane and I sanded and oiled and waxed, hour upon hour, until the surface sang just like my kitchen floor.

We eat queer food, it seems to me, sometimes big plates of nothing but vegetables, buttery beets leaking ruby juice, kohlrabi with caraway seeds, green beans, fat slices of tomato sprinkled thickly with freshly chopped basil. I've grown up thinking that a proper meal consists of a pork chop, a mound of mashed potatoes, and frozen green peas, and no matter how much else I eat, I can't feel full without some meat. Frankly (and I have to say this in a whisper), I'm not that crazy about vegetables. In later years, as my diet becomes increasingly vegetarian, I'll dream back to those meals. I'll buy a bunch of basil and plunge my nose into its voluptuous aroma, carried instantaneously into the yellow kitchen, hot on a Sunday afternoon, steamy from all the cooking vegetables, children and adults swirling in and out, half a dozen conversations going at once, squeaky children's voices and fluty women's voices against the basso continuo of the men. All this from a whiff of basil: the most erotic smell I know.

Houseguests entail hard work, I discover. I log countless hours in front of the old white sink, plunging one brown-and-white plate, one heavy white mug, one pot after another into a battered tin dishpan of frothy hot water. Never alone, though. At this hotel the guests grab towels and dry the dishes. Here I first meet Ellen, down from Tilton with her husband and five children. I've written a poem with the line "truth is the pulse in the palm of your hand." It's a bad line, but Ellen doesn't say that.

"Do you really feel a pulse in the *palm* of your hand?" she asks me instead, discarding a sopping towel for a dry one. I'm startled. I don't think it's yet occurred to me that one may not only make a poem but also discuss the way it's made. And Ellen's tone is serious, matter-of-fact, not in the least condescending. She doesn't sound as though she thinks it's cute that I write poems. She just seems to want to make sure I've gotten this poem right. What that line states is, I guess, a biological impossibility. And yet. . . .

"Yes," I say slowly, sensing my palms as they dip beneath the soapsuds and raise a handful of forks, coming to awareness of my body through the words I've written. "Yes, I seem to."

"Well, then," she says, sounding satisfied, "if you really do, that's fine."

At this hotel the guests don't merely dry the dishes, they

critique your poems as well. I'm much too young, and too confused about my desires, to believe myself a writer. A writer is what I "want" to be, "hope" to be, "some day," when I "grow up." When I finally recognize, nearly twenty years later, that I'm all the grown up I'm going to get, so if I'm going to be a writer, I'd better just call myself one and get on with it, I'll remember Ellen's sober question as a kind of initiation: she thought I was a writer right then.

Except for the name, this isn't a real farm, of course, but a summer place. Still, the ebb and flow of vegetables confers a farmlike rhythm: from Early Curly lettuce and strawberries through zucchini and beans and corn, if the raccoons ever leave us any, straight on through pumpkins and parsnips. We keep Rhode Island Reds, too, in the musty little hen house, with a rooster named Lucky Pierre, so every day we have warm brown eggs to soft-boil for breakfast, sprinkling their sunny contents with fresh chives. And one summer, after my time, there's even a heifer named Black-eyed Susan, borrowed as a lawn mower.

Once a summer the Potters mow our alfalfa field to have hay for their cows over the winter. Round and round goes the tractor with its whirring blades, the circles smaller and smaller, and once John Potter brings us a pheasant, its legs accidentally lopped off, to roast for dinner so as not to waste it. Then comes the clattering baler, which binds the hay not into the blocks I'm used to but into giant rolls, "like the things Nancy puts in her hair," Jonny observes. When the bales are loaded, I jump with the workers onto the truck, smothered in the fragrance of half-green hay, and jounce down the dirt road to the Potters'.

Helen and John Potter and their five children live in a white farmhouse a little newer than ours, statelier and more spacious, with a sturdy barn, square on its foundation, where John keeps a half-dozen or so dairy cows. Thus, he's much more a farmer than we are, though he can't make a living at it but works as an engineer at Raytheon down in Massachusetts. We toss the sweet prickly bales one after another up into the barn loft. The cows are out now, grazing in the pasture to the east, but their reek mingles with the golden hay-dust in the thick air.

Around us slink and scamper the barn cats, not house pets but real workers, spooky and suspicious of people. One has a nest of kittens, and I fall in love with a tiny orange and white male, which Jane says I may take home if I promise to bring him back at the end of the summer. The cats at home—aloof Mister Black and his tabby grandmother, Jenny Lind—are polite but clearly not thrilled. Pêcheur, our young black moyen poodle, is transported, however, the light of motherhood glowing in his eyes. Scrabble keeps me constant company, and I weep when, true to my word, I take him back to the barn at the end of August. On a visit later in the fall, I find him again, rangy now and as skittish as the rest of the cats. He doesn't seem to recognize me at all.

I am happy here, so happy that I think now and then, with a little start of guilt, that I ought to be paying Jane and Kip twenty-five dollars a week to let me live in my red, white, and blue room, sleep in my sleigh bed, gather fresh eggs and handfuls of basil, make the kitchen floor sing.

v

I do not, for the most part, know that I am happy at The Farm. I'm not yet prepared for happiness. I'm always going to be happy as soon as . . . As soon as school gets out for the summer. As soon as Caleb falls in love with me. As soon as I can go to college. Just now, I'm waiting for marriage. As soon as George and I can be together all the time, I'll be happy.

I have no means for seeing that "as soon as" is a signpost pointing to no place, *ou topos*, black hole devouring dream and desire. I am following its direction in good faith. I have been schooled in deferral: "You may wear lipstick when you're a bigger girl," my mentors have told me. "You may wear nylon stockings next year." "You're not quite old enough to use Tampax." "You can't drink alcohol until you're twenty-one." "Don't have sex until you're married." I believe that, by waiting, I'll finally get somewhere: elsewhere: to that infinitely mysterious, infinitely seductive realm of adulthood. Avalon, the island of apples, where that which was forbidden may be partaken of freely.

But *there* is *nowhere*. *There* one can never be. Only *here*. I can be happy here, or I can be unhappy here, or I can be something other than happy or unhappy here. Those are my only options. Life happens only in the present tense: here, now. I can say, I *was* happy once/before/then/whenever I plunged my face into apple blossoms/on Wednesday, April 8, 1959; but I'm really saying, in shorthand, as I recall events right this minute, I believe myself to have felt happy about them. If I've been very orderly (as I once "was"), I may even corroborate my current belief from an old diary: "Everything is perfect & I'm so happy I could burst." That too, however, is a record of a present moment. I may also say, I *will be* happy as soon as something happens which hasn't happened yet and isn't happening now, but beyond a vague faith in my own continuation, I can mean nothing by it. Its corroboration depends solely on the slow sifting of presence into the intransigent absence of the future—on the destruction of future, that is, through its transformation into this woman, now: happy, unhappy, neither, both, who believes the future to be not some Blessed Isle of Ever After but the following page in a hilariously Byzantine novel. What on earth, she thinks to herself, could happen next?

During my summers at The Farm, I am not so readily amused. George and I are not married, so we can't be together all the time, so I can't yet be happy.

In fact, however, we are together a surprising amount of the time. Jane takes to him instantly, to his dark, downcast eyes and gentle manners and verbal playfulness, and welcomes him whenever he can make it up from his parents' home in Massachusetts. She says this is to keep the hired girl from jumping out of her skin. A few weeks into the first summer, as he is lighting her cigarette, his fingers trembling almost as wildly as they did the night we first met, Jane looks square at him and says, "I think you've known us long enough now that you can stop shaking." He stops.

The Farm provides an ideal setting for courtship, much better than the "dates" we've been having in college. Occasionally we still go out, one night to hear the Weavers at Castle Hill, another to wander the streets around Harvard Square, but these lack the formality, the pressure to "do" something, that traditional dating imposes. Much of the time we just hang around home. The influx of weekend houseguests generally guarantees more liveliness and peculiarity than we could cook up on our own, anyway. It also provides natural occasions for checking one another out as future partners and parents. You can learn a lot about a person by watching him deal with the dripping chocolate ice cream cone of a four-year-old in the back of his parents' Renault Dauphine.

When we're apart, I pine, though he writes me engaging letters to while away the time. They don't come every day, however, and nothing less would satisfy me. Daily I tune my hearing to a finer and finer pitch till I catch the rumble of the mailman's red pickup truck. Then I amble, or my best version of ambling under conditions so trying to the nerves, out to the mailbox across the road. Sometimes there are wasps in the mailbox. Occasionally even a mama field mouse. More frequently, a letter from George. If not, my pining escalates, sometimes reaching a level so virulent that it infects Jane, who comes down with a case of sympathetic pining, and then we make a sorry pair.

"Did I tell you about free-carding?" George writes of his summer job as a door-to-door salesman.

This is a means of finding prospective clients for Cutco and ensuring entrance to their homes. You stop a young woman on the street and inquire whether she has received her free gift from Cutco. If she doesn't give you a glassy stare and walk on, you get her to fill out a little card—name, address, where employed, and most convenient hour for delivery of the gift.

Yesterday a young housewife from South Boston took the bait and filled out a card. Today I drove through the Sumner Tunnel to her address—a housing development, brick boxes among the warehouses and factories.

There was a green wooden door that wouldn't quite shut. Light in the corridors came from a window at each end. Walls were yellow tile with gray cement between. The floors were cement spotted with stains. Brown steel does not make a very handsome door; some had cards on them and some did not. There was no directory of tenants' names and I did not know her apartment number. One individual had put a woolly green mat in front of his ugly steel door.

There were flies, so many flies, humming in the air and crawling on the walls. From one apartment came the noise of a television set, very loud. *The Price Is Right.* I knocked and the noise stopped and there was a great deal of shuffling about. Finally a toothless old woman opened the door.

"Sorry to bother you, Ma'am, but could you tell me where I might find Mrs. Rivera?"

She mumbled something about the top floor and I climbed the stairs, following her directions. At the end of the corridor was the door, behind which a baby was crying. Next to it was a window overlooking the tar courtyard. Fifty yards away was another brick box, and behind that, a very tall factory building. There was a little grass and dirt around the tar and a spindly tree, protected from the neighborhood dogs by a chicken wire fence, but dying anyway.

Inside the baby screamed and a little child talked loudly and excitedly. Mrs. Rivera was trying to quiet them. There were flies around the window. I stood for a few minutes in the hallway and then walked down to my car and drove back home through the Sumner Tunnel.

I can quote George's letters at length not because I have a photographic memory (mine is eidetic, a quirkier and less reliable mode) but because I save every one of them, which will eventually form a jumbly stack about five inches high, sorted roughly by period: Brown, junior year; Summer 1961. . . .

He doesn't return the favor. He can't, he says. He'd drown. So when he's preparing to leave his parents' home, he weeds them out and eliminates huge chunks of my past. What criteria he uses to determine which are worth saving and which can go I can't imagine: most of the ones he keeps strike me as pretty dumb. How could the others have been worse?

He doesn't just toss them into a trash can. That would be disrespectful, he says, but I suspect he's also afraid they might attract his mother's curiosity. So he pours himself a glass of sherry and squats on the rug in front of his parents' fireplace, reading each one and tossing it on the flames until they're all reduced to a little pile of ashes. When he tells me what he's done, I pretend to be offended, but actually I kind of like having occasioned an impromptu ritual. In some ways he takes me more seriously than I take myself.

Leap. Leap. Leap. I am bounding across the slope below the garden where George is riding the lawnmower, to fetch him to dinner. He always finds some chore as thanks for Jane and Kip's hospitality. Over his sneezing and the roar of the little tractor's engine, he can't hear the resonant *bing-bong* of the Bermuda bell we tromp on to call everyone to meals, but he can see me springing across the mown grass, rising through the yellow early-evening air, tumbling to the ground, writhing in pain. He cuts off the motor and runs to pick me up.

"What's the matter?"

"Ow-ow-ow-ow-ow!" Actually, nothing much turns out to be the matter, though the initial pain masks the fact. Descending to earth, I've caught the toes of my left foot under me and come down full weight on the big one. I've probably broken it, Kip says with doctorly insouciance, but nothing can be done for broken toes. They just have to heal on their own. It turns a vivid spectrum of colors, pale yellow through turquoise right down to purplish black, and I limp for several days. Then it heals.

Was this the first sign of "foot drop," I'll wonder years later, the earliest and most dramatic symptom of my multiple sclerosis? "Foot drop" and my pernicious, inexorable fatigue. Who knows? There's no definitive test for MS, and even if there were, a stumble in the garden would hardly call for a neurological evaluation. Just as well. There's nothing to be done for MS, either. What I don't know, in this case, really can't hurt me. I've got ten good years left.

George has been helping Jon and Lars build a fort in the woods out of a big hole Pêcheur has dug, surrounded with logs from a fresh-cut tree. Here, armed with wooden cannons and rifles, they've been shooting air-Germans. Now they've returned to the kitchen for cold drinks. George holds the bottle of ginger ale Lars is about to pour up to the light and squints.

"Oh no, Lars," he says, "I don't think you should drink out of this bottle. It has little orgasms in it." Conveniently, he's standing in front of the bathroom so that, as Jane and I let out whoops of laughter, he simply and rapidly steps backward, closing the bathroom door behind him, and stays in there a very, very long time.

"Mmmmph," Jane gasps, doubled over, waving the paring knife in her left hand in the direction of the closed door. "I wonder what he gots on his mind."

That's it, all right. What we've both got on our minds. To use a ridiculous cultural metaphor.

We have a nightly ritual. When all the plates and mugs and pots have been scoured and dried and stowed in cupboards, when the boys have brushed their teeth and had a story and been tucked into bed, we announce casually that our chores are done and we're going for a walk. And we do walk a little way, into the sheep pasture or across the alfalfa field, dewy grass stroking our bare calves, fireflies blazing their coded seductions, greenish and eerily still in the muggy air. As soon as we feel invisible from the house, we drop to the ground and clutch each other like drowning sailors going down, who cares, for the last sweet time.

This sequence of actions generally provokes interventionist hysteria on the part of Pêcheur, who has appointed himself my duenna. Gender roles aren't one of his main concerns. His nervous protectiveness can come in handy, like the time, being a country girl and not knowing any better, I took him for a walk along Boston's Esplanade at night. I'd let him off the leash for a run when a man approached from my left.

"Have you ever seen a hard-on?" he asked, really quite conversationally.

"Oh yes," I replied in my politest tea-party tone, "lots of times." This wasn't strictly the truth. Actually, it wasn't remotely the truth. I had, by this time, felt a hard-on under my palm through a pair of trousers (the pulse in the palm of my hand?), but I assuredly had not seen one. I don't think I even knew it was the sort of thing you could look at with the naked eye.

"Would you like to see one now?"

"No," I said, my tone flat, perhaps a little weary. "No, I don't think I would tonight." I'd turned my steps toward the lighted pedestrian overpass that would carry me back across Storrow Drive to the Hill, but I couldn't see the damned black dog in the black shadows. And I couldn't whistle. I mean, I'd never been able to whistle anyway, and I knew I wasn't about to master the skill just now with my sandpapery lips and tongue. "Pêche!" I called out, my voice surprisingly strong. "Come on, boy! Time to go!" And bless him, out of the darkness he gamboled, big and dark and woolly, right up to have his leash snapped onto his red collar.

The man with the precious wares veered back toward the dark. "Well anyway," he called over his shoulder, "good night."

The trouble is that Pêche can't distinguish between that encounter and the one George and I are having now. Whither I go, there will he be also, jumping right in to join the frolic, so that some of our most passionate kisses land on a damp nose or a curly flank. This will turn out to be good practice for the particular future we're going to have, the hours of rocking and grunting under the round feline stares of Ho Tei, Ho's Anna, Balthasar, Gwydion, Vanessa Bell. . . .

As George learns about my body, I learn with him. This body I've treated like a piece of embroidery wrapped in tissue and laid in a bridal chest turns out to be very much alive. George tugs my shirt out of my shorts and reaches under it to rub my back. He unbuttons it and strokes my breasts. He pushes his hand under the waist of my shorts and touches my belly. He doesn't ever actually reach down there, but down there has waked up; I can feel it as I throw my legs around his and press my thighs together, in, out, in, out.

I want to go all the way, I'm ready, but here he balks. I never quite figure out why. Certainly he's excited enough. But he's also, though I hate to admit it, absolutely conventional. He's saving himself for marriage. Maybe saving me for marriage, too, since I haven't the sense to do it myself. Our mothers would be proud. I never quite forgive him.

All the same, we cherish these arousals in the sweet prickly grass. We come into the house limp and weary, chilled in our dew-soaked clothes, itchy with mosquito bites and sneezy with hay fever, our mouths swollen, eyes unfocused in the sudden light, as near to bliss as we are ever likely to be.

The rhythm of our summers: arrival and departure. Together and apart. George often leaves while I'm still asleep. I wake and stumble around in the hole of his absence.

"Monday morning out near the end of Skimmilk Road," he writes to my pining self, "two cows had broken out of pasture and were walking along in the gutter. They turned to watch me approach. Twenty-five feet between me and them. They kick up their heels and jump in front of me. Brakes. 'You dirtygoddamncowssons-ofbitches!' I'm moving up on them slowly, stealthily. They honest-to-God grinned at me. They turn their dainty cowasses to me. They feel the hot breath of the Renault on them. Voom. They jump apart and I start through. No. They gallop full tilt up the street and block me off again. Cows and poodles accelerate faster than Renaults. I come rushing at them—fierce car with horn bleeping (country horn, of course) and fierce driver glaring and swearing. They skip apart and I'm through and rushing away and they're grinning maliciously after me."

It's not so easy to escape The Farm.

Once when I answer a knock at the kitchen door, I see beyond the canopy of wisteria not George but Caleb, and my heart sinks. I ended my relationship with Caleb not long after I met George, well over a year ago. What I don't understand, and won't understand for almost twenty more years, more time than I've even been alive till now, is that Caleb hasn't ended his relationship with me, that that is quite a different matter and in a queer sense none of my business, in the bossy and meddlesome manner in which I define "my business." He's spent the past year at the University of Chicago, from which he wrote me a good many muddled and often miserable letters whose witty and affectionate tone went clear over my head. Reading them merely made me feel tired and sort of sad, as I feel now at the prospect of spending time with him. I haven't any erotic energy left over.

I'm surprised to see that his body is taller and thicker. His face looks older, too, still handsome in a broody way: blue eyes set deep above high flushed cheekbones, thin pouting lips. The day is overcast but muggy, and his rumpled blue oxford-cloth shirt is open over his smooth chest, the armpits stained dark. His face is also wet.

"You look fagged," I say.

"I hitched. Took me hours. Had a hell of a time getting a ride." Hanging from the belt of his jeans is a good-sized blade in a leather sheath.

"Well, for God's sake," I say in my mother's most exasperated tone, "who's going to pick you up with that thing in plain view?"

"At least it's not concealed," he shrugs. He's got a point, though I'm not about to concede it.

"Come on in." I push back the screened door.

Jane welcomes him with her unstinting hospitality. Any friend of Nancy's . . . His tone and his actions ("actings," I've come to call them) are as stilted as ever. *Drop the damned accent!* I still want to shout, shaking his shoulders. *Just speak as yourself!* Only now my impatience is softened only by a kind of reflexive affection, not by passion. And I don't know what "self" I have in mind. This is the only Caleb I've known.

After the others have gone to bed, Caleb and I sit on the green cotton cushions of the bamboo couch in the living room and drink beer and go on talking. This has always yoked us: the ability to entertain each other endlessly in conversation. A few times he drops his German accent and glances at me straight and I think I detect pain in his eyes, but not anger. Not even when I tell him that George and I plan to get engaged at Christmas. By Christmas Caleb will be long gone. He's dropped out of Chicago and plans to go abroad in September for a long time. Maybe forever. He sounds lonely when he says it, possibly even scared, but firm.

"I'm exhausted," I say at last. "It's almost four. And the boys get up early." We take our beer bottles and dirty ashtray out to the kitchen, then climb the front stairs and part on the landing, he into Granna's room, I into mine. I tumble onto the sleigh bed, where Scrabble has already curled up, impatient with my lateness.

I'm not sure how much later I wake. Probably only a few minutes, because my brain has that itchy feeling it gets as soon as I fall asleep after drinking too much beer. Caleb has climbed onto the bed and is yanking the sheet aside. Does he still have on his clothes? I'm not sure. He pulls up my nightgown, presses my thighs apart with his knees, and pushes his penis through my hymen.

I suck in air through my teeth. It *hurts*. I twist my face away and press my hand across my mouth. I'd like to wail, shout, shove Caleb's heavy thrusting body off me, but I can't make any noise because Jane and Kip are asleep in the next room, their bed perhaps six feet from mine, only a warped door between. It doesn't take very long. Caleb sinks briefly on top of me, rolls off, walks out, pulling the hall door to behind him.

I lie flat on my back, staring into the dark, for a few minutes. I feel sticky between my thighs, but I don't reach down to touch myself. Before long I thud into sleep as though pushed from a cliff. No dreams.

The boys do wake me early. When I get up, I see blood on the sheets, still quite red, and think my period must have come a couple of weeks early. Then I remember. I've known that virgins sometimes bleed the first time, but I haven't thought of myself as a virgin in so long that I'm a little surprised at this technical evidence. I strip the bed and get the sheets into the washer before anyone else is up. Though frowned on during summer's drought, bathing isn't forbidden outright, and so I take a bath, too. I don't feel dirty the way rape victims are said to feel dirty, scrubbing themselves time and time again without being able to get clean. I just feel dirty-dirty, dried blood and semen on my thighs, and since George is coming up later in the day, I want to freshen up. I dress in a clean red shirt and blue shorts.

When Caleb comes down, I don't speak to him. Not a word. Not even a glance. I'm not about to give him the satisfaction of thinking that what he's done has touched me in any meaningful way. In fact, I don't feel touched in any meaningful way. But what do I know? My body feels like a stone among stones, my mind wheeling high above the scene, a sea gull over the shore at low tide. This lucid anesthesia likely reflects a state of shock, but since I've never yet found myself in a state of shock, I don't recognize it. Believing that Caleb's act has meant nothing to me, I don't wonder even once what it means to him. The questions don't come until years later.

What did he want when he did it? To punish me for abandoning him? To bind me to him forever? To express his continuing love? To pollute me, like a rotting carcass in a well, for all who came after to drink? What did it feel like to him? Was he glad to have reached inside me at last? Did his orgasm bring him pleasure? And what kind of response did he need? Rekindled love? Cursing and spitting? Surely something beyond this lithic blankness that reduces his heat, the weight of his bones, his mouth and hands, and even his cock to a hole in the air?

He hangs around for a while in the silence, and then he sets out. I don't watch him go. I don't call out, "Good-bye." This will turn out to be the most poignant failure of my life, the omission of that one word of blessing and separation to that man at that moment. If I'd said it, perhaps he would have walked clean out of my life, as he no doubt believed he'd done, instead of lodging here, plaintive ghost in the bone house, making my doors swing unexpectedly and my attic floorboards creak at odd moments of my days and nights.

My period is due on July 31. When it hasn't come by the time I leave The Farm at the end of August, I'm panic stricken. A calendar hangs inside the bathroom door, where I can peer anxiously from it to the crotch of my underpants every time I sit on the toilet. Nothing there. A blank. My heart crawls up and lodges at the back of my throat, choking off my breathing. My thoughts scurry through the dark inside my head.

I can't think what to do. I can't possibly tell Mother, whom I'll hear a few years later giving Barba the message I too have heard all my life: "Yes, a woman can have a baby without being married, but it's a *very terrible* thing to do." I don't want to tell Jane, either, mostly for fear that she'll blame herself for not protecting me. I'm still having trouble sorting out responsibility in the matter, and I always will, but I know it's not Jane's. And I'm certainly not about to tell Caleb, even if I could. Since by this time he's probably already left for London, headed for Cairo, later Beirut, the point is moot.

The only person I trust wholly is George. So I tell him. His response is characteristic, as I will learn more and more clearly in the years to come. His face goes still, his brown eyes blank and perfectly steady. He brushes at my tears and then licks his fingertips one by one, as though he could swallow my sorrow. After a long quiet moment, he says, "I love you." He'll marry me, he assures me, but that seems like a terrible idea. He's working as a handyman until he goes to Naval Officer Candidate School in January. He wouldn't have the time or money to take care of me. And anyway, I don't want us starting out married life with Caleb's baby. Abortion is literally beyond thought. We never discuss it. The only possibility I see is to go to the Florence Crittenden House, have the baby, and put it up for adoption. This is what girls of my age and class do, I understand, though I've never known one. Their families say they've gone off on long vacations.

First, however, I've got to determine that there is a baby, which means going to a doctor. Not my own, who went to high school with Mother and whose mother is one of Granna's best friends. I call one in another town. But how to get there? George works days, and I still haven't got my driver's license. Enter—or reenter—Frank, who, despite my impatience and even outright rudeness during his high school courtship of me, has remained a steadfast friend. He listens to my tale. He drives me to the doctor.

The doctor shoves the fingers of one hand up inside me and prods into my belly with the other. He's frowning—not mad, just intent. I've never had a pelvic examination before, and I want to weep with nervous humiliation, but I've decided that if I've got myself into an adult mess, I'm going to behave like an adult, which for some reason entails speaking in clipped sentences and keeping my eyes dry. The doctor doesn't laugh at my affectation.

"I'm not sure," he says when I've put my clothes back on. "Your uterus is very soft and enlarged, and you might be pregnant. But we should do a test to be certain." The next day, Frank drives me with my little yellow bottle of pee to the hospital laboratory, where they tell me, "Oh dear, no, this isn't enough, you'll have to bring us more tomorrow, a lot more," so I line Frank up for the next day. When I squat over my bigger bottle the next morning, though, what comes out is not pee but a great rush of bright-red blood, initiating the worst period I've ever had.

"I'm not pregnant after all," I tell the doctor over the telephone, but of course we'll never know for sure whether I was. Later problems with Rh incompatibility will suggest that I was sensitized by the Rh factor before my first child. At this point, however, I just want to forget the whole experience, the grief and bitterness and despair and degradation Caleb's act has belatedly, through the threat of pregnancy, aroused: go back to college, plan my wedding to George, maybe at long last come to life.

vi

When they're not at The Farm, Jane and Kip live on Beacon Hill in Boston, in a house I gradually come to think of as another home. I've always loved to visit them in the city. On my first visit, when they were still living in a third-floor apartment on Beacon Street, I recall waking early and going to the window to stare across the April-muddy yard at the alley lined with gray metal ash cans beyond.

"That's an alley," I told myself with a kind of mental pinch to make sure I wasn't dreaming. "I must really be in the city. I'm looking at an *alley.*" Ever after, Boston has remained otherworldly, glamorous, with the power to confer its magical qualities on me, so that when I'm here I become something other and more than myself.

Throughout junior high and high school, I spend part of my vacations in Boston. This is the old Boston, on whose skyline, as we drive in over the Mystic River Bridge, the highest point is the Customs House Tower and the tallest building is the old John Hancock, twenty-four stories with a weather tower on top: steady blue means clear; flashing blue, cloudy; steady red, rain; flashing red, snow. This doesn't strike me as a particularly useful device, since if you can see the tower, you can also see the weather going on around you, but I memorize the signals nonetheless. On this skyline you can still see the gleaming gold dome of the capitol building at the top of Beacon Hill. From the Hill you look out past the Salt-and-Pepper Bridge, across the Charles, to the buildings of MIT, one a brick so dark it looks like dried blood, another creamy white with a squat green dome.

In this enchanted city in the spring we walk the boys down the steep brick sidewalks of Joy Street and stroll across the Common into the Public Gardens, between beds of yellow and scarlet tulips, around the pond where the swan boats are gliding and the mallards are nesting once again. On a fine day I sit out on the front steps and simply gaze at the houses across the street which, unlike ours, have front gardens, the greens of the leafing plants still so light and fine they look like haze, the long buds of the tulip trees pale and slender as candles.

If we want to go farther than our feet want to carry us, we ride the MTA or take taxicabs. Jane and Kip take me to the Old State House for a lecture and tour, to the Athenaeum and the

Museum of Fine Arts, to Chorus Pro Musica concerts at Symphony Hall. They even let me have a little sherry, and I'm surprised that it tastes so nice. Even after I've grown accustomed to these activities and have started to run around the city as though it's home, Boston retains a little residual exotic tang, like Chartreuse at the back of the tongue.

When Jane and Kip bought the Boston house, it wasn't in much better shape than The Farm, though it did at least have indoor plumbing, including a huge claw-footed bathtub and a marble sink and a toilet with a cracked mahogany seat that pinched your bottom painfully if you didn't lower yourself just so. The third and fourth floors were renovated into apartments, and from time to time the basement apartment was rented as well. The first and second floors have always belonged to the family.

Now it's the most beautiful house I know, with its high ceilings, tall many-paned windows, marble fireplaces, wide yellow walls hung with Haitian paintings and Scheier weavings. Kip has a genius for rescuing and resuscitating other people's discards, and he hangs out at the Morgan Memorial, bringing home hardly worn oriental rugs, heavy chests and dressers, queer little tables to tuck here and there in the vast rooms. One later find, a cracked white mug showing a voluptuous woman in a chariot drawn by butterflies, labeled ECSTASY, will so charm me that he'll let me take it, and it will live ever after on the Edwardian sideboard in my dining room. My favorite room is the paneled library, where I spend hours stretched out on Kip's bizarrest purchase, a faded greenish velvet couch known as Cleopatra's Barge, alternately plunging into one of the hundreds of books that line the walls and staring through the jungle of vines draped across the French doors into the back gardens beyond.

Finally, when I'm in college, I come in and out so often that I'm given a key of my own. Now I am thoroughly at home. Even on autumn and spring weekends when Jane and Kip and the boys have gone to The Farm, I have a place to change my clothes or to flop for the night. When I get to the empty house, I slide comfortably into my mother's helper mode, scrubbing away the tracks of peanut butter and jelly Lars and Jon have left on the table, defrosting the refrigerator, tossing dirty socks into the laundry basket. Miserable at college as I am, I find this domestic retreat a godsend.

On one such weekend, George finally succumbs to my seductions. I'm never quite sure what overcomes his scruples, but I'll later surmise that Caleb's trespass into virgin territory had something to do with it. The boyish desire with which George has regarded my body has been checked, nearly smothered, by the mingled terror and awe inevitable, I suppose, in the only child of terrifically repressed parents. At least as late as the seventh grade, he believed that you could get a girl pregnant by hitting her in the stomach, and he went around with his elbows clutched to his sides lest an inadvertent jab throw him into untimely fatherhood.

For him the maternal body was wholly shrouded. His mother is the sort of woman who would have buried her box of Kotex in the back of the bottom drawer of her dresser, slipping a fresh one under her dress before tiptoeing into the bathroom and probably carrying each soiled one, carefully wrapped, all the way down to the trash can in the garage. When George was five, her only other baby was stillborn, but no one explained this tragic event to George then and at the later intervals necessary to help a child grow into understanding of life's mysteries. He came away knowing only that something dreadful had happened to his mother's body which made her cry and cry. When I first suffered menstrual cramps in his presence, he seemed convinced that I was going to die, and since they always make me feel as though I am going to die, I was hard pressed to allay his fears.

He has shrouded his own body from me in similar ways. On our second or third date, as he drove me along the foggy narrow road back to Wheaton, he suddenly pulled off at a roadhouse, leaped out of the car, and raced inside. I couldn't imagine what he was up to, though I suspected a hidden drinking problem, and he said nothing to enlighten me when he emerged. It didn't occur to me that he needed to pee, because I assumed he'd have told me that. He pulled a similar but scarier stunt some months later when we were making passionate, though fully clothed, love in my room in Providence's shabby Crown Hotel. He leaped up and raced into the bathroom, slamming the door behind him, and emerged without explanation. I thought I might have inadvertently done him some genuine damage. Long afterward I learned that he rushed off to ejaculate without suspiciously wetting his clothing. Natural events like peeing and coming were for him unspeakable.

Beyond fear and embarrassment, though, has remained the matter of purity. Years and years later, watching a film about Christian fundamentalism, when a teacher tells her young pupils,

"Your body is a temple," I will recoil at the perpetuation of this boundless source of shame, self-alienation, and pain. "Your body is not a temple!" I want to shout at each wide-eyed child whose body has just been snatched from her and set on a hill, remote from the grubby reality that she is hungry for lunch already with a whole hour to go and the boy behind her has just dropped something squirmy down her blouse and she'd like to whirl around and give him a good smack on the nose. "Your body is a *body*. Not a holy place of worship but a person. Not a structure 'you' occupy like a maidservant in her master's house but you, yourself. Make yourself at home."

For George, I think, my body is such a place set apart, access to which he is not yet entitled. That's what marriage is for, like passing papers on a house, after which the escrow agent hands you the title and the keys to all the doors and you are free to move in your furniture, your potted plants, even three cats and a dog if you like, and to set up housekeeping, as the saying goes. If you try to get in before the papers are passed, you can get arrested for criminal trespass. Only the situation is even more severe, since this place has been set apart by God Himself, and to set foot in it without proper title is not merely to trespass but to pollute holy ground. With no word or act can I desacralize my own body and dispose of it according to my desire. Without the Father's permission, George cannot bring himself to enter it wholeheartedly.

All the same, he does enter it one autumn night in the little gold room of the Boston house. This is a queer space above the outer and inner front halls, scarcely big enough to hold a narrow daybed, a chest, and a table, papered with the gold-leaf papers out of old tea tins, darkening now but still intact. George and I climb the curved stairway and cross the landing. By the glow of a small lamp we take off our clothes and look at each other. George's body is skinny, still pale in spite of a summer of outdoor work, with dark curly hair across his chest and on his forearms and legs, and a great bush of it between his legs, out of which his erection rises. My first view of a naked penis. I'm struck dumb but not, at least, dead. He lies on his back on the bed and I straddle him. Thanks to Tampax and Caleb, the terra is no longer entirely incognita, and his penis slides into me nice as you please.

The encounter is brief but, on the whole, satisfactory. Afterward he has to put his clothes back on and go home, of course, since he's still living with his parents and has already begun the lifelong task of protecting them, in one way or another and with varying degrees of success, from the truth about me. At home, he will tell me later, he stands for a long time gazing at his naked body in the mirror, as though it has somehow been transformed (sanctified, perhaps?) by sexual contact with mine. For my part, I snuggle down as best I can on the lumpy little daybed and drift into sleep, relieved that we've had sex at long last and pleased to have begun here in the Boston house.

vii

In the following years, as I'm caught up by marriage, motherhood, and madness, both the Boston house and The Farm slip from my possession, or perhaps more accurately, I slip from theirs. I go there, but as one of the houseguests now, a good enough role and one that suits my present circumstances, but different. And then, more than fifteen years later, The Farm takes me up again and witnesses, maybe even triggers, my transformation from what I have come to call the Gifted Girl with Lots of Potential into an ordinary, plainspoken, working writer.

I return as a kind of exile, since I've moved almost as far away as one can go and still be in the United States, not Mexico or the drink. During the summers of 1979, 1980, and 1982, Jane and Kip provide me an intensely needed room of my own at The Farm where, in finishing a book of poems and later beginning a book of essays, I shift at last fully into writerhood.

The room of my own is not the one I had when I lived here before. That one I think of now as Ellen Norton's room. Mine is directly below it. Papered in a fine geometric print, it has sheer orange curtains at the three windows and a pair of twin beds with orange spreads and perfectly serviceable headboards rescued by Kip from the Kingston dump. Most important, it has a large work table, with a ginger jar of fresh flowers on one corner, and on it I spread my typewriter, my package of white typing paper, my yellow legal-size pads, my black fountain pens. Ready to work.

Days here are even more tranquil than they once were. Lars and Jon have both graduated from Vassar and headed out into the world, though they visit now and then, and my own children, who are often with me, are old enough to require little attention. (Too little, Kip would no doubt say after discovering Anne and her friend Sebastian, both about fourteen, asleep on adjoining cots in the shed. "Nothing happened, Mom," she assures me, and since she's in the habit of telling me the truth [though she's not exactly fanatical about it], I believe her and think the whole incident a little funny. Kip does not.) Often Jane and I are alone. Sometimes Ellen joins us in an amiable writerly threesome. Off and on all day we talk, but just as often we don't: three silent women at the long pine table, darkened now with use, chewing reflectively at carrots with mint or newly dug radishes, passing each other bread and cottage cheese, each absorbed in some snarl of writing left on her desk. At least, I assume that's what the others are also absorbed in. Who knows for sure?

Jane rises first, often just as the sun is edging up over the alfalfa field. Later Ellen and I join her in the kitchen. Ellen has marvelous dreams, which she recounts as I drowse over my fruit juice and shredded wheat. After breakfast we disperse to our rooms. I spend the morning at my desk whether or not anything is happening. Usually it isn't. At this point I'm still an undisciplined writer, dependent on inspiration, and my lack of productivity frustrates me horribly. But I keep reminding myself that Flannery O'Connor spent her mornings at her desk just so that if anything did come along, she'd be there ready for it. This habit of being strikes me as a good one, even if a lot more strode up to her desk than ever flits around mine.

After lunch I don't usually try to write anymore. Sometimes what's on my desk calls me back, but if it doesn't, I carry a Coke and a book out under the pear trees above the garden and sit in the dappled shade. I go through almost all of Virginia Woolf here, as well as a peculiar assortment of Jon's college philosophy books: Heidegger, Whitehead, Sartre, Binswanger. Through these books, chosen for no lofty reasons but simply because they're on the shelves in my room, I will begin to develop that sense of my self as a cultural construct which will propel me all the way into a writer's being. I don't know that. I'm just reading, and sipping, and smoking, and gazing out across the garden where poppies and zinnias tangle in my vision with bush beans and pole beans and squash vines and leeks in the amiable riot that characterizes Kip's gardening *gestalt,* and reading some more.

If we're going to chat, we usually do so during preparations for dinner. Our conversation is haphazard, associative, full of silences and quick shifts, a kind of writing itself, that spinning out and spinning out without any need to begin or finish—no "once upon a time" to "happily ever after"—which women do as they mince the garlic, crack and peel the hard-boiled eggs, stir cream into the soup, rummage in the refrigerator for the leftover rice that isn't there anymore. Jane and Ellen have been best friends since they met at Wheaton. Their past is like a large embroidery canvas on which they work and rework the designs of their tellings. I have known Jane all my life and Ellen nearly as long. My tellings weave into theirs. The girlhood in Jamaica. The lost lover. The dead lover. The straying child. The possibility that every atom in the universe knows instantaneously what is happening to every other. The black cat. The other black cat. What does it matter who "owns" which particular thread? Our lives tell one another.

When men come, on weekends as a rule, we have to do something else with our tongues. Not use them as tapestry needles. Our fits and starts of language drive men nuts. Especially the silences, which make them think we're mad at one another. They leap in to rescue the machine run amok, to cut through the tangle and clear up what this conversation is "about," to get it headed somewhere, buzzing steadily.

The champion helmsman is Alex, a tall, rangy, bald urologist of international reputation from D.C., who has known Kip as long as Ellen and Jane have been friends. In Alex's capable hands, no one need wonder uneasily what the conversation is "about." It is about Alex: his patients, his medical students, his fabulous collection of modern art and the expense of insuring it, his viola, his new Volvo. Fortunately, he's a fascinating raconteur, whose wit and insight and occasional wisdom lend shape and sometimes shadow to his tales. But they are tales, not tellings. I don't know how to explain the difference. In fact, I'm certain that I *can't* explain the difference. Inexplicability is what permits the telling to exist. All explanations belong to the tale.

On Mondays other poets in the area gather at The Farm for an informal workshop, six or eight of us, carrying cups of coffee or glasses of iced tea with our sheaves of poems out under the pear trees. If the weather is gloomy, we build a fire in the dining room and sit instead around the table. Oddly, though, in view of New England's quirky weather, the day is generally fine.

By this time I've spent several years taking workshops in one of the largest academic creative writing programs in the country. I've even got a degree in creative writing. I'm pretty well "workshopped out." For better or worse, writers have sought legitimacy and the means of making a living within the academy, that male model of ceremonial combat based on the boast and the *flite*, on the strife for excellence, the mastery of material, the control of language, on the probing analysis and the penetrating insight. The possibility that a workshop will become an arena full of strutting cocks, each one pecking at another's mixed metaphor, is all too real.

At the Monday workshops something else is happening: an attentiveness to the poem not as an artifact but as a human statement, still connected with its maker in a vital sense, this fragile bond requiring our gentleness, our care, and certainly our nourishment. I don't mean to imply that we sit around under the pear trees praising one another's poems regardless of their quality. On the contrary. Each of us wants to write perfect poems and wants the others to write perfect poems as well. We listen to and read each poem closely, trying to understand what it is doing. If we can't tell, we ask the writer. If she can't tell us, she takes the poem away and brings it back reworked another time, and maybe another, and another, and there is great rejoicing when she finally gets the poem right. On the other hand, if the poem is right from the outset, we rejoice then and there, without looking for small ways to pick at it and put it down and thereby establish our poetic mastery.

At the end of a couple of hours of such delicate and intensely focused work, we're limp. We climb into our swimming suits and troop out to the pool for a dip. Then we spread a feast on the dining-room table. We all cook at least as well as we write poems (and with considerably more consistency). Everyone has brought something. Zucchini quiche. Cream of asparagus and mushroom soup. Thin, hard, salty salami on crusty bread. Tabouli with ripe tomatoes and fresh mint. Lemon bread, eggy, sweet-sour on the tongue. These voluptuous flavors, whetted by our delight in one another's company, freshen us for another week of the solitude writing inescapably demands.

At The Farm Kip plants flowers everywhere. Many are naturalized now and pop up on their own in due season, but he always buys flats of annuals, too, for pots of jaunty petunias on the front step and beds of pansies, more petunias, alyssum, around the listing, silvery henhouse, used now for pool machinery. There are a lot of old-fashioned flowers, bouncing bet and bachelor's button and phlox. Four-o'-clocks unfold and fold, yellow and dark rose. Gloriosa daisies spring up at the bottom of the garden. Zinnias and marigolds grow by the lettuce. Under the kitchen window, fragrant nicotiana.

My favorites are the hemerocallis, the day lilies or, literally, day beauties. Tolerant, hardy, resistant to infection and infestation, they propagate year after year, pushing up dense mounds of sharp, slender, dark-green leaves and then long bare scapes tipped with clusters of buds. One at a time the buds enlarge, burst, then wither and shrivel. If the bees have done their work, a fat seed pod may swell at the flower's base. The first to come out are the old-fashioned single orange ones by the stone wall into the sheep pasture across the street. By the pool grow other single ones, the dull red of old bricks, and also some frilled double ones, light orange streaked with crimson, too fancy for my tastes. Some Kip grows from the seeds left on the stalks in autumn, bred at the whim of the bees, and it's anyone's guess what they'll look like. One turns out to be the loveliest I've ever seen, pale peach, the surface of the petals glistening as though sprinkled sparingly with diamond dust. For Christmas Kip gives me some seeds which I plant in an old whiskey barrel by my front door, and then every desert spring I witness a microcosmic enactment of summer at The Farm.

How can I not grieve at the certainty that I will never return to the Boston house, with its steep stone front steps and second-floor bathroom, and the likelihood that I won't return to The Farm either? I grieve.

All the same, my grief is modulated by the knowledge I gained when my parents sold the house at 236 and retired to Arizona. Barba, though grown by this time, was disturbed at their abandonment of the ancestral home in a way that I was not, and I tried to fathom the difference. Perhaps it was that she'd lived there from birth straight through adolescence, whereas I'd been dislocated several times in childhood and many more since my marriage. Perhaps it was only that I'm so much older than she. I know, as she doesn't, that a house once loved can never be lost. Never. Sold, yes. Moved out of. But not left behind. The house builds itself somehow into your tissues. Its floor plan, the color of its walls, its smell of fir and candied orange peel at Christmas, the summer light banding the kitchen floor, the chill of September that strokes its way up under your nightgown when you throw back the covers etch themselves into the whorls of your brain. It belongs to you in a sense no title can confer. You have metabolized it. It lives in your bones.

In a way, I am always, always at The Farm.

Shelter

i

IN THE photograph, the girl and the boy are smiling from
the car and waving good-bye. The boy, behind the wheel,
has leaned forward to peer around the girl's broad-brimmed
black straw hat. Only his face, the shoulder and sleeve of his
tweed sport jacket, and his slender splayed fingers are visible.
The girl wears a pale green orchid on the lapel of her heavy
cream-colored wool suit and black cotton gloves to match her hat;
you can't see them, but she also has on black lace pumps with
stiletto heels. The two are framed by the rain-streaked surface of
a red and white 1955 Chevrolet sedan loaned to them by the girl's
stepfather. I know that the orchid is green and the car is red and
white, even though the photograph isn't in color, because I am the
girl and George is the boy, and we've just gotten married. The
photograph will lie, with a couple of dozen others, between white
leather covers on one bookshelf after another in one house after
another for at least a quarter of a century. Longer if we're lucky.

As weddings go, ours isn't much. Until right before it, I've
been at college and George has been at Officer Candidate School.
Immediately afterward, I've got to go back to take my final exams
while George heads for Naval Supply Corps School in Georgia.
We've got to get married now so that I can join him in Georgia
for the summer. I know myself too well: if I don't go with him, I'll
find somebody else before he returns. I marry him not so that I

won't lose him but so that I won't get lost. A few years later and I could simply have gone along, without the rush into matrimony; but in 1963, People Like Us do not live together without benefit of clergy.

The wedding itself seems jammed into our lives, a distraction, almost an intrusion. We can hardly pay it attention. Mother has sent out the invitations and counted the guests. She has ordered a cake and flowers. She has opened the wedding gifts and arranged them for display on white tablecloths in the little den at 236. We drop in, towing our friends along to attend us, just in time for the rehearsal, like flustered actors who have almost missed their cues.

On the day itself, I feel too sick and too ugly to get married. "Nerves," Mother says, and everyone nods sagely. I've never admitted to anyone that I spend most of my life feeling like this. It's almost a relief to have an excuse for once. Daddy rushes out into the steady, cold rain that falls hour upon hour to buy a bottle of Kaopectate. My friend Judy tries to rescue my hair from the tortured style the hairdresser inflicted on it yesterday. I sit on the toilet, my hair bristling with rollers, and shiver. Finally, I get pushed out to the car, driven to the church, and dressed in my finery like a giant unwieldy doll, the kind I always coveted when I was little: a bride doll.

True to form, I wear the wrong dress—not the one I wanted, which was slender and lacy, but the one Mother said looked best on me. The night after I bought it, I wept with disappointment, and my roommate Puff urged me to get the one I liked, no matter what Mother said, but I didn't know how. I'd always bought the dresses Mother said looked best on me. And the situation was complicated by my sense that Mother was having, at last, the wedding first the war and then widowhood had cheated her of. Married twice in blue suits, she was finally getting a chance to choose a wedding gown. I owed her that, somehow.

So I wear white taffeta, with a scooped neck, long pointed sleeves, a waist dropped to a point in front, and a wide skirt with a ten-foot train that can be drawn up into a bustle at the back. The skirt is held out by a hoop, and my figure is molded by a padded long-line bra and a panty girdle. Once I'm dressed, my skinny frame enveloped by wire, I feel as startled and betrayed as a bird trapped for the first time in an airy but intractable cage. Over my eyes, a fingertip veil attached to a wreath of artificial orange blossoms mutes my view of the outside world. When I see my sisters, first Sally and years later Barba, dressed in the same gown, then I'll know that I was wise to adopt Mother's choice after all. It's perfect on them. But at nineteen one is not given to foresight.

My attendants wear plain gowns of pale yellow satin with yellow picture hats and carry bouquets of marguerites. On a pretty spring day they would look sprightly. In the murky light drizzling through the eight tall windows into the white and maroon interior of the First Church in Enon, Congregational, they look as stiff and chilly as the draggled jonquils on front lawns all over town. Twenty-five years later, I'll chance to sit in that church on a day just as dim and almost as wet, and in spite of the same brave illumination from the same brass chandeliers, not to mention my own burgeoning capacity for delight, the gloom will seep into my spirit once again. I am constitutionally incapable of singing in the rain.

Daddy guides me down the left-hand aisle and gives me to George, quaking there in front of the looming wooden pulpit in his stiff morning clothes, just as skinny as I am, his hair shorn appropriately for a newly commissioned naval officer, his eyes dark and panicky. I have to be given by one man to another because I am not my own woman. Later I will become my own woman, and then this giving business will appall me, but at the moment I'm really not—not at all, you might say, myself—so getting handed over like a string of cowrie shells or a plump cow pretty well suits my reality.

If you were going to hand your daughter over, however, you might just as soon give her to someone who at least looks as though he's graduated from high school. George has, in fact, graduated from high school, and college, and OCS, but he still looks scarcely seventeen. When we review the pictures in the coming years, we'll gasp and laugh: "Would you let those two children get married?" But of course we don't think we're children. And whatever our parents' secret misgivings, they know they can't stop us. We say our brief *I do's* and then nothing can stop us. We're pronounced man and wife.

On our way up the right-hand aisle, I catch my toe in my hoop and start to trip. You can see it in the picture: both of us laughing, the bulge of my left foot behind the hem of my dress, my upper body canted forward, George's arm tensed underneath my clutching fingers to stop my fall. All the other photographs record the ceremonies and sillinesses of that day. This one depicts the way our lives are going to be.

After our stark little ceremony, we move across the street for a stark little reception in Burnham Hall: the same space, with its white walls and dark beams and brown linoleum floor, where I danced with Buddy and Davy and James, beloved James, my first true love, in Mrs. Warner's dancing school. Mrs. Warner is here today, though no one is dancing. James wasn't invited. We've been out of touch for years. I did invite Caleb, because Mother said it was proper to invite old suitors, a gesture of friendship, but he didn't even send his regrets, although by now he's returned from his first overseas jaunt. (I was going to say, his first odyssey, but of course it wasn't an odyssey: no Penelope at the end of it weaving and unweaving her designs to hold off the importunate suitors until his return.) Mother is cross at Caleb's rudeness, but I can forgive it. Today I can forgive everything. I can afford to be generous. I have my heart's desire.

My heart's desire wants to get the hell out of there as soon as everyone has passed through the receiving line.

"What shall I do?" I hiss at Mother. "George wants to leave already."

"Stall him," Mother hisses back. "You can't leave *yet.*"

I ply him with white-wine punch and tea sandwiches and then some wedding cake, real yellow cake with butter-cream frosting, baked by a local woman, not one of those cardboardy jobs bakeries turn out. No miniature plastic mannequins on the top, either, just clusters of little sugar bells. Because she remembers me as a schoolgirl when she worked in the cafeteria, Alice has wreathed the base with fresh white roses.

At last I toss away my bouquet and we drive home to change our clothes and flee, through pelting rain and grains of Minute Rice, to the red and white car.

Just before we leave, as I'm hugging Mother good-bye, she whispers, stricken, "Oh no! Our talk! We've been so busy that we never had our talk."

What would she have told me, I wonder. I don't really need information, since George and I have now had intercourse eight times. (I've kept a tally: eight.) But of course she doesn't know, or doesn't permit herself to know, that. All the same, I wish I'd found out what she had to say.

"Don't worry," I laugh into her ear. "I'll be fine!"

We stop for dinner at the Winding Brook Lodge. Too dazed to feel hungry or remember my own preferences, I order turkey, even though I'm not especially fond of turkey. Noticing my corsage and the sprig of stephanotis in George's buttonhole, the waitress asks the occasion. When we say we've just gotten married, she offers to bring us champagne.

"Oh, thank you," I blurt, "but I'm too young."

We arrive in the dark to a cold house. This is George's parents' summer home. The Lodge, they call it. They've welcomed me here as their houseguest several times, but I still don't feel quite at home. If the place were on the seashore, I might grow fond of it, but it's halfway up a hillside in Vermont. The cramped proportions of the house and the encroaching woodland on three sides persistently make me edgy and breathless.

George turns up the heat to drive off the musty damp, pours us glasses of scotch, and starts to work a crossword puzzle while I put on the bridal-night finery Granna bought for me: white gown and peignoir, blue satin scuffs trimmed with lace. The style isn't flattering, especially now that I weigh barely a hundred pounds, but the gift made Granna happy. Shivering in the thin nylon, I sit by George and sip my scotch.

After a while, he puts down his glass and stretches. "Well," he says with elaborate insouciance, "I think I'll turn in." I go along.

He is fervent. He's put up with the whole long day, the silly collar and striped trousers, the felicitations of people he's never seen before and probably won't see again, the long drive through relentless rain, just to get here, between the clammy sheets of his parents' bed, between my legs. I do my best to match his mood, but I'm chilled and weary. And, in a dim corner of my being, a little bitter. He's never made love to me without reservation before. A kind of grudgingness in his manner has made me feel that he wouldn't be doing it at all without my insistence. Something beneath the trappings of this day has accorded him the right to make love to me freely. My giving myself was never enough. He needed permission from some higher authority.

I really do feel handed over.

After a couple of days, we go down to his parents' winter home for a last night before I return to Wheaton and he heads for Georgia. There, for some reason, we are given his narrow boy's room, with its student desk and switch plate reading "Outen the Light" and single bed, instead of the guest room. His parents have often reported, with obvious pride, that they've never slept in separate beds. If given a room with twin beds, they always occupy just one. As a consequence, throughout our marriage, George will view my occupation of the second bed in a hotel or guest room as a betrayal of the marital vow, one step short of filing for divorce. Two in a single bed seems normal to him.

He has already staked out his portion of the little bed (most of it) and I'm about to join him for a night perched on the edge of the abyss when we hear a knock at the door. I open it to see his parents, in their nightclothes, hovering outside.

"Your Dad gave me this," Mum says, extending a book, "when we got married. Now we'd like you to have it."

"Thank you." I take the book. When they've said good night, I carry the book to the bed. It's bound in red cloth, hardly worn, with gold letters stamped on the spine: *Sane Sex Life and Sane Sex Living.* George and I browse in it for a while before we "outen the light" and get on, as sanely as possible, with our sex life.

ii

My final exams are over. For the past two summers I've been a mother's helper at The Farm. This summer I'm going to Georgia to be a wife.

George calls with last-minute instructions for my rather complicated trip. "And when you get to Athens," he says, "don't take a Black and White cab."

"Why not?"

"It's just for Negroes."

Negroes have their own taxicabs? I think. That doesn't sound very practical.

I take an Eastern Airlines flight that gets into Atlanta at three in the morning. It's cheap. Until now, my solo traveling has entailed train rides thirty miles to the north or south of Boston. Period. For anything more adventuresome, like a ferry ride across Boston Harbor to visit my grandfather and his new wife, I've at least had Sally with me, and in her sturdy presence I've never felt afraid. I haven't been on a plane since planes had propellers. I've never been to Atlanta in my whole life. By the time I get off the plane, I'm so scared I can't draw a full breath.

Riding a cab from the airport to the hotel, I see an enormous Coca-Cola sign, still glittering against the darkened city, and my thudding heart slows. They've got Coke here, too. I must still be in civilization. This is 1963, and except for Coca-Cola signs, and a few brands of gasoline, and the orange roofs of Howard Johnson's, such cultural signals are rare. One can go to a new region of the country and really feel like a stranger in a strange land. Not, I think, until the spread of golden arches (the first McDonald's we've ever seen opens in Athens this summer), followed by buckets of chicken, sleepy bears in nightshirts, and the striped asphalt parking lot of at least one shopping mall at the edge of every town, will one have the reassuring sense of traveling without ever actually going anywhere.

Buoyed by the Coca-Cola sign, I catch a few hours of sleep at the Hotel Henry Grady and then board a bus for Athens, where I find a taxi (not, of course, Black and White, which isn't both) to take me to Oglethorpe Avenue, where my new husband has been languishing, sustained only by Campbell's Tomato Soup, peanut butter sandwiches, and beer, for his new wife.

The temperature is about ninety-eight degrees, the humidity about ninety-eight percent. I don't know it yet, but these figures will remain virtually unchanged throughout the summer. I'll nearly kill myself dashing around at my Yankee pace until I discover that every task takes half again as long in Georgia. Speech, too. I burst into elaborate explanations that meet only silence, followed by a lethargic "Ma'am? Would you repeat that please, ma'am?"

The taxi drops me off at a tall white Victorian house that may have been gracious, even elegant, in its day. Soaked and rumpled, I make my way around to the back.

We share the ground floor with our landlady, Miz Chase, a large lumpy woman of a certain age with ruddy skin and faded fuzzy hair. The second floor has been converted into three more apartments, also occupied by newlywed navy couples. Miz Chase is given to sudden, inappropriate questions, like what kind of birth control we're using. I tell her I'm on the pill, which in 1963 is still pretty avant-garde. In truth, I've hardly given the various methods of birth control a thought. I just asked for what seemed easiest. A door in our bedroom opens into her part of the house and, even more oddly, a little window high in the wall connects our bathroom to hers. Sometimes we have the prickly sense that she's crouching on the other side, all ears, though we never catch her at it.

The apartment has little to recommend it but its proximity to the Supply School campus, essential since we have no car, and the price: seventy-five dollars a month, furnished. No air-conditioning, only a fan in the bedroom window. No shower, only a claw-footed tub we leave filled with tepid water to rinse our sweating bodies several times a day. At the back, in what must once have been a sun porch, a narrow kitchen sags away from the house at such a pitch that all my cakes come out crooked, scorched on one side and soggy on the other. We move the table and chairs out onto a little screened porch, where armies of ants carry off the sugar but at least we occasionally catch a sticky puff of air. The living room is so tiny that you really can just about stand in the center and touch all four walls. The bedroom, by contrast, is cavernous, with murky green walls and ponderous dark furniture. The carved headboard is so tall that, standing on tiptoe on the bed, I can scarcely dust the top of it. When we make love, it sways ominously and I'm afraid it will pitch forward and squash us like cockroaches, but George assures me it will catch on the footboard first. All the same, I keep half a wary eye on it.

Our lives center on this bed. We make love whenever we have a free moment, sometimes even on George's lunch hour, our kisses sweat-salty, our drenched skins sliding against each other, our wet naked chests meeting and parting with great sucking sounds. One rainy afternoon the rector of the Episcopal church comes to call. We can see him, through the blades of the fan, pounding at the porch door. We slap our hands over each other's lips and rock with stifled giggles until he gives up, slides a card under the door, clomps back down the steps. Does he guess? We never know.

On Fridays we go to happy hour at the Officers' Club. Drinks are a quarter apiece. This summer I'm drinking Tom Collinses. When we leave, George slips his glass into his pocket, dumping the ice as soon as we get outside. Half a dozen of these glasses, emblazoned "Naval Supply Corps School," will travel from home to home with us ever after. We weave, hands clasped, up Oglethorpe Avenue, barely making it through the door before we start peeling each other's light clothes away and tumble onto our hulking bed. Sometimes we get up later and eat some tuna fish salad. Sometimes we forget to eat at all.

Otherwise, our lives have little enough charm. George spends his days in classes with names like Mess Management and Disbursing Afloat and his nights memorizing mounds of information he feels no interest in at all. He joined the navy to avoid the draft, and the navy stuck him in the Supply Corps because he's got a heart murmur. Most of the other Pork Chops, as Supply officers are nicknamed, at least majored in business or finance or accounting in college. George majored in English literature. When he's not studying, he fiddles with his uniform, but no matter how often he rubs spittle into his shoes or Brasso onto his belt buckle, no matter how carefully I starch and press his shirts, he seldom gets through an inspection unscathed. He's the sort of man who's going to go through life with chalk dust on his coat sleeve and his trouser bottoms crumpled around his ankles. And I'm the sort of woman who marries that sort of man.

Occasionally he takes a break and we play pinochle or bridge with friends. Once we even borrow a car and drive up to the Smoky Mountains for a couple of days, where we get food poisoning. But most of the time I'm left to my own devices, a wholly new situation for a schoolgirl who's been propelled through her life by bells for sixteen years. Delighted to be keeping house for myself rather than for Mother or Bernice or Aunt Jane, I sustain a positive orgy of domesticity, shopping and cleaning and washing dishes and clothes, even diving under the bed to retrieve the discarded socks George has never had to retrieve for himself, and cooking, cooking, cooking.

Eager to keep a perfect house for George, I have to find some model other than my mother, who has accorded her housewifely duties decent but desultory interest, preferring a book to a dustmop any day. "My mother has returned from her Women's Club meeting and is in the kitchen doling out food," George wrote to me one night during our courtship. Here's what he's accustomed to in a woman. Here's who I'll be. His mother makes and serves two desserts a day, fruit and cookies for lunch, pie or cake or jelly roll for dinner. Out in my steamy little kitchen I bake up a storm of crooked cakes.

One day, with George's money but without his permission, I buy a dress. It has to be with George's money since, without a job this summer, I haven't any of my own. It's a good dress, a collarless shirtwaist of heavy cream-colored oxford cloth with a small blue print, and I get it for a good price at an end-of-the-season sale. All the same, the boldness of my action makes me feel nervous and guilty. The only money I've spent so far is on groceries, which is okay because George eats them, too. But he can't wear the dress with me. And I haven't yet figured out that he takes real pleasure in my appearance.

He's not at all angry. In fact, he laughs at me and says the money belongs to both of us. I love clothes, and I'll go on buying them long after I have an income too, and no longer keep track of whose money is which. Even so, with each purchase, hundreds and hundreds of them over the years, I'll feel a little rush of daring and guilt, as though decorating my body were a frivolous, a slightly disreputable, possibly even an illicit, act. "Handsome is as handsome does," my mother and grandmother always said in order to counter self-admiration. A good woman needs no decoration.

George and I never come to understand this place at all. We catch disturbing glimpses: the Black and White taxicabs; Rosa, Miz Chase's black maid, slipping into the house each morning and out again, heading who knows where, at the end of the day; the way the middle-aged white couple who take us to church worry that we might swim in the same pool as coloreds. The navy insulates us so thoroughly that we never have to understand it, however, and we haven't yet learned how to find out what we want to know on our own.

All the same, as the years distill the summer in Athens to its essence, two crystals precipitate from the humid medium of southern summer, homesickness, cultural disorientation, languor, naïveté: sexuality and social conscience. They seem structurally dissimilar, maybe even alien. How could those hours, daylit and dark, of pumping and sweating and grunting in a tangle of soaked sheets, one on top, then the other on top, be yoked in any way to the quick, almost furtive thrust of a brown paper sack filled with old clothes or soup bones into the hands of a little black woman hurrying for the bus?

I don't know how. But in us, they are yoked, forming the axis on which we turn, first toward one another, then outward to the world, back and forth, back and forth. Although sometimes one will be eclipsed, sometimes the other, by the loom of financial distress, illness, troubled children, or infidelity, they are the elements that emerge time and again, the durable ones, the ones that bind us together. We make erratic progress in each, getting better, on the whole, with practice.

My major accomplishment of the summer is getting my driver's license. One of the couples upstairs has a new white Valiant convertible with red upholstery, and one afternoon they drive me to the county courthouse. There I take a written test. One of the items is an octagon with the letters $S\ T\ O\ P$ in the middle.

I'm supposed to tell whether it means "stop" or "slow." After determining that I've passed the written test, an officer who looks even younger than I escorts me outside for the road test. His eyes widen when he sees the car, and if I were more acute in reading human rather than road signs, I'd know that the license is mine already. All he wants is the chance to ride around in this car. Unfortunately, the town seems deserted, and I don't think anyone sees him as I creep around the square and out the road he points at. Immediately the town disappears. It seems to be only one layer deep. The only maneuver he asks for, a Y-turn to get us back to the courthouse, I do wrong.

Nevertheless, when we're inside once again, he asks for a dollar and hands me my official Georgia driver's license, which is honored, I'll discover, in virtually no other state in the union. When it expires, I'll have to take the road test all over again, the day after an eight-inch snowstorm, in a brown and white Karmann Ghia that clearly does not thrill the Maine trooper at my side. When I fail to parallel park properly, I blame the snow heaped in the streets (Maine doesn't get the plows out for a mere eight inches). I couldn't parallel park on the Fourth of July, but of course the trooper can't be sure of that, so he reluctantly issues me a Maine license. This is honored, I'll discover, in virtually every other state in the union, so I never have to take the road test again, a good thing, since snowstorms almost never occur in southern Arizona.

After I get my license, just before I leave Athens to return to college, George and I buy a baby-blue 1960 Volkswagen bug. When I come back for his graduation in November, we drive it in tandem to his new duty station in Davisville, Rhode Island, and in the eighteen months or so we own it, I log nearly twenty thousand miles, most of them alone, as though making up for the four extra years I took to get my license. I never do learn to parallel park, but otherwise I take pride in my driving. This license, even more than the marriage license, seems to confer a sense of competence and independence. If I want to (which of course I don't), I can go my own way.

iii

George has just come home from a picket. That's what they're called, these three-week forays of the USS *Guardian*, AGR-

1, into the North Atlantic to sweep the air for signs that the Enemy has transgressed the DEW line. Actually, the radar on shore is now so sophisticated that it can pick up signals sooner than the radar picket ships can, but bureaucracy hasn't caught up with technology, so the ships continue their senseless voyages. To avoid boredom, or getting dizzy, or something, they sail in huge circles in one direction for half the picket, then switch to the opposite direction. They never land anywhere. They never even see land. They see gray water, a three-hundred-sixty-degree horizon, empty sky. Sometimes gulls. Sometimes another ship. Sometimes fish. They catch a shark with a hunk of bologna, and George brings me one of the cruelly serrated teeth.

Now he's home for ten days before another picket starts. It's February, and the house is cold. Coming in, we toast ourselves by the only source of heat, a large gas space heater beside the dining-room table. During the winter, I stray from this location as seldom as possible. I suppose this is my version of sailing around in circles.

As usual, we are a little shy of one another. This schedule is very taxing. I just begin getting used to his absence when he returns to port, and just before I'm accustomed to having him around, he puts out again. Our times together pass in a blur of suppressed anger and sexual frenzy, punctuated by the long gray weeks of separation. I'd rather he were gone for six months and then home for six months. As it is, we've been married for going on two years without ever really living together.

"How does September sixteenth sound for a birthday?" I ask, glancing sidelong at him as I rub my hands over the whirring heater.

"Uh, fine." He sounds puzzled. His birthday is in January, and mine's in July. Only my mother's is in September, but it's not the sixteenth. Then he sucks in his breath. "You don't mean . . . ?"

"I think so." We're almost whispering, though there's nobody else in the little house but the cats. "I went to the doctor last week, and he's pretty sure."

"Oh, sweetheart, that's *wonderful!*" He puts his arms around my bulky coat and hugs me tight. "A baby. We've done it! We've made a baby!"

He seems prouder than I feel, as if my pregnancy proved something he's been a little worried about, though he's never mentioned being worried. I guess I've always assumed I'd get pregnant whenever we decided it was time. Maybe that's what having your period month after month does: documents your reproductive capacity. If so, women who menstruate but can't get pregnant must feel somehow betrayed, as though false promises had been whispered monthly in their ears.

At the moment I feel pleased enough but also scared. What if I lose it, whatever "it" is at this point, some imperceptible little lump stuck precariously to the inside of my uterus? What if my body doesn't notice it's there and sloughs it off, thinking it's just the same old uterine lining it's been dumping out regularly for nearly a decade now? I walk around nearly on tiptoe, half holding my breath, willing the baby that might or might not be there to exist, to take hold and occupy me until September sixteenth, like a tenant with a lease I don't want broken.

George and I live in a rose-covered cottage of weather-beaten shingles with white trim in Saunderstown, Rhode Island, population four hundred fifty in the summer, one-fifty in the winter. Truly, in the summer, roses weave themselves into the trellises around the front door and along one side of the cement patio, where, on the rare Sundays George is home, we sit reading the *Boston Globe* and sipping coffee until we're groggy from the sun. Most of the time it's not summer, and he's at sea.

The house itself never ceases to charm me. To the right of the central hall with the bathroom at the end opens a long room with dining-room furniture on one side of the French doors opening onto the patio and living-room furniture on the other. The landlord and landlady, who turn out to be the elderly parents of one of my college classmates, are almost as refined as they think they are, and the furnishings, though worn, are tasteful. On the left of the hall are the bedroom and the kitchen. From the window over the sink, looking beyond the landlord's handsome white colonial, I can glimpse Narragansett Bay. Something about this space, its small scale and graceful proportions, inspires me to scrub and polish and dust as I never will again, not for decency's sake but for love. If I can't be happy in this cherished spot, I should know something is the matter not with the external facts of my existence but with my self.

Yet I am unhappy here, too, and I haven't the faintest idea why, or what to do. At first I blame my misery on college, which does indeed complicate matters. While George is in port, I live with him here in Saunderstown and drive the Blue Baby an hour and a half each way to attend classes three days a week. By the end of the year, I've cut some classes nearly as often as I've attended. While George is at sea, I move back into the dormitory, where I keep a room so bare and tidy that one friend likens it, in horror, to a monk's cell. Shuttling between the roles of wife and schoolgirl, I remain detached from each, living in a kind of gray suspense, waiting until school ends and my real life can begin. During this period, I seek relief wherever I can: in alcohol, in the arms of drunken men I scarcely know, in the tranquilizers prescribed by the college physician. He, at least, is on the right track, though for the wrong reason (he wants to pacify me) and with the wrong substance (I need an antidepressant, not a tranquilizer).

After graduation, I wait to become happy, but nothing happens. With no training or experience, I take a job teaching fifth- and sixth-grade English and social studies in a private school. Most of my students, I discover, are here because they can't handle public school, or public school can't handle them, like sixteen-year-old Larry—taller and heavier than I, let alone his sixth-grade classmates—who has been in an institution since he was four. This is his first experience in an ordinary classroom. Guilt-stricken at my own ineptitude, I plead health problems and quit after a single semester, only to realize later that I was probably doing a better job than anyone they could find to replace me. I'm not quite lying about the health problems. I feel like death most of the time.

I've started having night terrors. I've always been afraid of the dark, but now that I have to sleep alone in the cottage while George is away, my fear swamps me. I lie hour upon hour on my back staring into black air, rigid, sweating under the pink flowered quilt. For a while I even sleep with a paring knife under my pillow. This is the same bed in which we make love feverishly, trying to make up for the time the navy has stolen from us, when George comes home. It's the same bed in which we missed the Sonny Liston–Cassius Clay fight on the radio, still noisily arranging pillows and quilt and snacks during the one minute the fight lasted. I know that. It doesn't matter. The dread returns as soon as he's gone.

I'm seeing a psychotherapist now, at the University of Rhode Island, a kindly man, quite young, probably a graduate student, who listens to my woes without shedding light on them. At his suggestion, I try staying with another wife while our husbands are out, but the loss of privacy plagues me worse than my anxiety. The cats bring me a little relief: the Mino, a handsome blue male who vanishes in adolescence, probably through somebody's back door, the first of several who will prefer some other woman's company or kitty kibbles to mine; then a couple of seal-point Siamese, Ho Tei and Ho's Anna, who curl around each other on the bed beside me. But the baby's presence at last brings real surcease. I'm never alone in the house anymore. As soon as I know the baby is there, my terrors dwindle, though they'll never vanish altogether. Well into middle age, if George goes away I'll have to sleep, fitfully, with the hall light on. By then, however, I'll be resigned to my weirdnesses, still scared of the dark but no longer scared to be scared of the dark.

The baby has definitely made itself at home, and except for a few weeks of queasiness at the beginning, I've never felt better. My body loves its new houseliness. I stop fretting that the baby will abandon me before its appointed departure. I nearly stop fretting entirely. The tensions of college and the Rocky Hill School recede pleasantly into the past. The gray, sodden year is turning once again toward spring, the pungent odor of cut grass on the salt air, buds on the climbing roses.

I stand naked in front of the mirror above my dresser and stare at the shape of the Venus of Willendorf. I have real breasts. To be sure, they're completely overshadowed by the protuberance below, but they're there. Because I have a protracted pelvis, I carry the baby not between my hips but in front of them. From the back I don't even look pregnant. Across my swollen front the skin stretches tight and shiny as an apple. My belly button has popped inside out. My God, I think, how can I get any bigger? It's now May.

When we go to parties, I cover the baby with a black cocktail dress dropping wide from a sheer black yoke. The rest of the time I wear cotton shifts made for me by Mother. When the weather warms, I buy a swimming suit we call the Red Balloon, red calico shorts with an elastic panel in the front and a matching tunic. The baby and I bobble around in Narragansett Bay or in the river at The Farm. The rest of the time, it bobbles around in me, its faint, finny quivers growing stronger until I feel as though I'm harboring a porpoise.

iv

The navy decides to put the radar picket ships in mothballs and send George ashore. After four months of wicked competitive pressure at OCS, and another six at Supply School, he's served his eighteen months at sea under a captain we've found every bit as bonkers as Captain Queeg in *The Caine Mutiny,* and we both look forward to beginning a normal life together at last. At least maybe he'll sleep through the night. At least he'll stop throwing up his breakfast before he leaves for work. What doesn't occur to us, of course, is that we have no experience of what we're calling a "normal" life, the two of us sharing the same house day after day forever. And within weeks of setting up this new structure, we'll be joined by a third person neither of us has yet met.

That this is a recipe for disaster—a new job, a new location, a new living arrangement involving a new baby, all tossed into the emotional stew at once—I haven't had the chance to learn for myself, and no one, not even the nice young psychotherapist to whom I'm saying good-bye, suggests it to me. I'm the sort of woman who wears the same bathrobe for seven years until the puppy chews a hole in the backside (and even then for a little while longer), who drives the same car until it's collapsing into scrap. Change is anathema. And for the next few years, my life is going to be in a state of continual flux. There's nothing I can do about the changes themselves. They come with the territory of being a young wife, mother, career woman in modern America. But if I knew that they were stressful, and that my troubled responses to them were normal for a woman of my constitution, perhaps I wouldn't be as frightened as I'm going to become. Perhaps I wouldn't crack up.

To exacerbate the problem, the navy first assigns George to Newport, just across Narragansett Bay. On Jamestown, a charming island in the middle of the bay, we find a cottage almost as pretty as the one we've been living in. George will have to commute to work by ferry, but I'll be able to have the baby in the same hospital I've been going to. Then, just as we're ready to move, his orders are changed to the Bath Iron Works, a shipbuilding installation in Maine. We drive up and search hastily for an apartment, but nothing is available. In desperation we settle for a farmhouse in North Edgecomb, half an hour's drive from Bath, and order our household goods shipped up.

Spring Hill Farm is a ramshackle house, not quite old enough to be quaint, set among broad fields in the middle of three hundred acres of woodland. In later years, we'll wish we'd had enough money to buy it for a summer place. At this point, it suits us badly. It's enormous, with a primitive kitchen, a dining room, a living room with a vast fieldstone fireplace painted white and red, and two small empty rooms off the living room. A broad, open stairway dividing the dining room from the living room rises to a second floor with four bedrooms and a large bath. In August we find it comfortable enough, but as fall comes on, almost immediately we find that the heat thrown up from a wheezing oil furnace in the cellar through a single grate in the front hall rises to the bedrooms, which grow stifling, bypassing the first floor almost entirely. A winter here would be intolerable. Even September is damned brisk.

We've traded in the Blue Baby for the Karmann Ghia, in which George bounces down the long dirt drive every morning, leaving me in almost preternatural stillness. Finishing my coffee at the breakfast table, I watch a red fox lope around the side of the house and head for the woods. I prowl from room to room. I lie on our bed, curved on my side to rest the weight of the baby on the mattress. I sit on the couch reading books George fetches from the library while Ho's Anna, the little female Siamese, who survived feline distemper against all odds as a kitten but never grew fully, perches on the mound of my belly, riding up and down, up and down, as the baby lurches and heaves. On the weekends, George and I sit on the front porch, overlooking a field of milkweed above which flit clouds of monarch butterflies, and play Scrabble. Ho's Anna rides patiently up and down, up and down, ignoring our laughter.

I'm terrified that I'll start having the baby while George is gone. I'm not sure what labor feels like, and I'm afraid I won't know it when it comes. One Sunday I start leaking amniotic fluid, but the contractions I feel are mild and infrequent. They persist until I see the doctor on Tuesday, however, and he declares that he will induce labor the following morning. Though I've known him only a few weeks, I like this portly little man with the fringe of silvery hair. I trust him. Because of my protracted pelvis, he recommends a cesarean section, but when I object, he says reasonably, "Okay, let's try labor and see what happens." I doubt that a busy city doctor would have acquiesced. I'm about to kill a full, bright September Wednesday on the golf course.

I don't, however, like the idea of inducing labor. Perhaps for that reason, the contractions grow stronger and more frequent until, nervous about the distance to the hospital, George bundles me into the car and drives through the night to the Bath Memorial Hospital. There, I am put to bed in a dim green room to endure my travail. To endure is all I can do. I've had no childbirth class. I've never even heard of one. I've gathered a considerable quantity of textbook information about childbirth, but no experiential knowledge beyond my mother's reassurance that "labor is just like having very bad cramps." Well, I've had very bad cramps since I was twelve. And labor, it turns out, is nothing like having very bad cramps. It's much, much worse.

It's the very worst thing that's ever happened to me. I think if it doesn't stop this instant, I'm going to die. But it doesn't stop, this instant or the next. It goes on, a great racking swell of pain, another, another. I think my bones are going to burst apart. I howl. I grab George's arm and dig my nails into his flesh. I dig my nails into my own flesh, raking my face, yanking out handfuls of hair. I gasp and pant until I pass out. I'm so tired I've begun to doze between each contraction, roaring at each new pain without fully waking, groggy with nightmare.

Dr. Fichtner is true to his word. He lets as many hours go by as he dares. Then he says, "Well, it's either the operating room or the delivery room. Let's try the delivery room first." Leaving George behind, we roll into a cramped room with dark windows. It's night. A different night. I get a spinal block. As the pain leeches away, I look up in bliss at the nurse who's been holding my head and hands off and on for hours.

"Oh, I love you!" I breathe.

"That's what they all say when the shot hits," she laughs.

Dr. Fichtner has inserted forceps, he tells me. Beyond the tent of my knees, I can see his face, red and sweaty, as he leans his considerable bulk backward. Since I can no longer feel the contractions, I don't know that I'm pushing as hard as he's pulling. My God, I think, he'll pull its head right off its shoulders. Behind Dr. Fichtner's head is a wall clock, the kind you see in schoolrooms, big black hands on a white face. I'm looking at it when the baby wails: 7:14 P.M. on September 15, 1965.

The nurse thrusts the baby's crumpled face up under mine. "It's a little girl," she says. "Look at all the hair. Just like Ringo Starr!" Everyone laughs. I reach out and poke at the baby before they take it away for a bath. Her. Before they take her away.

After the baby leaves my body, my life gets all scrambled up. Everything seems to be going on around me, just beyond my reach: nurses bringing the baby to me, taking the baby away, the baby sucking at my tender breasts, George putting the baby and me into the car and driving us back to the big silent house. The nurses haven't taught me how to nurse the baby. They may not be too sure. No one here seems to do it. One of my nipples cracks painfully, and George buys me a pump that looks like a bicycle horn so I can put milk into a bottle to feed the baby until the crack heals.

Mother comes, capable and reassuring. I've seen her with newborn babies of her own, and now she seems to find it natural that I should have this baby of my own. The house has no hookup for my new washing machine, so Mother washes the baby's diapers by hand. She bathes her. She makes funny chirping noises and the baby smiles at her. Then she leaves and George's mother comes to take over the diaper-washing and bathing and cooing. Then she leaves, and it's just the baby and me.

I peer into the lullabye crib, the same one Granna used for her babies, and stare at the baby while she sleeps. I say her name to myself: Anne. Anne for my mother, Eldredge for my father. My tongue tries to get used to it. In the night I get terrible sweats. I wake every couple of hours to the baby's thin wail. Anne's wail. She sounds just like a Siamese cat. George picks her up and changes her diaper while I shift to the rocker. Soaked, shivering, I nurse her in dim light until she sleeps again. Once while she's nursing she has one of those copious soft bowel movements common to breast-fed babies, which squishes out of her diaper and plastic pants, all down her legs and up her back. I strip off her wrapper, her undershirt, her diaper, and start swabbing.

"My God," I say to George, who is handing me balls of cotton, "what does a new mother do who's never taken care of a baby before?" I'm grateful for the gifts of feces and vomit Chip and Barba so generously provided. "She must want to throw it back!" I don't have any problem with this aspect of motherhood. It's only that the baby seems so strange. A stranger, I mean. I don't know her. I don't love her. The baby I loved, the one in my belly, has moved away, and I am bereft.

George finds us a new home, an apartment in a huge converted sea captain's house in the center of Bath, with a washer hookup and plenty of heat. Charm, too. We have a spacious bedroom with a bay window and fireplace, an even larger living room, also with a bay window and fireplace, a tiny room for Anne behind the living room, and at the end of a long hall, a large kitchen and pantry. It has one decidedly queer feature, however: the toilet and sink are in a closet under a flight of stairs, so small that you have to back in and bend over to sit on the toilet, and the shower has been installed in Anne's room. Throughout her earliest months, her dreams must be punctuated unpredictably by the gush of water.

The exertion of moving, so soon after childbirth, triggers a hemorrhage, and the doctor sends me to bed. Mother arrives straightway by bus and puts everything to rights, even if I can't find anything in the kitchen for weeks afterward. By the time she leaves a couple of days later, there are clean sheets on the bed, the dishes have been stacked in the cupboards, and I have begun, in an odd way, to love my daughter.

This love is wholly other than I expected. I was waiting for some surge, a tidal wave of maternal adoration, the sort of suffusing emotion you see depicted on the faces of all those Renaissance madonnas painted by men like Bellini and Caravaggio. This love doesn't overwhelm me. It undermines me, gets me from below, as though I were a tree, and Anne were another tree, whose roots put out tendrils that wrap themselves around my roots, down there, out of sight. I'm suspended, sustained, in a vegetable tangle. A thicket of love.

v

The winter of silence, George and I will come to call it many years later, when we've healed enough to be able to refer to it at all. The winter of icy silence. We speak to Anne. We speak to Ho Tei and Ho's Anna and their four kittens. But the two of us pass days at a time without exchanging a word except essential grunts.

"More stew?"

"No, thanks."

These episodes grow out of my recurrent inexplicable rages, but what fuels the rages I can't understand. I only know that, once one is triggered, as a rule by some apparently trivial disagreement, I refuse to speak, and once I've stopped talking, I don't know how to start again. I feel shut in, shut up, shut down.

George, temperamentally uncommunicative anyway, matches silence for silence. Emotional rescue is not his task. Emotional work of any sort is not appropriately his, for that matter. Our families have not provided models for communication, since in both of them the expression of feeling, particularly negative feeling, is discouraged. But what little emotional work gets done—comforting a bereaved friend, say, or cajoling a sick child—falls to women. Both Daddy and Dad Mairs return from work every day expecting solace and succor to be extended to, not demanded of, them in return for their public labors. They don't wash dishes, and they don't launder clothes, and they don't retrieve dirty socks from under the bed, and they don't help wives or children work through their rages, either, though they may listen indulgently and even pat a shoulder as long as the woman or child isn't making an unreasonable scene. As far as George is concerned, if I feel upset, even at him, then I've got a problem I need to straighten out. He is capable only of right action, and if an action of his infuriates me, then I must be misreading it. In sum, I'm on my own.

I'm willing to take the blame. In fact, I can't help assuming, any more than he can, that it's naturally mine. But self-castigation doesn't tease out the ravel of my misery. I am at the beginning of a new and unutterable loneliness, worse than any I've experienced before. The Maine winter is so bitter that, even in her fleecy, hooded pink bunting, Anne shivers, and so we hardly leave the house at all for days on end. We haven't any place to go, anyway. I have no friends here, except those dealt me arbitrarily by the navy, with whom I have little in common but babies and bridge. But, even more alienating, I can't confess my unhappiness to the family and friends I have elsewhere. As far as they're concerned, I'm married to the perfect husband and we're leading the perfect life with our little baby, who is also perfect except for her crossed eyes.

"What do you have to complain about?" they'd only say. And really, what *do* I have to complain about? How can I feel disappointed? I've done everything I told myself I'd be happy as soon as I'd done. I've married George. I've graduated from Wheaton. I've had Anne. What's left?

There *is* something, but I scarcely think of it because it's an answer illegitimate to anyone I can imagine announcing it to, except possibly Aunt Jane. I was going to be a writer. Since my wedding day, I have started only two poems, both listless and as flaccid as my breasts now that I've weaned Anne. Witness:

At first it is little more than an idea,
Only dimly recognized and quite unreal—
That it is, and a positive result in a chemical reaction.
Nothing else. Except that in its first, insistent
Burrowing, it lodges beneath consciousness
And becomes, before knowledge, beyond knowledge,
Mine. And mystery.
Frail subaqueous creature, searching
The depths, embedded and feeding and growing . . .
And finally stretching. Suddenly,
Beyond academic question, scientific explanation,
Beyond calendars and pink pamphlets, chemicals,
Icy instruments—alarm! it lives! it has me!
I am possessed.
Eyeless, armless, without skin or skeleton
(All graphic illustrations to the contrary),
Personal poltergeist, it is disembodied
Motion. It has nothing to do with names,
Smiles, gestures, talent, but it demands
Knowing, so I fashion it a covering
As the tiny yellow garment on my knitting needles.
It is a boy, brown-eyed and slender, named perhaps
Brian—a poet? sports car driver?—
It heaves and a hundred unknowable arms
Flail impatiently. Perhaps the sweater
Will fit whatever comes to fill it.

And it comes. Reluctant and insistent,
Irreversible, tormenting and terrified,
We are helpless, it and I. We are losing
The tenuous balance we achieved, each veiled,
Accepted without meeting. In blood, with violent
Shouts, hating, clinging, we are torn apart
And held up, face to face. Confrontation.

Mother. Daughter.

Gathering its nebulosity into a compact
Radiant wet whimpering form
With hair—my God yes!—and blue eyes—
And those were for real elbows and knees
Knocking at my doors. And out of the red
Recesses of my shelter, freed and startled and firm
It becomes incredibly, immediately Anne.

200

Chewing on my yellow pencil, I could weep with impuissance and loss. During this winter, I type up old poems from college and submit them to a few magazines, but none is ever accepted. I revise a few, but I don't write any new ones. I no longer feel the slightest creative urge, any more than I feel sexual desire.

Marriage has strangled me, choked me on my own ashes.

Inside and Outside

~~~

i

AN ITALIAN restaurant in Boston's North End. Dark woodwork, red brocade walls, stiff white table linens. I am sitting at the end on one side of a long table, George opposite me. It's winter. We're here with Aunt Jane and Uncle Kip and a group of other friends.

All of a sudden I feel as though I need to swallow and can't. For one shuddering moment I think I might vomit. Not long ago, I got drunk at a party where a nasty little psychiatrist tried to make love to me, and I was horribly sick the next morning. George held my head over a stainless-steel mixing bowl while I vomited for the first time in my adult life. For the first time since I had that stomach flu the day after Mother and Daddy got married and left us to go on their honeymoon. Since that dreadful hangover, I've felt very nervous that I might vomit again, without warning, in public.

I can't swallow. I can't catch my breath, either. My heart is pounding so that it seems to fill my whole chest and squeeze my lungs flat along my rib cage. The room recedes, and everything in it takes on a blackish silver cast, as though reflected in an old mirror. The sharp clatter of dishes and the hum of voices roll in waves. My head whirls. I feel hot even though my skin is shivery with sweat. The fingers clutching my napkin feel frozen, the long nails biting my wet palms. I can't swallow. I can't breathe.

* * *

Until this night, I would say that my life was now thoroughly satisfactory. True, the winter in Bath was trying, all those days of blizzard or icy wind off the river which cooped Anne and me in our apartment, spacious and sunny, to be sure, but a little stifling nonetheless, just the two of us all day, and the two cats with their four kittens, plenty of warm bodies, but only one of us yet able to talk. I got tired of the sound of my own voice. So sometimes I stopped using it, shut up for hours and days at a time.

But spring brought George's yearned-for release from the navy, and with that ordeal behind us, we were bound to be happy. We moved to Waltham to be near George's mother, who promised to take care of Anne while I went to work to put George through graduate school. At first we lived in an impossibly cramped apartment, the rooms so tiny that when we opened the Hide-a-bed for my sister's visit, it clunked into the opposite wall of the living room.

Now we've found a great place on the third floor of an old apartment building. The location is poor, right off Central Square, with the ambulances and police cars shrieking through at all hours. But the space! A railroad flat, they call this sort of place, large, high-ceilinged rooms strung out one behind the other: a living room and a study off the enormous entry hall, then a long skinny hall like a bowling alley, with our bedroom, the bathroom, Anne's bedroom, the dining room, and at the back a kitchen with two pantries. All this for a hundred fifteen a month, heat included. It looked pretty bad when we moved in, but we've painted every bit of it, and even though the furnishings we've scrounged are sparse and shabby, we're happy with it.

I didn't know what kind of a job I could get. What is there for an English major besides teaching, and the Rocky Hill School had soured me on that. Then I found an ad in the *Globe* for a junior editor at the Smithsonian Astrophysical Observatory. I knew I wanted the job as soon as the head of the department asked me what books I'd read lately. Who wouldn't want to work for a man who wanted to know something like that, instead of what I was going to do with my baby while I worked. I guess I'd been reading the right things. After all, I'd just spent the whole of a Maine winter in hibernation with a baby and a tumbling bunch of kittens. I'd reread all of *Kristin Lavransdätter* and then *The Master of Hestviken* as well. *The Hobbit* and the three volumes of *Lord of the Rings*. Jane Austen's six novels for the third time. *The Feminine Mystique*, the radical message of which I reduced simply to permission for working outside the home in order to educate my husband. Anyway, Nelson hired me, and I've been spending my days happily reading about the greenhouse effect on Mars and checking esoteric references in Harvard's libraries. Recently, I've been promoted to research assistant to the Assistant Director for Management.

After this night in the restaurant, however, my life unravels swiftly. The attacks of nausea and breathlessness recur with increasing frequency, often together with sickening abdominal cramps and diarrhea. I can no longer bear to go to bars or restaurants, to dinner parties, to movies or the theater, even to the Stop and Shop for a carton of milk. In the spring, I get into my parents' car for the drive to Wheaton for Sally's graduation, but before we've gone a block, I whimper, "Take me home." A couple of weeks later, I'm supposed to be Sally's matron of honor. I already have the pretty green dress, the silk shoes. I can't do it. I crouch at the back of the congregation. When the photographer gathers the family for a formal portrait after the ceremony, no one remembers that I should be in it, too. There stand Sally, on whom my wedding dress has become perfect, and Peter, with Mother, Daddy, Chip, and Barba, smiling against the sun of a breezy June afternoon in the backyard of 236. Nancy's gone: a naught, a cipher, the difficult child effaced.

I think if I don't have to work, I'll feel better. In a sense, I'll come to realize one day, I'm on the right track. The satisfaction I feel at leaving home each day for work I'm good at triggers a conflict I can't yet identify, and none of the professionals whose help I solicit with increasing desperation is equipped to recognize and help me learn to deal with it. On the contrary, I note in my journal, "I have the feeling that Dr. Julian and George and everyone who's trying to 'help' me are just cramming a way of life down my throat": the life of a contented young matron. But although I got a job in order to put George through graduate school, I've discovered I *like* my work. I like it better than cooking George's meals and taking care of Anne and sweeping the dust kitties out from under the bed. A lot better, if the truth were known. Which it isn't, even by me. All I know is that husband and child and house are supposed to form my fulfillment. My agoraphobic attacks ensure that I have to stay home to care for them. Or else I'll gag to death.

As soon as George has finished graduate school and found a summer job as a parking-lot attendant at a nearby department store to get us through till he begins teaching in the fall, I quit my job. Only I don't get better. I can no longer eat in anyone's presence except George's, and even then I can't swallow much. My weight drops to a hundred pounds, ninety-nine, ninety-eight. The panic that used to strike me outside has moved into my apartment. It blots out everything around me. I feed and bathe and dress Anne as though she were the Rubber Baby I had in Exeter. A sunny, imaginative child, she prattles to me, the cats, the television, spinning out her own entertainment. After a while I can hardly hear her voice. My own thoughts have begun roaring and echoing in my ears. I see things, dark shadows, out of the corner of my eye. Even my own movements startle me, so I stay as still as I can on the couch in the bay window overlooking Common Street. It's August. Puffs of sticky air come in through the dusty screens, carrying bleep of car horn, keen of siren, jangle of the bell at the intersection telling the blind couple next door it's safe to cross. Breathless, I telephone George at work: "Come home. Please come home."

ii

I am a character in a Victorian novel: a young girl living with her aunt. Aunt and I are lying under a heavy red velvet counterpane. I tell her it is too heavy for April and she begins to change it to a lighter but identical one. They are amazing—dusty and a little faded with long satin fringe.

Suddenly I am in a different setting. There are details from the Victorian novel; but now I am in a family—my own family— and we are blind. Then I am no longer blind but pretending to be. I have a yapping little terrier for a Seeing Eye dog, whom I don't like. I go to the door of my family's house, because someone is there. A blind man looking for his son. I send the child out to get in a waiting car, feeling danger for him.

I go out, and it is cold and icy. I walk to a street corner and wait for the school bus. A car speeds by, driven by James Hopper, with some friends. I wonder if they will notice that I am blind (which I'm not). I go back to the house, and Chip and Barba are there, home from the first day of school. School was almost closed because of snow. Barba is glad it wasn't, because she had such a wonderful first day. I think, "I had a wonderful first day, too."

When I sign myself into Metropolitan State Hospital on the advice of my current psychiatrist, who suggests I could use a rest, I think I'll be there for ten days of observation, but in fact I stay for over six months "on the Hill," as the local residents put it in their jokes. "Watch out," they say if you do something foolish, "or the little men with the butterfly nets will come and put you on the Hill." When I was young, we said the same thing about Danvers State. But no one ever really expects to wind up on the Hill. It's only a joke.

Once I go, I make myself at home up there as I would anywhere else, in a brick box at the top of a winding drive through spacious grounds. Waltham is an ugly city, the ugliest I can think of. At Met State I've found the loveliest spot in it, softly rolling open fields surrounded by woodland, but of course no one comes up to enjoy it, so we loonies have it to ourselves. Even George's parents, who have lived much of their lives only ten minutes away, have never been here. When I'm in the Intensive Care Unit of the city hospital after a suicide attempt and it's not yet clear whether I'll pull through, they visit me. But they never come to Met State.

Their shame at my condition intensifies my fear that I have now forfeited my place among the ordinary human lives I fitfully long to rejoin "on the outside," as we inmates put it. It exemplifies the attitude I expect to meet if I venture back out there: nice people, the kind of people you'd have in your family or among your dinner guests or on your payroll, simply don't go nuts. The others, the ones who do, need careful watching. Ever after, their affection will be tinged with anxiety, as though I were some unfathomable and tricky bit of technology that might go off if you jostled it. Danger: UXB.

My only consistent connection with that outside world I fear and desire is George, who braves the loonies and the locked doors night after night, and drives me on weekends to visit Anne, who has gone to live at 236. "I can talk with you in my head better than with anyone else," I tell him. "As I am now, you're the only person at all real to me." Even *his* edges are blurred, however. I can never quite conceive his life, how he drives into Boston each morning to teach boys with few gifts but great expectations at the Huntington School, which I've never seen, and returns to our echoing apartment, empty except for Ho Tei and Ho's Anna skittering up and down the bowling-alley hall, their loneliness welling into ebullience in his silent company, eats alone, then sets out for Met State to spend an hour with . . . who? Me?

It's still *me*, I'm sure, no one else, but I don't know this person, who feels like a transparency among transparencies, insubstantial figures smeared against the ward's green walls by the light seeping through the small-paned windows. Lit by our flickers, George looms solid, bearing a chocolate ice-cream soda from Brigham's in one hand. Through him, and through Anne, whom Mother is raising to expect her mummy to come home for good any time now, I am tied, however tenuously, to the world I've fled, and tugged through the door, down the long gray flight of stairs, out to the parking lot, into the car, off the Hill, as though one day I could go for good.

I am to be a car salesman, selling Fords for Uncle Robert. He gets me a beautiful car to use, very new, sporty, and powerful. I am driving it through the center of a city—supposedly Boston but it looks like Waltham. I have a good deal of trouble getting a cop to let me through a busy intersection. I have it on my mind to pick up George, yet I never do. Instead, I park the car and go into a building to speak to Uncle Robert, who is at a pharmacist's filling a prescription for Aunt Lucy. I am worried that I have left the car radio going.

Cut off from the outside world, my waking life flattens out, breaks up, takes on the eerie cast of a landscape blurred by fog. Only in dreams do I continue a coherent and often cheerful existence, filled with family and plenty of activity, as though a healthy and humorous Nancy had gone to ground to wait for the miasma above to blow away.

Breakfast: soupy Maltex with milk and a piece of corn bread. Lunch: salad, spaghetti, lumpy butterscotch pudding. Dinner: beans and hot dogs. And bananas. Eternally, infernally, bananas. The charge for a day at Met State is $7.50. When they see how little money George and I have, they don't make us pay anything at all. Probably most of the people here aren't paying. Everyone looks poor: shapeless, somehow, and faded, not just their clothes but their skin, their eyes, their bodies slackened by the white and yellow and blue pills, and the translucent green ones at bedtime. We dissolve slowly, slowly, swimming through murk, even at night only a few small unshaded bulbs lighting our wavery courses: cafeteria to day room to toilet to iron cot and back again, round and round, poor and drab as guppies in a muddy tank.

Maria wants to die. Ted wants to die, but then he gets better and leaves. I want to die. I think of the nearly full bottle of

Darvon I have. I wonder if it could kill me. Then I feel afraid, thinking of George and Anne. It would be very bad for them. But sometimes I think, How wonderful for me. At first Al doesn't want to die, but later he does. Herbert wants to die. Brian wants to die. He goes out into the snowy woods and hangs himself from a tree.

I am at my family's house, upstairs in Granna's apartment with Granna and Mother. We are talking about various things—my cousin Helene, my new job, the effects on children of having three generations in a home. Mother is treating Granna as though she is practically senile again. We talk about Peter Johnson and his wife, though I don't think he's married. They are involved in an experiment using LSD for birth control. They've been using it wrong—it seems to have something to do with the positioning of the feet—and she may be pregnant.

After three months, when I've taken the Darvon and thrown it up again but I still don't get well, I'm transferred to the "best" of the wards for chronic patients. On the first day, awash in the clatter of metal trays and beneath it the hum of drugged voices, I hear my name shouted by a stranger.

"Hi, Nancy!" He grabs my hand, and I start to pull back. His face is nearly white, green eyes fringed by pale stubby eyelashes. He has no hair at all. At either temple a reddish purple welt pouts like an angry little mouth. "Don't you know me? It's Ted!" Ted? Yes. The line of nose, the curve of jaw take on remembered shape. Ted, who got better and was sent home.

"Ted. My God. What are you doing here?"

"I tried to kill myself. Shot myself through the head." He turns his face from side to side. Bullet in. Bullet out. "I missed my brain. Missed the optic nerve. I'm not even blind."

"How long have you been here?" This appears to be the polite form of address in the back wards. Not your name. Not the work you do. Your Met State credentials.

"I was on R2 for three months before coming here," I tell the girl with dark curly hair, the only person on the ward who's spoken to me. "How about you?"

"Oh, I've only been here two years. Harold has been here six. Everyone else has been here a long time." She speaks softly because no one else in the day room is talking at all. Even our whispered conversation resonates oddly through the dim space littered with old Windsor chairs, painted lilac and Pepto-Bismol pink, and their motionless occupants. "They have to keep me here because I keep trying to kill myself." The satisfaction in her voice resonates even more oddly through my skull.

I am not this crazy.

On our way to a dinner given by the Ures, a group of us run in gray light down a city street, brandishing clean, fresh mackerel. Puff is there, as well as Al, a man with a crippled arm, and many others. The dinner is held in a vast, elaborate palace, each course in a different room. First shrimp cocktail, then many different kinds of meat—lamb, turkey, beef.

Dinner over, a relief because I'm afraid to eat, we adjourn to a room where Mrs. Ure suggests playing some game involving spirits. There are a lot of young people, and we veto the idea, wanting to dance. George is there, but Al asks me to dance and I leave George. We dance and keep falling to the floor, as gracefully as though the fall is part of the dance.

I am a mental patient. I do not act; I endure. I receive, but do not participate in, my treatment. When I resist, I'm accused of not wanting to get well. No one interprets my resistance as a sign of health. They may recognize my desire to control my own well-being, but if so, they assume that such control would be dangerous.

No one sits down and talks to me about my treatment woman to woman. Since my psychiatrist at Met State is female, such a talk would be possible in theory. But she doesn't say, "Nancy, we think that the biochemistry of your brain is screwed up and that medication combined with electroconvulsive therapy can correct the imbalance." Maybe psychiatrists don't yet know enough to say that. She doesn't even say, "We don't yet know what the hell causes depression, but we've observed that people who take certain kinds of medication and have shock treatments often get better, at least for a while." What she says, in essence, is, "You are sick. If you do as I tell you, you can get well. Otherwise, you will be here forever in that chronic ward I sent you to."

I hate the chronic ward. And I am, by preference if not by expectation, a good girl. When the nurse gives me my meds in a little paper cup, I don't spit them on the floor. I swallow them: Stelazine and Artane, chlorpromazine, imipramine, amitriptyline. I don't even ask what they're for. I attend group therapy. I attend individual therapy. After one session, I draw the line at occupational therapy. I can half believe that fabricating fifty minutes of talk may be therapeutic. But potholders and pen wipers? I attend the Christmas party put on for us by a group of good-hearted beauticians, who give us each a trinket and waltz us around the day room to "Jingle Bell Rock." How many times I've made little gifts and sung carols for shut-ins, I think as I return the strained smile of my partner, and now I am one. I lie down on the stretcher and go to sleep so I can have a convulsion, though the aide promises me that only our toes twitch these days.

What "cures" me is probably a combination of medication and twenty-one shocks to my brain, a kind of gigantic biochemical rearrangement like putting all the furniture in your house in new and more interesting places. What propels me out of Met State, however, is not a cure but boredom. As the depression abates, I grow less tolerant of my drab surroundings, the routine of meals and meds separated by long hours in which no one demands a single thought or act from me, the company of people with whom I have nothing in common but psychic pain. Even poor sad Al, with whom I've been having an affair in the hope of rousing my body to some sort of desire for the world, looms as a tedious obsession to be thrown off rather than the wide-eyed young druggy with his wrists sliced to ribbons who has come to love me in his mizzly way. I take on the task of editing a doctoral dissertation, a glossary of musical terms found in Shakespeare and his contemporaries, boring and badly written, but I rejoice in the demand it makes. I need hard work, which I'll have to venture outside to find. Nothing here is hard.

When I got here, I felt such revulsion against the terms of my life out there—dust rags and shrieking babies, meals to cook, evenings of bridge with nice young couples—that I was terrified of puking every moment. "I want to play," I complained. "What a drag the real world seems." It still does. I still suffer from attacks of nausea. I feel dizzy and disoriented. I don't know it now, but I will continue to have these symptoms forever, both when I'm clinically depressed and when I'm not. I'm an agoraphobe, I will discover for myself long after Dr. Julian has released me from her healing clutch, and these are called panic attacks. Once I figure that out, I learn to survive them, though I hate them just as much as when I thought they meant I was crazy.

In my forties, I'll meet a psychotherapist interested in phobias, who mentions that most of the people she treats seem to have at least one hypertrophied sense. At that chance remark I recollect the childhood label "hypersensitive" that triggered muddy feelings of shame and satisfaction. Now that I reject the label as a metaphor for social deviance, it's free for helping explain my panic attacks. My senses let in, in even the most tranquil setting, floods of information that threaten to drown me. That's what a panic attack feels like: being a five-year-old girl on the sandy beach at The Port when the great glassy-green wave tumbled over my head and tugged me forward into the icy water. I go rigid. I can't breathe. My body simply doesn't know what to do under the weight of all that water. That day on the beach, I bobbed to the surface, however, and gasped a lungful of air, and then some grown-up hauled me out of the foam like a striped bass. In the twenty years after Met State, I learn that you can't avoid swimming in treacherous waters, but you don't necessarily go down for the last time.

As I depart Met State, I'm given a chance to participate in a longitudinal study of the children of hospitalized mothers. The researchers, a team from Harvard, are delighted to get me because many of the women they've approached have resisted the idea of prolonged prying into their private lives. They have no private lives at Met State, but once they get home, apparently, their lives become their own again. For my part, I'm thrilled to be asked because I feel certain that, by deserting Anne for six months, I've harmed her in some way. Here's a chance for experts to monitor her and let us know how bad the damage is. They do monitor her for four years, until we move out of state, but all they can ever say is that she seems cheerful and extraordinarily bright. Thanks to Mother's steady, matter-of-fact care, Anne's life was disrupted surprisingly little; and she has, she will demonstrate time and again, an unusually resilient nature. Between them, the two Annes made the best of a bad thing.

I am, of course, immensely reassured by these assessments. But the study offers me, purely by chance, another kind of reassurance. To observe Anne and me at home, a social worker pays us regular though infrequent visits. After the first one, she probably thinks even a six-month sojourn in Met State would be preferable, because she turns out to be terrified of cats. If she glimpses Ho Tei or Ho's Anna, even if they pass through the next room, she blanches, then flushes, a line of sweat breaking out on her upper lip, her chest heaving, her fingers clenched around the ballpoint pen with which she's been making notes on my condition. Clearly she's on the verge of scrambling up onto the blue tweed seat of my Swedish swivel chair, there to revolve like a dervish, though she never quite takes the leap. I make soothing noises. I make an elaborate display of shooing the bad kitties away. I refrain from collapsing into giggles, at least until after her hasty visit, at the incongruity of sending an ailurophobe to check how the agoraphobe is coming along. The whole encounter leaves me feeling terrifically well.

"What were you doing there?" Lisa, my editor, will ask one day. "What was happening to you? Why did you stay so long?" Lisa, my dear, if I understood these things, I would explain them. I have told you what I know.

iii

In spite of my fears, after my long confinement I'm anxious to resume an ordinary life with George and Anne in the high, bare rooms of the Common Street apartment, to return to my work at SAO, above all, to start another baby. What with putting George through graduate school, and then having a prolonged nervous breakdown, I've fallen way behind schedule. Anne's second birthday, on which the new baby ought to have appeared, has long since come and gone.

Actually, I don't feel any personal yearning for another baby. Anne is immensely entertaining on her own. Yet never for a moment do I question the necessity for a second child. An only child himself, his one brother stillborn, George has been raised by his grieving parents to feel impoverished. If I refused to provide Anne a sibling, he would doubtless leave me for a willing woman. This would not be faithlessness on his part, or cruelty, but absolute need. But I never think of refusing, because the socially approved quota for our generation, regardless of George's urge to fill some private lack, is two children, two years apart. I am still a good girl, even though I've screwed up. I can't bear any more deviance. On Anne's third birthday, during a holiday at the Lodge, I get pregnant.

My body is thrilled to be pregnant again, evening sickness and all. It throws off an attack of the Hong Kong flu and otherwise never even sniffles. Unfortunately, however, it falls into the hands of a coercive bantam cock of an obstetrician intent on controlling it. "No salt!" he snaps. "Gain no more than twenty pounds!" So I eat unsalted tuna in unsalted white sauce on unsalted toast, the true equivalent of library paste on cardboard, and blow up anyway. I gained thirty-five pounds when I carried Anne, weighing a hundred forty-two when she was born. I weigh a hundred twenty at the start of this pregnancy and come up on a hundred forty-two with two months still to go. Then I stop gaining. It's as though my body thinks a hundred forty-two is the appropriate pregnant weight. Unfortunately, Dr. Arno doesn't believe in carnal wisdom.

As with Anne, my belly swells prodigiously. At six weeks, Mother asks if I'm pregnant, though I hadn't planned to say anything yet. A couple of weeks later, I go into maternity clothes. By the time I reach six months, people are helping me across the street as though afraid I'll whelp in the intersection. I have to make a sling of my arms and lug the bulge up the two long flights of stairs to our apartment. I can't find a comfortable position to sleep in. Night and day the baby tap-dances exuberantly on my bladder until I'm so exhausted that I fall asleep in the dark sitting on the toilet.

Despite my weariness, I keep my job, which makes me happy. The people in the editorial department don't seem to mind my pregnancy, but we share a building with the business department, and those men have fits. Every morning I clamber into a maternity girdle and stockings, put on a dress or suit, curl my hair on electric rollers, make up my face so that I will seem the very model of a professional woman. To no avail. I have to march my bulk past their stiffened faces, their pinched nostrils, as they turn away in distaste. I imagine they've all got women in my condition at home, and at home is where they think I ought to be, too. It's the 1960s, and I'm still scarcely aware of the women's movement. I certainly don't consider myself part of it. But those stares and hisses following me down the hall to my office are my dues. I'm a member long before I join up.

At seven months the pregnancy goes awry when, in my blood, the level of antibodies against the Rh factor begins to rise. This isn't supposed to happen, says Dr. Arno. Only 10 percent of women with Rh incompatibility develop any problems, and of those, only 8 percent have them in a second pregnancy. I've lost the numbers game. Later I'll lose others, until I come to feel a certain resignation, at once ironic and comic, as though losing numbers games was somehow my task, maybe even my genius. At this point, however, I'm ill equipped for loss.

Suddenly I am no longer sheltering a baby but poisoning it. It's not sufficiently developed to breathe on its own, so I have to hold onto it. But the longer it dwells within me, the sicker it will get, until it dies. The trick is to guess the critical moment and snatch the baby free in time. Three weeks before it's due, Dr. Arno announces he will induce labor the next morning.

Once again the threat of induced labor sends me into spasms, and in the dark hours George and I scoop up Anne and take her to stay with her grandparents before driving to Waltham City Hospital. This is not Bath Memorial. There's no private labor room where George can sit with me. Three women howl in the beds around me. Pretty soon I join them. This labor is much shorter, only about nine hours, but "real time," I discover, doesn't matter. I can't tell the difference between this one and the last. They seem to run together, effacing every other experience I've ever had. I feel like some female figure from a myth I'm making up as I go along, rocking in eternal terror and travail. I've always been in pain. I'll be in pain forever. No one comes to comfort me.

Abruptly the baby's heart begins to fail. I learn this later. At the moment, no one is talking to me. I'm just a heap of flesh to dump onto a cart and whip into the delivery room, where Dr. Arno yanks the baby out with forceps.

"It's a boy!" These are the only words he's spoken to me. I almost faint with relief. In my heart of hearts, warmed by my years of sisterhood, I've wanted a girl. But with the Rh problems, this is the last child we can have, and so I've hoped for a boy. One of each. A son for George.

"A boy? You're sure?" I croak. Dr. Arno laughs.

"Let her see him," he says to a nurse, who brings him up near my face. Sure enough. I want to touch him, but the nurse has whisked him out of sight, over to the pediatrician, who will test his blood.

"He's yellow," I hear the pediatrician say. "No nursing." I feel the sting of a needle.

"Stilbestrol," Dr. Arno says from between my knees where he's stitching and stitching. "To dry up your milk."

"Dry up my milk? I was planning to breast-feed."

"I know. But you can't because the baby's jaundiced and he'd be allergic to your milk. It has antibodies like your blood." More poison. Although we've discussed breast-feeding in the past, he's never once mentioned this possibility. Apparently it slipped his mind.

When he finds me a couple of days later with the tears sliding down my face as milk drips from my breasts and slides warmly over my belly, he's almost curt, though he masks his impatience with a jocular tone: "What are you crying about? Bottle-fed babies do just as well as breast-fed. Sometimes better." But what about bottle-feeding mothers? I want to say. You didn't even give me a chance to get used to the idea. I was in too much of a hurry with Anne, rushing her from stage to stage just to see what she'd do next. I weaned her too soon. I was going to keep this one at my breast for at least a year. I've been cheated. *Why didn't you tell me?*

I don't say anything. I don't howl out the raging disappointment inside me. I don't even whisper. I just try to smile and be a good sport, doctor's little cooperative and reasonable patient.

I don't have any baby to feed with either breast or bottle anyway. The pediatrician immediately took the baby away and exchanged a pint of his blood for that of a man from SAO I never meet. Later, the man comes back and donates another pint. The baby lives under bilirubin lights in an isolette in the crowded nursery. I can stand among the fathers and other visitors and watch him, wailing as I don't dare to wail, behind the glass. Except for the orange cast of his skin, he looks fine, good-sized despite his premature birth, his rugged arms and legs flailing vigorously. Nothing's wrong with his heart. That was a false alarm. I'm not allowed to touch him. Even the nurses hardly touch him. Every so often they poke their fingers into the limp rubber hands built into the isolette to feed him, change his diaper, jab his heel for another blood sample. No one picks him up. No one rocks him. No one puts her mouth right against his ear and whispers that he doesn't need to cry, she's right here, everything is going to be all right.

Hour upon hour I watch him through the window and murmur his name to myself, trying to get used to the sound: Matthew, Matthew. It doesn't seem attached to anything. After a couple of days, I'm sent home, still empty-handed and before long empty-breasted as well. When he's a week old, George and I are allowed to fetch him. I have him in my arms at last. But it's too late. Some connection has been blighted. They could have picked any baby at random from the nursery and thrust him into my hands. They could almost have given me a life-size doll. He's no more mine than any other baby is. But no less, either. As good as any other. I take him home.

Years later, I'll read about the bonding shown by studies to occur in the moments and hours after birth, and I'll begin to understand the true violence the doctors inflicted on Matthew and me, tearing us apart like this at precisely the moment when he should have lain across me while we smelled and stroked and stared at each other, while he got used to being outside and I got used to the absence within. I'll never forgive them for depriving us of that bond. Nothing else that happens to me—not my father's early death, not the nervous breakdown I've recently survived or the one that still lies ahead, not the multiple sclerosis that will soon begin crippling my body, not even the melanomas George will develop, giving us the real tang of our own mortality—nothing wounds me like this botched pregnancy and childbirth. It acts like the bite of the brown recluse spider, which inflames and necrotizes the flesh until it sloughs away, refusing to heal. It arouses an impermissible grief, one that has—unlike madness, illness, death—no social form to contain it. I never hear another woman utter it. In this sense, I spend the rest of my life in the dark and alone. Matthew's birth is the only episode in this book that makes me howl as I write it.

iv

Just as we moved right after Anne's birth, we move right after Matthew's, and once again I hemorrhage. Slowly I recover my strength, but no amount of vigor seems equal to the Augean task we've set for ourselves. We've long wanted a home of our own and now, by borrowing the down payment from our parents, we've managed to buy a duplex on Waltham's South Side, the ugliest section of this relentlessly ugly city. The homes in this largely Italian working-class neighborhood were probably built for low-level managers at the now-defunct Waltham Watch Factory. And built badly. Our floors, for instance, are hardwood around the edges, but in the center, where the linoleum carpets must once have been nailed, is a large rectangle of soft pine.

We may have managed to buy the ugliest house in the neighborhood, though they're all pretty bad: a tall, slightly sagging structure covered with faded gray asbestos shingles. Even after we've painted the front doors fire-engine red, to the dismay of our neighbors, the house retains a lugubrious air, as does life within it, a gray-asbestos-shingled sort of life, short of money, depleted of erotic energy. Driving past on a visit a couple of years after selling it, I will stare at it a long time, trying to stir in myself some flicker of the nostalgia the places of my past always fan in my soul, but I feel nothing. Quite probably, I will think, I lived in this house for three years without once feeling happy in it, except perhaps for the day I pruned the lilac (to its ruin, it turned out).

We get it quite cheaply in the settlement of the estate of the old man who died in it recently. He had a heart attack while using the toilet and fell forward against the door. They had quite a time, the tenants tell us, getting him out. The tenants, a man and wife and their teenage daughter, have lived for many years in the five-room apartment on the first floor, and we let them go on living there although the rent they pay is less than half the going rate. We have six rooms on the second floor and two more, as well as an unfinished attic where I hang the laundry, on the third.

For months we scrape off floral wallpapers, stained and dark, sometimes as many as six layers, and replace them with paint, white and Wedgwood green. The place looks a little better, though we're too poor to do the job properly. It always feels as though it's on the verge of crumbling around our ears. The one time I do something properly, however, hiring someone to hang a pale woven paper in the hall and down the front stairs, Anne almost immediately covers it with huge drawings in green Magic Marker. I don't quite commit infanticide, but I lose heart. We paint over the drawings, and the beautiful wallpaper, and eke out a shabby, makeshift existence furnished in finest Early Attic style.

Right from birth, Matthew is the loveliest baby I've ever seen. And the most miserable. Nothing seems to go right for him, although monthly tests show that his blood is now healthy. He doesn't tolerate formula or new foods well, spitting up constantly. Throughout the whole hot summer he reeks. "Barney Badsmell," George dubs him. During his first year he cuts sixteen teeth, each one accompanied by an ear infection. Except when his mouth is full or he's alone in his crib, he cries inconsolably, even between bites, so that feeding him is a frantic shoveling exercise to stave off the next wail. He can't bear to be held for more than five minutes. Once, we try a drive-in movie, which has become our staple entertainment since we can't afford baby-sitters, but we can't hear the tinny speaker over his shouts, so we give up and go home. If we take him visiting, he screams the entire time. One Sunday, at 236, after he's cried for five hours straight and I'm ready to jump out of my skin, I ask Mother if she could keep him for a couple of days to let me catch my breath. "I can't," she says sorrowfully. "I just couldn't stand it."

She doesn't have to. I do. And I have to do it alone. Because he's healthy and gaining weight steadily, the pediatrician decrees that he's thriving and brushes aside my concerns.

"But something's *wrong,*" I say to George. "Babies don't just cry like this."

"Don't worry so much," George replies, in what I'm coming to recognize as his Nancy-spent-six-months-at-Met-State-and-we've-got-to-take-that-into-account tone. "Matthew's just fine." He's going to give me the same line, with the same degree of condescension, in all the years to come. What he means by it is, *I do not* (or *do not choose to,* I'm not sure which) *perceive a problem here, and therefore no problem exists. If Nancy perceives a problem where no problem exists, then she's screwed up and may safely be ignored.* He sees in the situation not a conflict to be resolved but evidence of a defect in my maternal character.

What he never sees is that the fact that I perceive a problem in itself constitutes a problem. So *some* problem sure as hell exists, and ignoring it is not a reasonable response. It's easy enough for him to believe that Matthew is fine. For one thing, he's constitutionally inclined to leaps of faith. For another, he doesn't get home till an hour or so before Matthew goes to bed. One hour's crying may well seem less worrisome than eight. I wouldn't know. And he'll never find out. Not once does he say, "Look, Matthew's screaming obviously bothers you, but I don't mind it, so why don't I stay home with him and *you* go out to work." In all the years he'll accuse me, silently and aloud, of bad mothering, he'll never once offer to take over the task himself. He'd rather be the good father. So would I.

Since I can't nurse Matthew, and since he takes no more comfort from my company than from anyone else's, by autumn I mention tentatively that I'd like to hire a baby-sitter and go back to work.

"Good," says George with considerable zest. "You'll be less bitchy."

Anne doesn't seem quite sure what I'm doing at home anyway, though she figures it has something to do with the baby. Happily immersed in nursery school, she views my returning to work as getting back to normal.

The rest of the family is less composed. "You're deserting my grandchildren," Mother accuses. George's parents are less outspoken, but their faces furrow in the way they have that suggests that "Nancy's job" will become one of the problems they fret over by the hour when they're alone. "She'll soon get sick of it," pronounces George's aunt who married late and quit her secretarial job gratefully. I can feel their disapproval like soft, sticky little paws pulling at me, patting me into place.

For a while, it looks as though they have nothing to worry about, anyway. Smithsonian has lost its NASA funding and can't afford to hire me back. And even if they could, I have no luck finding a baby-sitter. For the next several months I find first a job but no baby-sitter, then a baby-sitter but no job. During that time, I find plenty to do. I take on a freelance editorial project on nuclear reactors for the MIT Press as well as hours of antiwar work. But these activities too seldom get me out of the house, away from Matthew's insistent howls, which pursue me everywhere, even up to the attic room I use as a study.

I begin to think that if I don't get some respite, I'll go bonkers again and have to head back to the Hill. Actually, I am pretty depressed, but since I don't feel crazy, I don't recognize the problem and won't for many years. No one ever taught me what signs to look for so that I could care for myself responsibly. They probably didn't think I *could* care for myself. They thought only doctors could do it.

I've got a doctor—for that matter, the same psychiatrist who sent me to Met State in the first place—but even he doesn't pick up on the fact that I'm depressed. He thinks I've got a lot of problems I need to talk about in order to work them out. So for a total of five years I spend an hour every week talking to him about my problems. He doesn't talk back. He's of the "mmm-hmm" persuasion. Now, I'm a terrific talker. And God knows I've got problems. I have no trouble filling an hour a week for five years. And I'll be almost as depressed at the end as I was when I started. Moreover, since we haven't talked much about depression in practical terms, I won't have gained any particular competence in living with a chronic mental illness. That skill will come much later, but not until I've almost died.

Meantime, here I crouch over a cup of tea and a Camel in my unheated study, puzzling over an article on the technology of nuclear reactor safety while the air from Matthew's extraordinarily lusty lungs wafts through the cracks in this rickety old house and burrows like an earwig toward my brain.

Then, a double miracle: simultaneously, an international program at Harvard needs an editor, and a pale, shy girl who lives near us drops out of school and needs a job. I won't actually make a living wage out of this arrangement. My gross pay will be a hundred forty dollars a week, of which I'll give Susan seventy plus Social Security, and child-care expenses aren't yet tax deductible. After expenses for transportation, clothing, and lunches, I'll be lucky to keep pocket money. But as long as I break even, I'm content. "Yes!" I say to Harvard. "Come on!" I say to Susan. On the first of April, I charge down the front stairs, jump into my old Volvo station wagon, and zoom toward Cambridge, leaving the gray shingled house in my exhaust.

v

"Run through the jungle! Run through the jungle!" The bass on the stereo has been cranked up so high I can't tell the difference between CCR's rhythms and my own lurching pulse. "Don't look back!" The face of the man I'm dancing with is indistinct in the bluish dusk, but as he turns, his wet face catches the light from the doorway. "Don't look back!"

"Another?" he asks as the beat resumes.

"No, thanks." I'm still breathless. "I've got to be going. We told the sitter we wouldn't be late."

"Too bad." He pulls me forward, out of the way of the dancers, and I lean briefly into the curve of his arm. Our bodies are damp. "I was enjoying our dancing."

"Me, too." I catch sight of George in the next room and wave.

"Would you like to go out for lunch on Monday?" he asks as I move away. I'm surprised. He's a visiting scholar in the program I work in, and more than once when we've arrived at the same time to retrieve our sack lunches from the refrigerator, we've eaten together. But we've never gone out.

"Sure," I say as offhandedly as I can. "I'd like that."

I spend all of Sunday sewing a hooded cape of pink and gray tweed. I'm an awkward seamstress, and the heavy wool is hard to work with on my little Singer, the one Daddy bought for Mother out on Guam, so it must be about as old as I am. All day I hunch over the broad dining-room table fumbling with pins. This is a good room to work in, lighted by a large bay window in one wall, but noisy. The floor plan of the house is basically circular, each room opening into another, and the children clatter around and around, Matthew on his Tike Bike, Anne on her imaginary horsey. When she turns thirteen, we'll tease her that it's time to retire her horsey, and for the most part she will, but every so often she'll break into a telltale prance. For all I know, she'll continue prancing through the jungle on her way to bathe in the river when she's moved to the other side of the world.

I hardly hear the children's shrieks. I hardly sew either, but since no one else in the household can sew, they don't know that. They think I'm concentrating on my mysterious craft. In truth, I'm feverish with sexual fantasy. I play my Credence Clearwater Revival record, then my Rolling Stones record, reliving every dance: the way our bodies almost touched, did touch a little, pulled apart, the burn of that touch along my belly, down my thigh. I recall a coffee break at work, how, standing behind him at the sink waiting to rinse my coffee cup, I was smitten all at once by the curl of dark hair on his neck, the slope of his shoulders. I was surprised by that onslaught of desire, and a bit outraged, as though my body were playing a trick on me, going all breathless and dry-mouthed over this stocky, rumpled man, his only handsome feature his curved, slightly pouting lips, a man who wears sleeveless undershirts, for God's sake, the vulgarest of garments.

The fabric crumples in my restless fingers as I jab at it with sweat-sticky pins. Under the folds of my long woolen cape, I'm trying to decide whether or not to have an affair. Not my first, true, but the others hardly seem to count: a single drunken encounter the night before a friend's wedding, and a febrile romantic interlude up on the Hill. I never gave either of them a thought. This time I want to know what I'm doing. But my head is swamped with images: hot dancing, black curls, straps of undershirt glimpsed through broadcloth, hot dancing. . . . Avram, I say to myself. Avram. Avram. My breath catches each time my heart stumbles over the name. My thighs tighten, loosen. At the end of the day, the cape and I are still in a muddle. I fold the fabric and clear the table for dinner. I'll leave myself open to whatever happens, I conclude. Maybe a relationship will develop. Maybe not. I don't seem to notice that my thighs have decided already.

"Will you come home with me?" Avram asks after we've finished our sandwiches and beer. His accent is so heavy that I often can't be certain what he's said. This time, in spite of the uproar of conversation and crockery in the Wursthaus at lunchtime, I have no trouble. "Now?"

I thought I was going to get some time to think about this. I thought I could try to decide whether or not to have an affair for a good long time. Perhaps indefinitely. Perhaps could even substitute the process of deciding whether or not to have an affair for the affair itself.

"All right," I say, reaching for my coat.

We take a taxi to the shabby apartment he and Naomi have rented for his six-month appointment. In the dusky light filtering through plastic window shades, we yank off our clothes. I want to hide my skinny body, grayish in the light, the bony washboard of my chest, brown hairs sprouting around my nipples. I want to cry. No man but George has ever seen me naked. Avram doesn't seem inclined to inspect me, though. He pulls me down onto the prickly couch and enters me quickly.

Most of our sexual encounters have this lunch-hour haste about them. One Saturday, both working overtime in the deserted building, we even make love on the floor of my office, throwing my coat down on the scuffed brown tile and rolling around, fully clothed, between the legs of my desk and the bookshelves on the opposite wall. For an adulterous couple in the dead of winter, Cambridge doesn't offer many opportunities for dalliance, and this is a particularly hard winter, one in which the temperature doesn't rise above freezing for sixty days in a row. One glittering noon, we drive to the Cambridge Reservoir and trudge around in the snow among unleashed rollicking dogs, stamping our feet and slapping our arms as we talk. There's no question of slipping off for a little roll in the bushes, though. We'd lose to frostbite the parts of which we're the fondest.

During our brief affair, just a couple of months before he goes on to New York, and then returns to his own country, we seldom find chances, even indoors, to make love with our bodies. We bundle them into coats and boots, wind them in scarves, and head across the Yard to the Fogg Museum, where they steam in damp clothing in front of the minute, tranquil faces of saints adoring their gold-leafed girded Christ. Or we stay in and retreat to a sunny conference room, seldom used, to eat bread and cheese and fruit while we argue amicably about my leftist tendencies and he tries to teach me a new alphabet. We learn to caress with glances, voices, the accidental touches occasioned by dropped napkins and spilled coffee. Our closeness is observed, of course, but not commented upon, at least never to us. In our absence the office gossips are probably having a field day. We don't care, as long as no one tells George and Naomi, whom we've agreed from the outset to protect.

One day we play hooky. I toss an empty suitcase into the back of my car, and we drive out into the suburbs to rent a motel room. There, from nine to five, we make love, stopping only to drive to a nearby restaurant for lunch: a queer inversion of our ordinary working day. No one knows where we are. Cut off in this way from George and from Naomi, from our colleagues, we drift in and out of one another's bodies, of one another's incomprehensible pasts and futures, of clothes and sleep. My thoughts stumble and blur and finally fall almost silent as the center of my being shifts downward. I grow stupid with sex.

Later in my life, I will feel some regrets about this affair, and about the ones that follow it. But I will never regret what my body comes to know of sensitivity and satiation in those hours absorbed wholly by sex. Really, Avram and I have nothing else for one another. Our time together is too limited, and our backgrounds are too incongruous, for us to do more than make a little love and conversation.

"If I hadn't been married," he says at one point, squinting down at me, "I might have tried to take you from your husband and children."

"If you hadn't been married," I reply, "I might have gone. No. I would have gone." But my words sound high-flown, romantical, false. We don't belong to one another outside of fairy tales. And we live, except for these brief hours, outside of fairy tales. I might leave my husband and children, but I wouldn't do so for him or for any other man. That's not what this affair is about.

What this affair is about, I will recognize only after I'm older than I now think it's possible for me to get, is writing. "This," my editor will chide me, "doesn't ring true." Lisa, my dear, that's life as opposed to art: so much of it, almost all of it, doesn't ring true.

Steeling myself against the pain of Avram's departure, I scribble on a sheet of white lined paper,

> When you return to your country of constant sun,
> may you lie one day motionless, the heated sand
> pressing your naked flesh, and thoughtless,
> drifting near sleep, drugged
> by the syrupy scent of ripened fruit. May your body,
> heavy and beautiful with rest, be washed in warmth
> and thick yellow light.
> And then, behind your eyes,
> may you go icy and grey with the bitter snow
> of a Cambridge winter. And may my face, white
> and worn to transparency by memory, hang
> against the pillars of Langdell Hall like the pattern
> of frost against a darkening windowpane.
> May the snow then sting your sun-gilded eyelids,
> though only for a moment, with cold tears.

I know right away that it's a terrible poem, but I don't mind too much. It is the first poem I've finished since I got married. Imagine that you've had aphasia for almost eight years. You've thought about speaking. You remember that speaking is possible. But no amount of straining produces a word. If, after eight years, you suddenly burst out, "Peanut butter!" would you mope because you hadn't uttered something beautiful instead, "calla lily," say, or "celestial mechanics"? You'd be so thrilled at the sound of your own voice that you'd forgive yourself a good deal worse than "peanut butter."

I started writing poetry at about the same time I started my period, just as I was discovering passion but long before passion was permissible. I wrote poetry to encode that excruciating ardor while it was prohibited, and its interdiction became an element in the code. That which I want, that which arouses me to the kind of needy pain I always call "being in love," though it's actually sexual desire, retains its power only as long as it remains forbidden. The erotic connection between the word and proscribed desire has never weakened.

By the time I meet Avram, I've long since stopped being in love with George, though I go on loving him in a stuttering sort of way even at the worst of times. Marriage, by lifting the taboo on our desire, ended my poetic impulses toward him, however. I can't want him because I've got him. His utility has ended, just as Caleb's did before him, just as Avram's would if he somehow managed to take me from my husband and children and regularize our relationship. I write only out of lack.

I will have several more affairs in the years to come, the last of which will almost kill me, but functionally, despite the variety of their delights, they are identical. I don't want lovers, I want poems, and poems I will get, though at terrific cost. And then one day, I'll give them up, the lovers, and perhaps, for a while at least, the poems. I'll stop reenacting tales of doomed love. I'll get too old to be turned on by interdictions. I'll plunge straight into the impermissible with no intermediary. All words will become erotic. I'll want everything. I'll take up writing essays.

vi

Aunt Jane sometimes teaches poetry workshops in her home during the winter.

"Why don't you come?" she asks me in the fall of 1971.

"Why not?" I say. Before this I'd have smiled and shrugged and turned her down, but my poem for Avram has stirred the memory that I once thought I'd be a writer when I grew up. I got so ensnared in the struggle to grow up that I pretty much forgot the writing part, and when I thought of it again, the drive and self-assurance I'd felt briefly in college had vanished. But my life seems almost stable now. George and I both have jobs we like. The children seem sturdy and content. My six months as a mental patient are nearly four years behind me, and recently I've given up psychotherapy. Perhaps I can risk a new exploration of old dreams. "Why not?"

After work on Tuesdays I walk to Harvard Square, take the T over to Charles Street, and climb the Hill. Sometimes I feel so exhausted that I can scarcely make it, even holding on to the iron railings driven into house walls at the steepest spots, and occasionally my left ankle turns under me without warning. These are definitely symptoms of multiple sclerosis, as I will know in another year or so, but for now I ignore them as, reaching Number 48, I burst from the icy dark into the lighted hall, filled with the fragrance of dinner wafting from the basement kitchen. Down the steep stairs I go, to set the table in the low-ceilinged room with brick and blue-painted walls where Jane is cooking and Mr. Black and Jenny are sleeping in rocking chairs on the hearth. Lars and Jon are teenagers now, with oddly elongated forms and funny cracks in their voices. We all pull up to the round table and eat together, and I feel slipped, as neatly as a brick, into some waiting gap just my size.

After cleaning up, Jane and I go up to the library to wait for the other students. I always take the same chair, a deep one in the far left corner near the fire. On the shelf behind it sit two alabaster eggs, which I always take down and hold against my pulsing palms all evening. We form a motley group, ranging in age from beautiful James, who's perhaps eighteen, to a Russian émigré named Isador, well into his eighties. In this room, warmed slowly by the fire and as many as a dozen bodies, the paneling and gold-stamped bookbindings glowing behind scattered lamps, Kip's jungle looped over the black reflective panes of the French doors, we talk about each poem attentively, courteously, and I feel myself shudder a little, like a frost heave, erupting in slow, slow motion into the woman who will one day learn to say, in the same ordinary tone in which she says, "I live on Mabel Street" or "My hair is turning gray": "I'm a poet."

Juices flowing once again, I take it into my head to go to graduate school for a degree in creative writing. The imagery in my poems reveals how much I detest winter, and for the first time I hear my own work as an authentic mode of communication, not the moony glossolalia I've always considered it before. So I choose a graduate program not on its merits but on the average annual temperatures and hours of sunshine at its location. The University of Arizona offers a Master of Fine Arts degree in creative writing and thirty-six hundred hours of sunshine a year.

Neither George nor I have ever been to Tucson. For a friend's wedding, I spent a couple of weeks in southern New Mexico right after college, where I was thrilled by the scoured, bony landscape and the inexorable light, but George has never even seen the desert. If we move to Arizona, we'll have to do it blind. That's how we open our sentences more and more frequently: "If we move to Arizona. . . ." Then George, always semantically more pragmatic than I, points out that unless we want to find ourselves one day lamenting, "If we had moved to Arizona," we had better say, "When we move to Arizona. . . ."

Except for Mother, no one thinks this is a very good idea. By the time she was our age, of course, Mother had lived a year and a half in the South Pacific, and as far as she's concerned, Tucson is practically next door. "Good!" she says. "I'll have to come visit you!" George's parents, however, have ranged no farther from Boston than Washington, D.C., and as far as they're concerned, their only child is not offering them an opportunity for adventure but abandoning them to leap off the edge of the world. "Why are you doing this?" Their voices are plaintive. "You have no *reason.*" The fact that I've been accepted to graduate school does not persuade them. It's just further evidence, like my returning to work after Matthew was born, of my waywardness and George's inability to control me. If George had decided to move, they'd have expected me to follow, but the reverse doesn't hold.

"I'll give you your exact words which we heard you say to George," Mum will tell me years later: " '*I'm* going whether you come or not.' What exactly were *we* to think of that statement?" One possibility might be: Nancy wants so urgently to escape this climate and begin graduate school that she's willing to take full responsibility for moving without forcing George to go along if he doesn't want to. But nothing in their experience has prepared them for the thought that a woman might determine her own outcome. I'm not really prepared for it, either. I probably couldn't make good on my promise if George balked.

They begin to wage a campaign of nerves, calling us at quarter of seven in the morning, though they know we don't get up till seven, to ask whether we've thought about everything from snakes and scorpions to cultural deprivation. Actually, we haven't thought anywhere near as much about snakes as we later will, because we've never really known any, except a mother boa constrictor and her brood we handled once at the Franklin Park Zoo. Scorpions are even more unthinkable; we've never met one. And as for cultural deprivation, we can't afford a baby-sitter, parking fees, and a pair of movie tickets here. We might as well not be able to afford them in Tucson.

Both parental attitudes serve us well, it turns out, the one by assuming an independence and a capacity for adventure we don't yet really have, and the other by resisting these qualities, so that we're forced to claim them for ourselves.

We jettison everything. Too much, we'll think later, but we have no way of knowing what we'll want or need.

We quit our jobs. I've been given a teaching assistantship for the fall, paying two thousand dollars for the year, but George has nothing so far. He'll have to look when we get there. In preparation for job hunting, he shaves off his beard.

"What did you do?" Matthew asks, scrutinizing him uneasily over his Alpha-Bits the next morning.

"I shaved off my beard." George strokes his naked chin.

"Well—" even at three, Matthew's voice is surprisingly deep and firm, nothing like Anne's reedy treble— *"shave it back on again."* Neither child objects to any of the other upheavals in their hitherto routine lives.

We sell our gloomy gray house. We ship some necessities, pack our few treasures into Mother's attic for the two years we believe we'll be gone, and sell off the rest. Through an oversight in feline birth control, we currently have three cats and eight kittens. We find homes for them all. Two people even take two apiece. We sell our battered Volvo with the antiwar bumper stickers that made our neighbors seethe with ill-suppressed hostility— both the Volvo and the bumper stickers, not to mention the beard and my long, straight hair—and replace it with a red Ford van we call Ludwig, into which we load the gear for a cross-country camping trip.

On the morning of my twenty-ninth birthday, we all clamber into Ludwig and, once again smiling and waving out windows, head off toward a sun that will set on some place we've never been.

The Desert

〜〜〜〜〜〜〜

T HE FIRST WEEK in October, two months after we settle in Tucson, the weather suddenly offers something we haven't seen here yet: days of steady rain. We've had rain before, in the late afternoon and evening after a day of sunshine scorching the desert floor: brief torrential bursts that turn the streets, unequipped with storm sewers, into rivers, illuminated by jagged streamers of lightning, thunder tumbling tumultuously down the flanks of the Catalinas at whose feet we live. Local residents call this pattern, appearing in July and August, the monsoon, with wry affection born in brains baked to pale ashes by a sun that burns every day for weeks, sometimes months. Today is different, however. The air has turned gray, obscuring the mountains and turning the desert's muted colors dun. I think the effect ugly, unlike the soft, silvery damp of New England, though later I'll come to see that it has a beauty of its own.

I sit on the edge of my bed in the Tucson Medical Center, watching the rain drizzle into a little courtyard outside the window. I am wearing a plaid nightgown trimmed with white lace and over it an Empire-style robe, dark green with white embroidery on the yoke, both bought for this occasion. We have very little money, and I feel guilty about spending so much on clothes I won't live to wear out. But dressing well has always been my way of preparing myself to encounter the world: putting on a thick skin to cover the thin one that holds my frame together. Despite the family injunction

229

against vanity, "handsome is" matters to me at least as much as "handsome does." I need a costume to act out good behavior, and at the moment I need to behave better than I ever have before.

Something is in the right side of my brain "which doesn't belong there," the neurologist says. Probably a tumor. When he first told me that in his office last week, he looked straight into my eyes. His dark gaze, though pained, didn't waver. I'm glad that if I have to entrust myself to a stranger, he's someone who can look at me without flinching when he tells me I have a brain tumor.

I know a little about brain tumors. A colleague of George's died of one last year. It took about four months. Toward the end, George went to the hospital to visit him, but he was gone already. There was just a skinny body sitting up in the bed, whose haunted eyes didn't even see George, let alone recognize him, speaking in snatches of English and French . . . "a' babbled of green fields."

I'm here to find out whether I'm going to die.

My first response to the possibility of a brain tumor, beyond the stab of terror, was a wail: "But I've never been to Europe!" To die before seeing England, at the least, seemed the worst possible cheat. But almost immediately that complaint seemed dumb. If I had a brain tumor, the fact that I'd never been to Europe was trivial. I'd have much further to go than that. And anyway, at least I'd made it to Tucson. This particular pattern of grief and solace in the face of heartbreaking loss will form the ground of my being ever after: at least, at least.

A brain tumor strikes me as monstrously unfair. We've just moved all the way across country to begin a new life in a setting that moves us strangely. I remember thinking, as we crossed the Texas Panhandle into the Chihuahuan Desert of New Mexico, the colors paling to buff and sage, the vegetation stunted, the mountains erupting raggedly against the enormous sky: "My God, what if George hates it?"

During my earlier trip west, I had the first intimations of a truth about myself that I'll suddenly see clear many springs later, driving between Tucson and Phoenix across a desert smudged gold and lavender by blooming palo verde and acacia. The hedgehogs and cholla and prickly pear have almost all gone by, but the saguaros are in bloom, wearing wreathes of waxy white flowers around their arms and heads, for all the world like green, ungainly brides. Later the flowers will turn into knobby fruit, and then they'll look like those slovenly women who wear rollers in their hair in the supermarket. Their final transformation will be grimmer, the burst fruit scarlet as blood on wounded heads and hands. Between us and the saguaros, white poppies and yellow brittlebush line the pavement. The hot air is tinged acrid with creosote. The truth is that, on most occasions, I prefer vegetation to people, and the vegetation of the Sonoran Desert, a jungle translated over time, above all. "You cannot be neurotic," Thomas Merton once wrote, "in front of a bunch of trees." Or cactus, I would add.

For George, love may come more slowly, but right away the desert pricked his curiosity. At dawn we crossed into southern Arizona, into a stretch of landscape so bleak it could truly have been the mountains of the moon, long shadows slashing the rubbly ground, and stopped at a rest area for breakfast. In the bathroom huge black beetles stalked around on legs tall as stilts, silent and menacing, and I was so scared I could hardly pee. They were only palo verde beetles, I found out later, harmless enough, though they can pinch if you touch them. But who'd touch them? When we drove into Tucson, the temperature was a hundred three in the shade. We drove down Speedway to a Whataburger, where we ordered soft drinks and checked the classifieds for apartments. Then we went to the bank across the street and opened an account. We were home.

We've found an apartment we can almost afford. With air-conditioning. It's in a huge complex that looks like a well-maintained prison, but it's okay for now. We've made a deposit on a sweet house down by the University. George found a job within three weeks of our arrival, teaching emotionally disturbed boys at a residential school. It looks like a badly maintained prison, which is pretty much what it is. I've started graduate school. I'm studying Old English, which I've always wanted to do. This gives the creative writing people fits. They don't want me to read anything written before 1950. I guess they're afraid I'll start writing another *Beowulf.* Life's getting interesting. I don't want to miss out on it.

Because I'm poor and it's uncertain what my student health insurance covers, I'm put in a room with three other women. Beside me lies a seventy-two-year-old Mexican woman who's had two cerebral hemorrhages. All day her children come in and out. They don't speak English, but they smile at me sweetly. Across from her, a sixteen-year-old girl who was in an automobile accident is strapped into a frame. The nurses turn her regularly, like a roast on a spit. For an hour or so she looks at the ceiling. For the next hour she looks at the floor. Across from me, a woman named Belva lies on her bed, picking her nails and muttering ceaseless tales of the murders her husband and son have committed with a shotgun. Sometimes she speaks to me, sometimes to people I can't see. Alcohol, a nurse confides in me. Large areas of her brain have atrophied.

I've known there was something wrong with me for at least a year now, in the way you have of knowing something without letting yourself know you know it. At first I started to drop things from my left hand, and the fingers, after hours of typing or knitting, felt too weak to move. I began to stumble, catching the toes of my left foot on cracks I could hardly see, and my ankle turned unpredictably. No one else seemed to notice, and I have such a long history of neurotic ills that I hardly paid attention. But after we got to Tucson, when a new acquaintance and I were going out for a beer after class one night, he asked suddenly, "Have you hurt your foot?"

"No," I said, startled. "Why?"

"You're limping." So someone else could see it, too. Alarmed, I went the next day to the Student Health Service, where a gentle elderly doctor, after tapping me with a rubber hammer and watching me walk a straight line, immediately picked up the telephone and made an appointment for me with a neurologist.

"Can you even guess what it might be?" I asked as I pulled my socks and shoes back on.

"No," he said. I thought his reticence a little odd, but I didn't know enough to be terrified.

When Dr. Buchsbaum told me a couple of days later about the brain tumor, I tried to explain my psychological history to him. Most likely, I told him, my condition was hysterical.

"Not this time." He softened his bluntness with a smile, but it wasn't a cheerful one. "This time there's something there."

A nurse comes in with a hospital gown for me to put on. Then an orderly arrives with a wheelchair. I'm not allowed to walk anywhere. In the corridor, I ask him to stop briefly by an open door while I breathe the unfamiliar air, damp and chill and rank with greasewood. Then we go down to the basement, to a small room where seven people are waiting to give me a pneumoencephalogram. Dr. Buchsbaum has been putting this test off because it's a little risky. But the CAT scan, which will render this procedure obsolete, won't reach Tucson for another year. And the X ray, brain scan, and electroencephalogram haven't shown what's going on. So now they've got to shoot bubbles into my brain.

I need a lot of information. That's my way of countering the helpless panic that the thought of having a brain tumor triggers. Some people don't want to know anything. "Just take care of it, doc," they say. For years my father-in-law will swallow the blood-pressure medication his doctor prescribes without once asking what his blood pressure *is*. I can't achieve that blissful ignorance. I once trusted an obstetrician and a pediatrician too much, and the damage to my soul has never healed. This time, I want to participate, and if necessary to balk, every step of the way.

The team assembled for the test seems to understand. They explain the procedure in detail.

"It will hurt terribly for about seven seconds," I'm told. "But you mustn't move *at all* or you'll spoil the picture and we'll have to do it again."

"Somebody better hold me then," I say, "or I might jump."

"Oh, yes," says a deep voice. He must have played football. From the vantage point of the cold table I'm strapped to, he looks like Jack's giant. "That's what I'm here for."

Dr. Buchsbaum punctures an artery in my groin. I feel only pressure, no pain, having had a local anesthetic, and I've been told to look away because blood spurts up. I'm watching television. On the small black-and-white screen, the catheter inches forward, spitting little puffs of dye that burn inside me slightly. It snakes up through my neck. And then the top of my head comes off and my brain bursts in brilliant shards all over the room. The pain is unspeakable. When my vision returns, the halfback's hands are clamped under my jaw and over my skull, his ruddy face close to mine. Everyone congratulates me. We should get a good picture.

They said it would seem like the longest seven seconds of my life, and they were right. I'd rather have both my children again, prolonged labors and complicated deliveries and all, than go through that another time. Only the brain has two hemispheres, so I have to go through it another time. At the thought, I panic and start to faint.

"Put some more Valium in the IV," Dr. Buchsbaum instructs. Almost immediately, the panic symptoms abate, and I lie still, tears washing into my ears, for the second picture.

After all, nothing is there. Nothing detectable, anyway. I go home under a shroud, not literally, thank God, but figuratively. I could have a tumor too small to see yet, Dr. Buchsbaum speculates, or a "demyelinating syndrome," whatever the hell that is. He doesn't elaborate. A few months later, during a regular checkup, I ask him, "Do I have multiple sclerosis?" I'm not sure how I know to ask about MS. I may have read about it in *Parade* magazine. I'm not the kind to pore over articles in medical journals.

"Probably," he says. "But you have to have another episode for us to be sure." There's no real test for MS at this point. It's only a clinical diagnosis. But neurological events disseminated in space (at different sites in the central nervous system) and time (over a period of months or years) characterize the demyelinating syndrome labeled multiple sclerosis. I like that construction: disseminated in space and time. It sounds like the way I live.

More than a year later, when I develop a scotoma (blurred spot) in my right eye as the result of a lesion in the optic nerve, he telephones. "Well, you've got your diagnosis," he says with his habitual bluntness. "Now go back to doing whatever you were doing before I called." His point is clear and, in an odd way, reassuring. There's nothing he can do for me. Most people with MS lead productive lives, however; and of those who don't, many are hampered more by attitude than by disease. Until I have to give up my activities, perhaps many years hence, I'd best get on with them.

Why didn't he just say it was probably MS in the first place? I wonder. I'm glad to have a name for it. There are strong cultural connections, not entirely without force, between naming and power. Perhaps he was merely being prudent, not wanting to risk misdiagnosis. But as I get to know this man, I sense that his diagnoses are seldom off the mark. He knew, I think, but he simply didn't want to say. I'll encounter this reluctance in other neurologists, as well as in the medical students I teach to give neurological examinations. They want to protect their patients, they think, from the shock of knowing what a terrible disease they have. But most patients deal with the knowledge pretty well; many, like me, are relieved to have *something,* something real, not a nameless mystery. In reality, doctors project their own fears onto their patients. For a neurologist, MS must be the worst possible fate, worse even than a brain tumor, since some tumors can be sliced out or blasted away with radiation or chemicals. The chance for heroic rescue is there, at least. With MS, they stare powerlessly, sometimes for decades, at inexorable degeneration. No wonder they sometimes practice denial.

Now I am who I will be. A body in trouble. I've spent all these years trying alternately to repudiate and to control my way-

ward body, to transcend it one way or another, but MS rams me
right back down into it. "The body," I've gotten into the habit
of calling it. "The left leg is weak," I say. "There's a blurred spot
in the right eye." As though it were some other entity, remote and
traitorous. Or worse, as though it were inanimate, a prison of bone,
the dark tower around which Childe Roland rode, withershins left,
withershins right, seeking to free the fair kidnapped princess: me.
My favorite fairy tale as a child turns out to have nothing to offer
my adulthood. Rescue from the body is merely another word for
death.

Slowly, slowly, MS will teach me to live on as a body.

ii

We live in a Chinese grocery. It isn't a Chinese grocery
anymore, but it was until World War II, our elderly neighbor, Mrs.
Prentiss, informs us. That's what the Chinese did in Tucson: they
ran not laundries but groceries. Mrs. Prentiss has lived in her tiny
bungalow across the street since 1929, before our house was built,
when the area just to the north was the University of Arizona
experimental chicken farm. Now it's the Arizona Health Sciences
Center, and helicopters buzz in day and night, delivering chilled
hearts for transplant and emergency cases for the neonatal unit.
The Safeway down on Speedway put the Chinese grocery out of
business over thirty years ago, before it got put out of business by
the bigger Safeway a dozen blocks or so to the north. Then the
Armenians bought it, Mrs. Prentiss says, and converted it into a
house.

The future yawning uncertainly before us, we retrieved our
deposit on the sweet house we'd found before my brain tumor tests
and let it go. I will remember it in detail forever, though: the pretty
red tiles on the carport roof, the French doors in the front bedroom, the queer furnace sunk into the floor, the long dark kitchen.
It was actually too small for us, and I try to envision our lives as
they would have been shaped by this cramped but charming space.
I can do the same, I realize, for many of the other places we almost
lived in, apartments unrented, houses unbought, on one side of the
country and the other, eidola of the lives we never moved into. In
an infinitely branching universe, of course, we did move into them,
and we are thus sealed off from any knowledge of life there. But
perhaps these memories serve as comforting intimations of possible

lives not exactly lost but shunted down the arteries of complicated time. I like to think about those other Nancys.

By spring, I hadn't died, and the abyss of uncertainty, though no less menacing, had begun to strike us as a feature common to all human experience, more visible in cases of chronic illness, perhaps, but not necessarily broader or more dangerous. The fact is that our apartment is too small, and since I may limp along for years, I might as well do so through a space adequate for the coexistence of two noisy and energetic children and their silence-greedy graduate-student mother. The space in the Chinese grocery, though peculiarly shaped, is ample.

Moreover, it feels right. We're not sure what we mean when we say that, but both George and I have the same sensation that Sunday afternoon in April when we stop at the "open house" sign and climb the steps into the dining room, with its coved ceiling and cantaloupe-colored walls. It seems to go on and on: a long, narrow house with a kitchen, a dining room, a living room, four bedrooms, two bathrooms, a hall big enough for a desk and book-case, five doors to the outside. The huge windows offer views of the Tucson and Catalina mountains. We don't think about the icy air they'll leak in the winter. We don't fret about the uninsulated wooden floors and the high uninsulated ceilings, either, or the elderly plumbing that will erupt periodically in geysers, or the cramped yard, so narrow you can spit across it, with its aged fruit trees and rickety wooden fence. These features will plague us in the years to come, but for now we are enthralled. We sneak a sidelong peek at the asking price on the listing sheet. $23,500. A good three thousand over our limit. We look at each other, but not for long, and then shrug. "We'll take it," we tell the agent.

It turns out, in spite of its many inconveniences, to be the right house, as we've sensed. In the way that the Robbins Street house in Waltham never felt right to me, this house, even in its most maddening decadence, never feels wrong. Do houses have spirits? Perhaps. Not haunts, I mean, though some might have those as well, but souls built up out of all the experiences sheltered by their walls. Maybe that's why I've never succumbed to that urgent American fantasy of "building my own dream house." I don't want to move into a gleaming spiritless space. I want to slip my life into a flow of life already begun. I'm not a founder, I'm a joiner. The soul to which I join my soul in the Chinese grocery is a good one.

We stay in it for thirteen years, leaving only when the

University of Arizona begins buying up the houses on our block in a protraction of the ruthless expansionism that "won" the West a century before. Even then, we move only half a block down the street. We can see the old house from the new. I am afraid the university will use the structure for something morally dubious, like an ROTC program, until they tear it down and turn the block into yet another parking lot, but in fact they house a music school there. Behind one of the great windows stands a grand piano. Tiny children with violin cases pop in and out of our old dining room. On summer evenings, we can sometimes catch the strains of chamber music wafting down the street, an umbilicus between past place and present.

Because we have ample room, we start taking in creatures, some human, some otherwise. This is a pattern already laid down in Massachusetts, where we put a Brown student up one summer while he volunteered, as we did, in the campaign of the Jesuit priest Robert Drinan, an antiwar Congressional candidate; and later hired as a mother's helper a German student eager to improve her English. Now the friend of a friend, a young woman recovering physically and financially from a car accident, comes to board for a year, leaving to make room for our new foster son, a fifteen-year-old who remains with us until he goes into the navy at eighteen.

This habit of sheltering sojourners suits me badly, though I won't recognize that fact for many years after Craig and Margret and Liz and Ron have gone. The trouble lies not in the people themselves, who possess the ordinary human mix of charms and deficiencies, but in my own intolerance for any sort of disturbance in my surroundings, which my senses elevate automatically to hubbub. I like the idea of sharing houseroom with those who need it. I especially like the message it conveys to my children, that a family is not an accident of blood but a deliberate and infinitely extensible construct. Anyone may—and ultimately does—belong. But at the pragmatic level, I'm simply not very good at living with other people, not even Anne or Matthew or George, let alone strangers. The slightest demands they make on my attention feel like a noisy assault on the doors and windows I've bolted and shuttered to keep my interior space bearably dim, uncluttered, still. Empty. I need to spend long hours of every day alone in my house in order to function even briefly in company. A household of five people seldom provides such emptiness.

All the same, I never feel easy having more space than I

need. It seems wasteful and greedy, especially as we become involved with Casa María, the Catholic Worker community in Tucson which feeds as many as five hundred homeless people a day. For me, homelessness seems an unbearable deprivation, although some of the people we know have chosen it. Those who have not, however, should be sheltered. We go on taking in whomever we have room for. I never get over my discomfort, but I do get over believing that comfort is a state worth desiring.

Here is the ideal antidote to the clamor of human company: a snake. All the dreadful behaviors in which human companions indulge—cranking the stereo up to eleven, leaving dirty coffee cups on the glass-topped table, wearing your black turtleneck on the day you were planning to wear your black turtleneck—are wholly foreign to a snake. Indeed, any sort of indulgence is foreign to a snake. Snakes are immune to any human connection. Cold-blooded.

We get our first snake by chance. Some of the boys at the school where George is teaching catch him in a wash and decide to see how long he will live without a head. This is a school for emotionally disturbed boys, but I suspect that that's beside the point. Anyway, George pays them a quarter to give him the snake instead and brings him home in a shoebox. Ferdinand the Bull Snake, we call him. A handsome creature, still less than two feet long and slender, with a long sleek head and supple creamy skin dappled with cocoa spots.

I haven't the faintest idea how to care for a snake, so I call a herpetologist at the Arizona-Sonora Desert Museum. I'm worried that if we keep him for a while, he'll get domesticated. The herpetologist almost laughs. Snakes, he explains, are all instinct and no intelligence. Even born in captivity and released years later, they'll function perfectly in the wild. Reassured, we buy Ferd a terrarium and he settles in. Because our hands are warm, he likes to be held, coiling in comfortable constrictor fashion around a wrist or nestling in a shirt pocket. He never grows attached to us, though, never offers the merest hint of communication. He doesn't mind being handled, but neither does he want it. Maybe that's what I like so much about him. He has no use for me at all. He gives me a feeling akin to the one I've known sometimes with men I love. For a moment I am extinct.

Snakes, we learn too slowly, are escape artists. Once, reaching into Matthew's top dresser drawer for a pair of socks, I come up with Ferd instead. Another time, he reappears during the visit of friends from out of town, who take this manifestation with remarkable composure. They were planning to spend the night in their camper anyway. Finally, just before we move out of our apartment, Ferd disappears for good, out the door, I hope, and not into the ventilation ducts, whence he might emerge into the unsuspecting bosom of the next family to move in. In the course of that move, we also lose our only other pet, a tarantula named Penelope, this one in the new house. We're creating haunts of our own, I guess.

Ferd is followed by three more bull snakes—gopher snakes they're called in the desert—Squeeze and Beowulf and Taurus. Also Hrothgar, a large Yuma king snake, black with yellow stripes; Winslow J. Tweed, a checkered garter snake; Crictor, a baby boa constrictor; a black racer named Jesse Owens, the only one who ever scares me, racers having an irritable and aggressive nature; and Little Greg, a California long-nosed snake named for Anne's boyfriend, who finds him wriggling around in the department store where he works. All of these we eventually release in the desert after we've observed their habits, except Winslow, who dies of starvation after a prolonged disappearance, and Crictor, who succumbs to complications of a respiratory infection. These we bury in the backyard.

This strip of land surrounding our house becomes, over the years, our private cemetery. One day archaeologists may believe they've stumbled upon a ritual burial site, and each burial was accompanied by a ritual, I guess: digging the hole, wrapping the little body in a pillowcase; covering it with earth; placing an inscribed stone over the spot. The better part of my bridal linens have gone to earth. Gradually the stones fade and sink and slide around, but they're still there somewhere. Under them lie Winslow J. Tweed and Crictor, of course, and the ancestral mice Spice and Vanilla, their scions having gone for snake food. The guinea pigs, Flower and Bubbles. Hot Cross Bun. The impetuous puppies: Terry and Clifford, who hurled themselves into the paths of cars, and Amelia Earhart, who drank antifreeze. The cats who died of feline leukemia virus before a vaccine was developed: Mimi the pastel tortoiseshell, who once gave me ringworm in places I couldn't scratch in public; Freya, black with a little white bikini; Balthasar, the seal-point Siamese who ate peaches and purred so ecstatically that he sometimes choked himself. Beloved tabby Burton Rustle, crushed by a car, is there too, and Gwydion, the cat with striped mask and striped stockings.

Others have fetched up elsewhere. Shaggy, lumbering Amaroq, whose father was a Labrador retriever and whose mother had sheepdog in her, once hurls himself at a car also, but the car stops and *he* hits *it,* careering away unharmed, though the driver is considerably shaken. He lives twelve years before all systems fail and he has to be put down. Lionel Tigress, another spotted tabby, is a borderline basket case from kittenhood; moving half a block sends her straight round the bend, pissing everywhere and howling like a banshee at four every morning until we take her to the Humane Society, the only creature we ever give up on. Bête Noir is hit by a car, her body carried off by the Humane Society before we know it. Rangy Eclipse, with the battered nose and broken rib, lets himself in through the car door one night and as good as shouts, "Ta-da! Here I am! Take me! I'm yours!" We take him, and he's ours for maybe a year and a half before he disappears as inexplicably as he arrived. I hope he goes off to make some other woman as happy as he's made me.

iii

My body
is going away.

It fades
to the transparency
of rubbed amber
held against the
    sun.

It shrinks.
It grows quiet.

Small, quiet,
it is a cold
and heavy
smoothed stone.

Who will have it
When it lies
pale and polished
as a clean bone?

The sentence of multiple sclerosis is not death but diminishment. I will lose and lose and lose: energy, strength and musculature, coordination, control of my bladder and bowels, eyesight, sensation. No one knows how much I will lose, or how fast. But mine is the chronic progressive form of this degenerative disease, and it moves in only one direction. Even the little I have will ultimately be taken away.

I submerge the grief I feel at my uncontrollable fate beneath a greed for bodily experience that leaves me feeling, for a couple of years, like an electrical storm spitting sparks of sexuality almost randomly in all directions. This condition generates a lot of poems, and they're getting better and better. To keep them coming, I sleep with professors, fellow graduate students, but never, at least, my own students. Although I love my students immoderately, more and more over the years as they approach the ages of my own children, they never turn me on. Except one, not at all my type, a golden triathelete who, at twenty-three, is smart, lazy, a terrific writer. He comes to class in tank tops and skimpy running shorts, invariably late, and at the sight of him my thinking stumbles and I have to go back to the beginning of whatever sentence I'm in the middle of. By this time, I'm nearly twenty years his senior, and this stutter of sexuality amuses me.

Saul invites me to lunch. We go to a Mexican place—a real one, all Formica and plastic flowers and Christmas lights looped from the ceiling, not one of those tiled jobs hung with sombreros and tinware for the tourists. I've seen Saul quite a bit in my poetry classes, but we've never really talked. I feel a little embarrassed, alone with him for the first time, and very excited, knowing that I'd go to bed with him in a minute if the chance arose.

The likelihood seems remote, however, and so I'm stunned when he asks me if I'll come with him to a motel right this minute. But of course I say yes. He's intrigued by the idea of making love to a cripple, and I think, Well, what the hell, I am one, so why not let him find out what it's like? It's easy to feel a kind of cynical generosity when what you have to offer has scant value on the open market. We climb into his old VW and drive through the winter rain, heavy and chill, up to Miracle Mile. In the shadows of a room at the Marilyn Motel, rain dripping outside and a faucet dripping in syncopation in the bathroom, we lose an afternoon.

I'm a cocky bitch, sure I can handle this sort of encounter

without entanglement. But Saul, it turns out, is the sort of man I could follow—bare-mouthed, bare-footed, bare-assed—anywhere and for as long as he wanted. It's not love. It has nothing to do with courtship or romantic ideals. It's bleaker and more basic: need and devotion. Need, perhaps, *for* devotion, outside all filial or conjugal or maternal bonds, to an object I can fathom only in my body's shadows. The feeling appalls me, the way it leaves me somehow un-intact, broken up, broken into. It reminds me of my relationship with Caleb, though Caleb I also knew and loved, at least. Since him, I've succeeded in avoiding such men, dark men, the kind who muddy me. This time, I let a man I didn't know touch me carelessly, and I suffer long after he's wandered off toward some new conquest.

I decide I must always first become friends with my lovers.

Rob and I are fine friends, humorous and sympathetic, and lusty lovers, too. He's an awfully pretty man, though: certain of his charms, reveling in the riches he reaps by using them, one eager woman after another. At first I figure, Well, what the hell? It's his right if he enjoys it, and I don't mind being part of a collection. After all, I don't belong to any man, but I am married and not looking for a permanent relationship, only as much sexual pleasure as I can get while I can still find men to want me, before my body goes all the way away. Why not enjoy the sunshine that he radiates? And he does radiate it. There's no malice in him, no darkness. But if I complained that Saul muddied me, then Rob bleaches me. I am washed right to the bone by that radiance, faceless, a skeleton. All skeletons look alike to me. I don't want to be buried in Rob's boneyard.

No, no, no. Not in love again, or whatever the hell this disease is called. I feel like an idiot. And it makes me so tired. I haven't the energy. Especially for something that's likely to tear me up for a few days and then come to nothing. But I am so charged that someone like Luke scarcely has to look at me, let alone dance with me at a graduate student party and kiss my neck with careless drunkenness. His dusky, tall, sculptured beauty—brown eyes, wide mouth, body smooth as stone—muddles my aesthetic and erotic responses. His favorite word is *percipience*. I have an image of myself, drowned, turning over and over in the sea.

Beer and sandwiches at Gentle Ben's, dark even in the middle of the day and calculatedly crummy: college dive. Luke and his friend Jack have just high-passed their doctoral qualifying exams, and we're celebrating. Except that Luke and I are fighting. Jack sits sideways on the bench opposite us and watches, very quiet. I think he knows what's going on. I don't. I ask him at one point, but his response doesn't mean anything. Everything is dark except Luke's face.

He is saying that he won't do anything with me because he won't practice duplicity against my husband. I respect him for that, for keeping George in focus when my own vision has grown so hazy, but I hate him. I hate the fact that because of a drunken kiss I have been obsessed by him for four days, not eating or sleeping or working efficiently, and I need to do those things. He says I could have spent four days doing something worse. I hate him for that, too.

He says, "You talk like it's a game and it's over."

"I think you think it's a game," I reply. He says he doesn't, but I don't believe him. I finally say what's been having to be said all along and I don't want to: "I want you."

"It's mutual."

"Okay," I say and go home to take care of my children.

One night, after I've given a poetry reading and we've both had a good many beers, I manage to seduce him, and so I bear forever the image of his body, even duskier in candlelight, curiously flattened, his erect cock curved upward a little. This image tumbles into my hoard along with all the others and works its way down toward the bottom. After a while, I seldom take it out, but occasionally I catch a glimpse of it when I'm pawing through looking for something else: a tiny, exquisite scrimshaw on a yellowed ivory of passion. This is all I am, in the last analysis, this collector and sorter of images piled higgledy-piggledy into the basket of my brain.

Some weary months later, George and I see Luke and his ex-wife on the patio of the Cushing Street Bar. "I'm half in love with him," I confide in George, realizing, in my ability to speak of it, the passion's ebb. George looks at him quietly for a long moment.

"I can see why," he says.

Other than this offhand remark, I say nothing to George about my infidelities. They consume quantities of psychic energy but relatively little time. I spend most of my life at home with him and the children, and if I feel trapped and stifled there, the fault is mine. These affairs strike me as my private responsibility. George hasn't provoked them, nor could he prevent them. Knowing about them would only cause him pain without remedy.

And yet, in the manner of a naughty child, I assume that I'm transparent to him. Like an omniscient parent, he must know everything about me without being told. So strong is this impression that, when I come to write about these affairs years later and he expresses shock, *I'm* shocked. The two of us stand staring at each other, mutually dumbfounded.

"I always thought you knew," I say. "God, I'm sorry."

"I feel like a fool," he says.

"The thing about you two," says Ken, the psychotherapist we've worked with off and on for years, "is that you've gotten so fused by now that you have trouble sometimes figuring out who's which and who knows what." In the glow this fusion bathes our lives in now, the affairs shrink, shadowy and desiccated as neglected house plants. We can't deny they happened. So we stick them out of the way, like the scraggly Christmas poinsettia you shove into one corner of the back porch after the red leaves have all wilted and dropped off.

In the midst of yet another tumultuous graduate student party, Ramona catches my hand across the kitchen table, and I twine my fingers among hers. If the people sitting around us see anything odd in this behavior, they don't show it. Maybe they don't even notice. Women can get away with a lot. I notice. The watcher that squats eternally in one corner of my mind, groggy at this late hour with beer and cigarettes and old Rolling Stones songs, springs awake at Ramona's touch and looks all around, startled, curious. When I stroke Ramona's fingers, my heart thuds.

"Come over to my house after classes on Monday," Ramona whispers as George and I prepare to go home.

"Okay, I will," I say, and I do. I drive her to the trailer she and her husband share, its shabbiness transformed by the handsome artifacts they brought from Tanzania when they came back from the Peace Corps. We put Waylon Jennings on the stereo, that dark voice that makes me feel as though a hand has just slid down the damp inside of my thigh.

Ramona wants me to make love to her. I've never made love to a woman before, I've never even wanted to, but I am suddenly willing to try. My time is running out. Whatever I'm going to try

I'd better try now. And she is so beautiful: much taller than I, with a long pointed face framed by wisps of hair. I unbutton the top of her shirt. Her breasts are perfectly round. I put my mouth on one of her nipples, and she moans.

"In here," she says, and we go into the bedroom. In the greenish light, we stretch out and I stroke her belly, downward to the springy dark bush. My fingers slip into the hot slit between her legs. I'm amazed. I never get wet like that, bubbling. She twists urgently against my fingers. It's no good, though. I don't know what I'm doing, and I can't make her come. And she doesn't seem to want to touch me at all.

Her husband will be home for dinner. We get up and go into the kitchen. She whacks garlic cloves under the flat of a long knife and peels them, pounds cutlets of veal until they're papery, chops vegetables, splashes wine. Each flick of her wrist—the tiny bones, the pale skin over blue veins underneath—makes me more feverish. Her husband comes in, and we sit around a little table, eating and drinking wine and conversing. We're all in a Beowulf class together, Rob, my other lover, too, and we're all teaching freshman composition, so we have plenty to talk about. I don't know what I am saying. I stroke Ramona's legs with my bare feet under the table. Donald sees nothing. The only light comes from votive candles in tall red holders. It makes me feel as though I'm inside a vagina. My own, its pellucid walls plumped and pulsating. I will never again achieve this absolute immanence. Afterward, I write her my most perfect poem.

"Let's go away together," I say to Ramona another time. "Let's move to San Francisco." This is the closest I ever come to leaving George for another person. But Ramona isn't ready to leave her husband. She's a lesbian, and struggling to come out. What I don't comprehend yet is that I'm not a lesbian, and so this kind of talk is easy, fantastical. What if she'd said yes? I'll wonder afterward. What if we'd flung our clothes into suitcases and hopped a Greyhound for the Coast? I try to imagine our free new lesbian life, but what comes to mind is inevitable bitterness: recriminatory shouts and hot tears and doors slammed shut, me stomping down the stairs and out into the street with my arm around some man.

In a little while, Ramona starts her lesbian life without me, drifting off to New York and Maine and finally Hawaii, dropping me a postcard with a new address now and then. Better that way.

Still, I love her always. My only woman. You just never stop loving someone you've loved like that, and you don't want to, either.

I fizzle. I'm not sure why. I travel with my brother, who is eighteen now, across country in his VW microbus. We're nearly killed a couple of times, but mostly we enjoy ourselves. I spend a month or so in New England, and when I return, I don't want to make love to Rob or Ramona or anybody else anymore. Since I don't explain this to either of them, they're hurt by what they perceive as my sudden coldness, but the truth is that I don't know what to say to them. I don't know what's happened. I've simply shut down.

Later, I sustain a protracted but listless desire for one of my classmates, a great bumbling ruddy man, not the sort that usually turns me on. I tend to go for the large dark ones. I try to think of how to set up a situation in which I can kiss him. I try to think of it for at least a year. Vegetable love. Except for a couple of clumsy embraces, nothing happens between us. If I touch him, he jumps as though my fingertips were flares. "Don't worry," I tell him, "I'm not going to *do* anything," but I don't think he believes me. I think about going to bed with him. His awkwardness and embarrassment and guilt would be too much for me, I decide. He's like a giant adolescent, and seducing him would seem decadent, wicked, like trying to turn on a younger brother. Even so, I spend another year giving up the idea.

The poetry fizzles, too. In its place I write syllabuses. Finishing an M.F.A., I teach in a Catholic high school with George for a couple of years. Then I return to the university to teach freshman composition and work on a Ph.D. I devote huge amounts of passionate energy to my work and dribble what's left out among George and Anne and Matthew. Sitting at the dining-room table after dinner one night, drinking coffee and smoking a cigarette, feeling done in, wasted, I suddenly realize, with a kind of passive horror and curiosity, that the only reason for doing anything is to fill up the time between now and death. I go to school every day to teach my reluctant darlings not so much in order to do what is good and right (serving students, serving society, serving God, even serving self) as to keep busy while I wait.

Perhaps some truths about MS are seeping through the denial my febrile sexuality once served. My body *is* going away, but at a more leisurely pace than I'd anticipated. Suddenly, life stretches out again before me, longer than it's ever seemed, crowded with alarming possibilities: wheelchairs and diapers and electric beds and nursing homes. George got yoked to this future through a vow spoken in trust when we were invulnerably young. If he broke it now, no one could blame him, I least of all, although I would miss his companionship grievously. But if he does leave me, no one else will ever speak that vow. Even if someone wanted to, I would never accept it now that I know I have MS. Either I spend my life with George, or I spend it without a partner.

This is not a productive revelation. It leaves me feeling sorry for George for having had the ill luck to marry me, and sorry for myself for being trapped by my failing body in a dependency I despise. After it, nothing changes. I go on waiting out my time.

"Come on, Mom, we're almost ready." Anne gallops into my room. At fifteen, she still hasn't quite put her imaginary horsey out to pasture. "What are you *doing?*"

I'm sitting on the edge of my bed, staring into a dresser drawer. "I can't decide what to put on," I say. I don't mention that for the past several months I've been sitting like this every morning, sometimes for fifteen or twenty minutes. It's not as though I have a vast wardrobe to select from. It's not as though it makes much difference what I wear. I just can't decide.

"Oh, for heaven's sake," she says, yanking a pair of jeans out of the drawer. "We're only going to the zoo." She tosses a long-sleeved jersey, some underpants, a pair of knee socks onto the bed. "Put these on."

"Thanks." Now that I know what to wear, I get dressed docilely. But I'll have the same problem tomorrow, when she's already gone to school, and the next day, and the next. Getting dressed is a commitment to living through the day, and I've reached the point where I can hardly make it anymore.

iv

I fall in love with a man because he eats a cup of yogurt with a fork. From the frailty of this pretext, you can guess (though I don't) how ripe I am for capitulation. Richard has come into my office to eat lunch with me, but he's forgotten a spoon and all I've got in my desk is a fork with twisted tines, kind of like the one my old school principal, Bessie M. Buker, used to rap the cafeteria door frame with to get our attention. The sight of Richard making do with that disarms me.

Well, there's more: smiles in the corridor and little compliments and witty notes in my mailbox, all the small singling-out gestures that signal the presence of an other on one's cluttered horizon. Slowly he comes into focus: a lovely long body with good legs, tight from cycling, and a deep chest below narrow shoulders, a shock of black hair, a dense beard framing sensuous lips, pale hazel eyes. I think off and on about having an affair with him, but the idea makes me tired. Having an affair, I remember, requires a lot of effort, a lot of attention to another person, and although sometimes I feel like bothering, as often as not I don't. It's been six years since the last one. I'm afraid I've lost the energy for turning anyone on.

But he gets turned on. A group of graduate students gathers on the last night of July under a chinaberry tree strung with tiny clear lights on the terrace at the Shanty. I sit beside Richard. We look at one another for a long moment, and he smiles a little.

"What?" I ask.

He starts to say something and then breaks off: "You know."

"I've been wondering," I say softly, laughing, "what would happen if I leaned over and kissed you." This is a dumb idea. I don't know most of the people here very well, but Richard does, and they all know I'm married.

"I think we'd better wait to do that on our own," he replies. "Soon."

"Yes," I say, "yes, soon," and go home.

Three months later, to the night, I nearly die.

Because I don't die, but go on living for many more years, I gain ample hindsight. I recognize that Richard and I entered one another's lives at the worst possible moments, he bolting from a ruined relationship, I teetering on the verge of a nervous breakdown. He couldn't help treating me badly any more than I could help cracking up. Reading over my notes from the time, I will see that an elegiac quality permeated the brief affair: I knew the ending before the beginning. I will feel grateful to have survived. For now, I hold *love* on the back of my tongue, bitter pill of a word, bitter as poison, determined to die rather than spit it out. That's just how crazy I am.

* * *

Richard is a careful, empathic lover and a humorous companion. After making love, he sits beside me, reading me bits out of Jacques Barzun, recalling his college sweetheart, who loves him still, recounting how he organized the Canterbury Recycling Association. I've been lucky in lovers. Most have been bright and entertaining. Richard, I feel especially close to, delighted by, because he likes to write, too. Still, in the years since my last affair I've grown increasingly introverted, and now his lovemaking lays me open to terrors I haven't felt before. When he puts his fingers between my legs, my insides explode, and I think, My God, how does he know how to *do* that?—as though he had violated my private self. "You like to make love, don't you?" he asks, and I don't want him to know that about me. I don't want anyone to know so much about me. I don't want anyone to have such power over me.

"You're different in bed," he says.

"How so?"

"Earthier. Simpler."

"Yes," I say. "Life seems simpler here. There's nothing beyond the edge of the bed." But of course there is.

In his journal, Richard says, he refers to me as "a woman I know."

"Please," I tell him, "please, in your journal, let me be Nancy." But does it matter, I wonder.

Almost immediately, the poems start coming, the strongest ones yet. Some short stories, too. I feel as though I've been boarded up, and my desire for Richard has thrown me wide open, images rushing in, words rushing out. The sense of trespass his lovemaking creates is the price I have to pay. Someone's got to break in, or the poems don't get out. I take to writing poems even in dreams:

Sometimes I just don't want to be good.
Too many of me have been good for too long. . . .

I may be in love less with Richard than with Richard's space. He has an apartment, really just one large room with a kitchen and bathroom, at the back of an old house downtown. The pungent smell of eucalyptus branches stuck in a jar on the bookcase permeates the dim air. He says the place holds what he needs to live, which doesn't seem to be much: a few clothes, a few dishes, shelves and shelves of books, a typewriter. Mostly, a typewriter. I don't know whether he needs that to live, but I suspect that I do.

My own house feels as filthy and chaotic as a bus terminal. George's working hours are long and erratic. The children wander in and out, trailing friends. If they notice me at all, they see the Big Meanie. The one who makes them wash the dishes and sets curfews earlier than anyone else's. I recognize that structurally, at this point in their lives, as a parent I have to be wrong, no matter what I do. That's not to justify my actions. Maybe they're truly dreadful. But I'm not sure it matters a whole lot. Whatever I do, they have to reject it—and me too, I suppose—in order to get on into their own lives. In the process, they're creating me, and I hate who they need me to be.

The house itself is too big for me now. I'm too weak to care for it properly, and no one else is willing, so I feel constantly as though it's falling down around my ears. I can't breathe here. "The quest of women writers . . . ," Janette Turner Hospital writes, "is a search not just for a room of their own, but for safe private space, for nontoxic air, for a place where the self can really breathe. . . . The search involves contraction into smaller and smaller space; frequently it leads to an ultimate withdrawal into the body itself."

The evening after Richard and I first make love, everyone happens to be out at once. Smelling of Richard, feeling soft and tired, I make myself an *omelette savoyarde* and sliced tomatoes with basil. I eat alone, drinking a glass of white wine and thinking how badly I want to live like this. As proof of my ability to live alone in spite of my physical limitations, I start to clean up my own dishes and promptly slice my left middle finger on the French cutting knife. Finger on ice, I take coffee and Amaretto to the porch to watch a storm boil in over the Catalinas.

And so, ignoring the omen of the sliced finger, I run away from home. Not far. About nine blocks. I find one little room, with a sink, stove, and refrigerator and an enamel table with two chairs at one end and at the other a studio couch, some bookshelves, and a desk. The closet and dresser have been built into the bathroom. I like its snugness, as though it were a ship's cabin or a camper, something miniature, encompassable, to carry me along. The landlord is taken with me, so he gives the walls fresh coats of paint, white and yellow, hangs yellow curtains in the windows, even puts a new corduroy slipcover on the couch. Here, I think, I will make my own life.

What I jot in my journal, however, rings a different note:

"I am deathly tired. Literally deathly tired. I wonder if I have not crawled away to this little space not as a bid for independence but in order to die."

Anne has given me a tiny black kitten with tufted ears and a kink in her tail. I've named her Bête Noir, my beloved Beast, the Beast of My Heart. When I move away, George insists that I take her along for company. At first I don't want her with me. I want no responsibility for another living creature. But I go to the Safeway and buy her Purina Cat Chow, tinned tuna, a pair of yellow dishes, a Ping-Pong ball with a fuzzy cover of pink and yellow stripes, and we settle down together.

My affair with Richard suits me badly. Since the evening at the Shanty, I haven't once slept through the night. Drained at the end of every day, I thud into unconsciousness as soon as I stretch out, but after an hour or two I surface, preternaturally alert, and often don't sleep again till dawn or later. My exhaustion leaves me groggy and ill. Flesh starts melting off me like candle wax. I weigh a hundred one, ninety-eight, ninety-five. I rather like this part, the way my bones jut up under my skin, the way my clothes hang off me. It makes me feel fragile and pellucid.

Then Richard ends the affair. He arrives at my door one Sunday afternoon. We sit out on a little wall under the cedar trees. He sleeps only with women he's in love with, he tells me, and he's not in love with me. I wish he'd given me that information a couple of months ago. Now it's too late. Too late for what, I'm not sure. But I know it's too late. After he leaves, I close my door and windows and bury my head in my pillows and howl the way I did both times I gave birth. Afterward, I grow quiet and begin to plan to die.

I'm not sure that the loss of Richard causes me all this pain. The loss of self seems at the heart of it, a loss I never experienced with other lovers. But I was younger then, prettier, and not so shy. I permitted Richard to see me naked, to penetrate me, surely in sexual terms, but also symbolically. I abandoned myself in making love to him, exposing myself horribly, and now I'm ashamed. The shame, as much as the loneliness, is doing me in. I want my self back, intact, untouched by Richard's careless fingers. When I think of my scrawny, crippled body, kicked now out of his bed, I feel as though I'd been stripped to the skin and then flayed.

* * *

The fact that I'm having a breakdown strikes me abruptly and with perfect clarity. I go on having the breakdown anyway. Knowledge is no proof against certain kinds of disaster. Maybe most kinds. Part of me knows I am ill; another part sneers incredulously, accusing me (in Mother's long familiar words) of dramatics. The first part gets me to my neurologist, who prescribes amitriptyline, and to the psychotherapist I haven't seen in years, who tells me that my psychic patterns no longer serve me and I must restructure my life to allow me not merely to pose but to function as a writer. The second part circles warily, sensing that José with his pills and Ken with his new structures may do me out of the urge to kill myself, and then I'll have to struggle on and on.

The day before taking an overdose, I meet Richard at the Shanty for a beer. The beer comes in sweating mason jars. Served like that, it always reminds me of pee.

"You misunderstand me," Richard says. He has a deep voice, and he drawls slightly. "I have nothing against you. Nothing against your body. You have an elegant body." I am tracing designs in water on the tan Formica table so that I won't have to look at him as he speaks. "It wouldn't matter to me," he goes on, "if you were Genevieve Bujold, Anne Tyler, Annie Dillard. I simply don't want a relationship with anyone."

"I *know* all that." Now I look up. "Knowing doesn't make any difference. Some part of me is so crazy it can't know anything."

Bête Noir trains me to play fetch. I'm a slow learner, but eventually it dawns on me that when she trots up with the ball in her teeth and drops it at my feet, she wants me to throw it so that she can retrieve it and return it for another toss. We entertain ourselves in this way by the hour. Paddling in the sink, too. That is, I'm there for the serious business of washing, but she's there for paddling. My sink grows a bloom of little black paw prints. She monitors the roaring ebb and flow of water in the toilet. The cascade of the shower is too scary, though, and she perches anxiously outside the plastic curtain until I reemerge.

Our apartment has only a small gas space heater, so it's always cold even though the winter is unusually mild. Bête sits in my lap with her head tucked into my sweater like a sleepy bird. At night we get into the sleeping bag and she curls between my arm and my ribs. In the morning she leaps out, onto the bookcase beside the bed, stretching her front paws up to the windowsill and chittering at the finches in the cedar trees. Daytimes, I sit in the sunshine outside the door, reading and watching her chase grasshoppers in the weeds. The ones she catches, she brings to me for admiration and then eats noisily. She is with me as I approach death, and throughout my return to life.

The telephone wakes me. Bête, too, who uncurls herself from my side and stretches. The room is dark. I don't know what time it is. I squint at the clock, but my vision is too blurred to make out the glowing red numbers. The tinny radio is playing rock music softly.

"Hello, dear." George's voice. "How are you?"

"Not too good." I'm awake. I'm talking on the telephone.

"What's the matter?"

"I took Elavil. A lot."

"Oh, my God." He draws the words out as though they really were a prayer. Later, he'll tell me that he's rehearsed this kind of conversation over and over in his head ever since my suicide attempt at Met State, but on this night he hasn't given it a thought. "I'll be right there. Unlock the door for me."

"I don't know if I can." I'm lying in bed now, but I have jumbled memories of trying to get up and go to the bathroom. I couldn't stand, couldn't even kneel. I squirmed forward using my feet and elbows, and when they were all bloody I turned over and scooted on my back, battering the knobs of my spine. The lock is too high to reach from the floor. "I'll bring a hammer to break the window," George says. "Just in case."

I roll off the bed and wriggle toward the door. I'm in a lot of pain but I feel stronger than I did before. I'm awake. Pulling myself up by the doorknob, I flip the bolt before tumbling backward.

The last time I tried to kill myself, after swallowing the Darvon, I put on my prettiest robe. This time, I'm wearing a tatty nightgown I've had for years, smeared now with blood and urine. George bursts in, grabs my coat, shoves me into it. It's after six at night on the first of November, chilly even in Tucson. George is shaking and swearing, madder than I've ever seen him.

"Why didn't you tell me?" he asks.

"I didn't tell anyone," I say. Only Richard, who forgot.

The next day, José comes by. With the suicide attempt, he tells me, I've finished something I had to do, and I'm safe now. This might be wishful thinking born of guilt at having given me the pills in the first place, but in fact, he seems to be right. Either that, or the whopping dose of antidepressant, not quite enough to kill me, blasted me straight out of my depression in a kind of shortcut to normalcy. In any event, although I go on grieving over Richard for a ridiculously long time, a year, maybe more, I no longer feel suicidal.

Richard helps by shaving off his beard, so that he no longer looks like the man I went to bed with, the one who threw me out. I eat greedily, packing weight on almost as rapidly as it melted off. I sleep through the night. I am already becoming the woman who will sit one day across from Richard in a little restaurant on the Gulf Coast, to which he has long since returned, looking at his photos, chatting about mutual friends, and forget until hours later to check herself for the pangs of love, the way people who've had cancer palpate themselves nervously for new tumors. When she does check, nothing's there but a scar, and she can hardly see that.

The poems and stories keep coming, and in the spring I start writing essays, too, which combine the delights of poetry and prose for me. They are carnal acts, enabling me to inscribe the earthly life I've tried to flee: its tricks, its sweet poisons. They dis-enchant me. I'm awake. And I will write my self into well-being.

One night at the beginning of February, Bête runs out when I open the door. I don't think much about it. She's done it before. But this time she doesn't come back. In the morning I call George, who comes to search the neighborhood. In a while he knocks at my door.

"Oh, sweetheart," he says, reaching for me, "she's dead." She was hit and killed instantly, he's learned, and someone called the Humane Society to take her away. So she's the only one who doesn't rest in our boneyard.

I have loved all our cats, all, perhaps, except an ungainly black and white one named the Princess Saralinda, and I will love the ones to come. But none like Bête. Aunt Jane says that for every person, there's one cat, and maybe she's right. Hers was Otello, the Black Man. Now I've had mine. Over and over I called her the Beast of My Heart, speaking in silliness more truly, I think, than I knew. We should all have, some time during our tricky lives, the thing we can love unconditionally, without measure, not because it is good and tries to please us but because it is beautiful and makes us laugh.

At school I don't mention her death to many people. I have no friends close enough to understand my loss. When I get home, I start to call out, "Is there a beast in the house?" before I recall that there isn't. Anne comes over. Leaning over the back of a chair, I talk and cry, and she lets me, and then we both laugh because I've wept a puddle on the floor worthy of Alice in Wonderland. She takes Bête's food and dishes away with her. I keep the pink and yellow ball awhile longer.

Beastlessness wears on me. Each return to my empty apartment wrenches my heart. I think of all the tears I have shed for cats. George and the children have shed them, too. Are they wasted? Are we foolish? I don't think so. There's something to be said for love no matter what the object. There are ways in which such love translates into the power to love ourselves and one another. I want to live with people who know what I've lost.

At the end of February, I move home. I've been away almost precisely the same months in the calendar that I spent at Met State, thirteen years earlier.

A few months after breaking off our affair, Richard invites me back into his bed. I don't know why he asks me here now. My charms haven't grown more fatal, and he's certainly no more in love with me than he ever was. Maybe he's just horny. It's spring.

We've been at a party, and on the way home, he asks me to stop in for tea. We talk for a while, and then I reach for my cigarettes and car keys, but when I stand up, he reaches for me. I lean into the lovely softness of his mouth.

"Would you like to make love?" he asks. I say I'm worried that he'll still be bothered by making love without being in love, so we make a pact: his terms are not to think that he's making any kind of a statement about love; I don't pay any attention to what my terms are, something to do with not killing myself, I suppose. We shake hands and go to bed.

By two o'clock I'm back in my own bed, feeling full and happy. It occurs to me that because he broke off with me without any warning, I never had the chance to make love to him for the last time. Now, unexpectedly, soothingly, my body has had time to say good-bye to his.

The tea was a bad idea. I lie awake for a long time in the moonlight spilling across my bed, the mockingbirds outside my open window singing feverishly in the sudden heat of a desert spring. Instead of thinking about Richard, I find myself planning a new essay, about my friend from Saudi Arabia, which I will start tomorrow.

Even without the pangs of love, the poems and stories and essays keep coming, in defiance of the patterns of desire long defined. It feels as though each affair—the excitement of novelty, the sexual urgency, the stab of grief and sometimes shame at its subsidence—were another turn of a vast engine made sluggish by some Arctic night. With Richard, for some reason, the engine kicks over for good and steams along on its own. I have fallen in love at last, not with yet another man, no matter how arousing his beauty, but with my true object: words.

Here at Home

～～～～～

i

A S THE CONDITION of my return to George and the children, I ask for a room of my own. I haven't any money, so I can't fulfill that half of Virginia Woolf's prescription for the woman writer. At least, however, I need my own space. I take the dim little room papered in a green jungle print, which we used to use as our bedroom. It's crowded, what with all those tigers and leopards and lions and zebras peering down with slightly stupid ferocity, and awfully accessible, having doors to the living room, George's room, a closet, the bathroom, and the backyard. But in addition to my dresser, commode, and Hide-a-bed, I have a desk and a typewriter and lots of bookshelves. I even think of putting in a little refrigerator, so as to be wholly self-contained, but I never get around to it. The fact is that I will be drawn increasingly into the life that fills the rest of the house, and after a year or so, under the weight of George's unhappiness with the arrangement, I move my body back into his bed. I cling to my desk, though. I cling and cling.

The pattern of my physical life continues: a couple of good days paid for by bouts of nausea, dizziness, headache, griping bowels. The fact that these are not symptoms of MS, and thus there is nothing medically wrong with me, increases my weariness and self-loathing. After more than twenty years of such inexplicable misery, and the struggle to carry on a productive life in the teeth of it, I'm wearing out.

"I don't think you're doing anyone a favor," I say to Ken, "by keeping me alive." It's a drizzly December day, and the light through the gauzy curtains gives a subaqueous quality to his high white office. He has a kindly young face, bearded, with pale, attentive eyes.

"I do it," he tells me, "for my own sake."

I've always believed that there was something wrong with me and that if I tried really hard I could get better. To some extent I was right, of course, because I've suffered badly from the symptoms of depression, and those can be controlled. But the fact of being a depressive is just that, a fact: who I am. No amount of wishful thinking or medication or psychotherapy can make me into someone else. I'm it. Here and now. If I keep taking my pills, I will survive in spite of myself. Good girl. Good, good girl.

A year or so after my return, George announces that he's thinking of leaving. Only fair, I say, thinking of the breakdowns, the affairs, the MS, the bitchiness, the joylessness, all the shit he's put up with over these long years. The only wonder is that he's stuck it out so long. He really ought to go, get out now, while he's still young, find a healthy woman free from black spells, have some fun. No one could blame him. I've brought this all on myself. I know that, and so will everyone else. "If anything ever happens between you and George," Mother once told me, years ago, "I'm keeping George."

Trying to ready myself for his departure, I feel the weight of our past heaped up behind me. Odd, unrelated flashes. Ducking drunkenly behind a tree in the middle of the Brown campus to strip off my pantygirdle, too giddy to recall that "behind" from one perspective is "in front" from another. Driving to a shopping center in Rhode Island to buy me a black maternity cocktail dress and deciding on the spur of the moment (was the weather bad?) to stay at the Sheraton in Providence, where we got fishy stares because we had no luggage. George in uniform, on his way to a Reserve meeting, bringing me a chocolate ice-cream soda at Met State. How can he leave this accretive process now, stop it, just walk out on it?

"What will you do?" I ask. Go back to New England, he tells me, get a teaching job, find another woman, start over. I think of him calling another woman "dear" and "sweetheart," kissing her, meeting her for lunch, driving around on errands with her, discussing what to serve friends for dinner, maybe even playing Scrabble, all the intimacies that have seemed peculiarly ours but that I see now are not peculiar at all but can be done by any one person with another. In some sentimental back corner of my mind, I've always believed that we'd grow old together, that he would make the trip toward death with me, that we'd ease that particular hard journey for each other. Now he's getting off at a way station.

I'm filled with rue. If only I'd behaved better, I say to myself. If only I'd slept with him more often. Hadn't complained about money so much. Been nicer to the children. Hadn't taken lovers. Kept a better house. I keep thinking of all the things I could have done to justify myself. If only I'd been healthy. If only, I find myself thinking as I stir a *ratatouille niçoise* in my old cast-iron pot, if only I'd prepared more interesting food. This thought is so wildly off the mark that even I find it funny. Of all the things I've failed at, cooking is not one.

After all, he doesn't get off at a way station. He comes along for the ride. Maybe he sees something in a woman who, wracked by grief, suddenly catches herself ruing her culinary inadequacies and gets a fit of the giggles.

"I'm so ashamed," I say to Ken, hunched over in the tweed armchair next to the door of his office mopping at my mascara with a soggy tissue, "ashamed and discouraged, to be sitting here saying the same things I've been saying to you for more than a decade."

"I've never claimed to be good at this," he says.

"I find you very difficult," George tells me. When I mention to Anne that her father finds me difficult, she sighs explosively: "Don't we all!" They do, they do, and the family counselor we've started to consult falls right in with them. Of course I take their word for it. What else can I do? A woman with a crippling disease who runs away from home and tries to kill herself is unquestionably hard to deal with.

But maybe, it occurs to me in a rush, I don't have to be all that difficult. Maybe their treatment of me, and Mother's before them, has thrown me into that architectural position, and I've been fool enough to occupy it all these years because it's what everybody, including me, expected. Needed. Maybe I'm no more problematic at heart than any other spirited human being. Maybe George's device for keeping me in my place in the family floor plan has been to show me how long-suffering he is to put up with me. And I've gone right along, flailing myself for putting poor George through the torment of living with me.

If living with me is awful, then surely no one should have to do it. But neither should I have to live with people who assume that I'm a madwoman, a bitch, a problem—the lexicon varies depending on the speaker but the message remains the same. People who demand that I play those roles. Who treat me as though I'm playing them both when I am and when I'm not. Surely I should be free to learn to think of myself not as a repository of misery but as an ordinary, decent, pleasant human being. Running away has never gained me that freedom. I'll have to plot out another route.

Why doesn't George leave me? Does he stay because he is, as one reviewer of my essays suggested, "a saint, staying through extreme mood swings, suicide attempts, severe illness, and a number of love affairs"? Maybe so. Certainly most people who know us have subscribed to this hagiolatrous view, I no less than the others, for most of the years we've spent together. It seems never to occur to any of us that he might stay in part because of those very events and even that he may in some instances have collaborated in them. He sees me as the "wild" one, he'll admit one day, and himself as "staid and sober," the one who holds things together. A person who conceives of himself as holding things together can fulfill his mission only if "things" are threatening to blow apart. And if they don't blow on their own, perhaps he'll just strike a match—thoughtlessly, of course, attention absorbed by loftier matters—and set off the explosion he needs.

The role of Saint George may or may not suit him. He says not. All I can be sure of is that it must long have suited me, for I have consistently presented him as a saint, sharing the construction of this fiction with him, his parents, my parents, my siblings, our children, our friends, and eventually my readers. How else could that reviewer, with only my words to go on, have reached his conclusion? Despising myself, I've grown convinced along with everyone else that only a saint could bear life with me.

As my depression has dispersed under medication and hard psychotherapeutic work, however, and I've begun to reimagine myself as a healthy woman, I discover I have to imagine George differently as well: no longer my saint, my perfect prince, my father come to earth again. Just George, my Scrabble partner, who for his own reasons takes some joy in being here, at home, with me.

ii

Anne is the one who leaves, though not because of me. Despite her impatient outburst, she tolerates me pretty well and even likes me sometimes, I think. But she was never along for the whole ride, and before we know it, we reach her station, the point of transfer we've spent eighteen years preparing her—and, less successfully, ourselves—to reach bravely. Circling and circling outward, she spins off toward college.

The night before she heads East, I hold her and rock her as she weeps her inevitable reluctance and uncertainty at leaving home, and then I want to call the whole thing off, to hold her forever, but of course that wouldn't make any difference. The Anne I want to hold here would vanish anyway into the smoke of some future, this or another. In the morning, through the window of the airport restaurant, George and I watch her little erect figure in a green-and-white-striped shirt and chinos, her blond head newly bobbed, over her shoulder a tote bag with her boyfriend's baby blanket spilling out the top, climb the steps and duck into the plane. We hold hands and can't speak.

Anne has irradiated my life. Not always with sunshine, mind you. Sometimes, rather, the smoky glow of banked embers or a sudden pyrotechnic flare. But light, always light. She is the child I need: sturdy, humorous, capable, self-confident. Once, when she was about ten, she found me doing one of those silly psychological exercises popular in the feel-good seventies where you list ten things you like about yourself and ten things you don't.

"Sounds like fun," she said. "Can I do it?"

"Sure," I said, handing her paper and a pencil. Off she went, returning in a little while to plunk her sheet in front of me. I still have it, tucked into the front of her pink baby book:

1. I am left-handed.
2. I am cross-eyed.
3. I like to read.
4. I like to play games.
5. I can run fast.
6. I like plants + animals.

7. I like long dresses.
8. I like to draw.
9. I like Social Studies.
10. I think I'm pretty.

"This is great," I told her. How much she likes her body, I thought, its capacities and attributes, even those, like being cross-eyed, which might cause another child shame. She likes being cross-eyed, she says, because she doesn't know anyone else who is. "And what about the things you don't like?"

"Oh," she said, her attention beginning to wander toward Gwydion, who had come in with a little blue-bellied lizard dangling from his jaws, "I couldn't think of any of those."

She has been my model of sanity.

"Okay," I say on the morning of my birthday, "here I am. I've made it to forty. Now, send me a sign." I'm speaking, roughly, to the Writing God, the one who has seemed to mock me at every turn, who makes certain, for instance, that when I apply for a fellowship, not only do I not get it but, out of all the applicants around the country, Richard does. I find it hard then not to revert to a primitive view of chance and accident, not to see an intentional pattern—ironic, cruel—behind such an outcome. It's such a neat one, designed to shaft me straight through.

I don't actually believe in a Writing God, or any sort of God who takes requests, like the disc jockey on KROQ, or hands out goodies according to one's deserts, just or otherwise. Life seems to me, in fact, a giant lottery, in which a man's receiving the very award his jilted lover yearns for is simply A Very Bad Accident. Still, I prattle on to the Writing God, if only for a sense of companionship.

And then in the giant lottery my number, like Richard's, comes up, just a few months after my fortieth birthday. The editor of a small press submits two collections of mine, one of poems and another of essays, to a competition for the Western States Book Award. The poems win, and the essays receive honorable mention. Within a year *In All the Rooms of the Yellow House* comes out; less than two years later, after being accepted as my doctoral dissertation, *Plaintext* is published, too.

The difference these events make in my life is immeasurable. For more than a quarter of a century I've been bleating about becoming a writer when I grow up. As the author of two books,

I am a writer and therefore must be grown up. This state scares me a good deal. It's easier to be the dreamy child than the active adult, responsible for her own well-being. All the same, I'm exhilarated. "No more pissing + moaning—ever," I scribble in my journal. It's a pledge I won't make good on. I'm a pisser and moaner by nature, who reads every denial of a Guggenheim, every rejected poem, every unfavorable review as a slap across my psyche from the Writing God. But if my successes don't transform my bad nature, they ameliorate it no end. To have, if only transitorily, precisely what one wants lightens even the most sodden heart.

By the time Anne leaves for college, Matthew has departed emotionally, although for several years he continues to squat amid fetid heaps of clothes and bedding, mugs growing greenish mold, sheaves of crumpled paper, and fragments of electronic equipment, emerging periodically to use the refrigerator and the telephone. He has joined what he refers to as The Movement, with its gospels according to Sid Vicious and Johnny Rotten, and wears its uniform and insignia, disfiguring his increasingly handsome body as much as possible: the sides of his head shaved and the rest of his hair shellacked into a ten-inch Mohawk dyed red and yellow; chains with padlocks and grubby camouflage bandannas and studded strips of leather wound around his neck and limbs; crosses and razor blades dangling from his ears; heavy combat boots with a knife stuck in the top. I am sick at the sight of these emblems of domination and bondage, and after he has thrown me to the floor in a temper, I am afraid as well. He steals from us, lies to us, despises us. I'm expected to endure him because I'm his mother and rebellion is an inevitable element in adolescence. But those judgments are based on cultural assumptions I'm beginning to reject. If he has to despise something, let him look elsewhere than to me. I don't think being despised is good for me.

"I was just like Matthew at his age," George tells me to quell my concerns. This strikes me as a queer statement, both arrogant (since in order to provide reassurance it must be followed by "and I turned out just fine") and fallacious. George's parents had wanted several children, and he soothed their disappointment by being the best only child he could be: attending church, getting good grades, playing in the band, winning essay contests, making friends from the right class, slightly above his own, going on to college. Like so many of us products of the fifties, he was practically a well-scrubbed parody of himself. Now, it occurs to me, he needs this furious, feckless child. Matthew is the crazy boy George repressed and resented repressing. In clenched silence he protected his own parents from him. But by God, the boy will now be set free.

I find their *folie à deux*, though increasingly comprehensible, excruciating, because it rests on premises that I will no longer accept. During one of our bitterest three-way confrontations—no, two-way: two against one—George says to me with the strained reasonableness that constitutes shouting for him, "I'm sick of your name-calling and bitching." Clearly, George views his labeling me a bitch not as name-calling but as a simple description of reality. This double standard makes me feel crazy.

But, no matter what George wants, I'm just not crazy anymore. I'm not even depressed, although I'm very, very miserable. And this inability to subscribe to my own craziness forces me to see that our situation depends on George's discounting or trivializing my anger without ever knowing what he is doing. Because he assumes that his perception of any situation is the accurate account of a single reality, the possibility of my rightness, in any instance where my reality deviates from his, is literally unthinkable. If I stay, I have to continue to operate, as this family always has, in the teeth of the premise that I'm a crazy bitch whose unreasonable demands and desires must be gotten around as best as anyone can, because George's reality depends on this premise. And if I am going to know any of this, I am always going to know it absolutely alone.

Oppressed by this role I have not chosen, I feel inclined once again to bolt, but Ken, who is rarely directive, says, "Don't. Don't let them drive you out of your home." And he's right. I'm the one who loves this place. George ignores it, Matthew defaces it, but I draw its space around me and, in spite of its growing shabbiness, continue to cherish it. If I'm going to leave it, I'll do so in good order.

It takes me the better part of two years, but I engineer a respectable escape. Actually, by this time the desire for escape is no longer keen. Life as the mother of a punk rock musician who's started to read Sartre has its amusing moments. Like the retrieval of Amelia Earhart's corpse. The occasion itself isn't at all funny but very sad. The foolish puppy has turned out to be an eater: of Anne's Seiko watch, of three pounds of freshly made fudge, and finally of antifreeze. As her kidneys fail and she slips into a coma, Matthew cradles her by the hour, but clearly she can't recover. Finally,

George drives her to the Broadway Animal Hospital to be put down.

He doesn't have time to take her home for burial, however, so he delegates that task to Matthew and me. We enter the Broadway Animal Hospital, I in my Mrs. Middle America persona, all made up and dressed for success, lurching forward on my cane, Matthew in his black jeans and black leather jacket, hair now dyed black, clanking in my wake.

"We're here for our dead dog," we tell the receptionist, and every human head in the waiting room swivels toward us, fantasizing who knows what satanic rituals. With the carton bearing its sad freight in Matthew's arms, we exit as coolly as we can, exploding into laughter as soon as we reach the car. Then we drive home and lay Amelia in the ground beside Burton Rustle and Gwydion. To console ourselves, we make *spaghetti carbonara* for dinner.

iii

What I need more than escape at this point is a "real" job, one appropriate for a writer with a doctorate and a dozen years of teaching experience. Since I can't find it in Tucson, I apply elsewhere, and after securing several offers, I accept a one-year renewable lectureship at UCLA. If I like it, George and I agree, then he'll join me the following year. Meanwhile, we'll fly back and forth as often as we can. Thus begins the Great Los Angeles Adventure.

"Oh, shit," I yell as, catching my toe on the front edge of the elevator, I pitch toward the concrete floor of the garage in my new apartment building.

"Do you realize," George will ask me later, "that you might have died in that fall, and then your very last words would have been, 'Oh, shit'?"

"Ignominious," I'll giggle.

Now, I open my eyes to a dim circle of faces high above me. My first thought is lucid and restrained: I may be dying. A paramedic, his face down next to mine, is strapping me onto a stretcher. "I'm . . . so . . . frightened," I whisper to him.

"Don't worry." Into the ambulance I go. "You're going to be fine." Does he know that, or does he just say it to all the girls? An IV needle stings the back of my hand.

In the emergency room, a young doctor bends over me. "Who did this to you?" he asks. On behalf of all battered women, I'm grateful for the question and for his skeptical expression when I tell him I did it to myself.

"In fact," I say, "I don't know anyone here. I only got to Los Angeles yesterday afternoon."

I've made a mess of myself, breaking an artery and pulverizing the skin and flesh above my left eye, but skull X rays reveal no fracture. I spend several hours in the emergency room, waiting for X rays, waiting for a plastic surgeon, waiting most of the time for nothing at all. Next to me, a black boy with a bullet in his butt howls to the doctors and his mother and the police: "I dunno who shot me. I was just leanin' over to get somethin' out my girlfrien's car when . . . blam!" Like hell, everybody says, but they bandage his butt, leaving the bullet inside, and send him home with Momma.

Eventually they find me a bed in the Michael Jackson Burn Center. After two days, they release me. A week later, still looking as though someone had rammed a California plum into my left eyesocket, the whole left side of my face tinted in iridescent greens and yellows, I meet my classes for the first time. "I don't always look like this," I tell my students. Like hell, they may think, but we get along fine.

Despite its inauspicious opening, I like this new life. I find the city, sprawled under its gaseous haze, beautiful. I have come to a point in my life where I can find almost anything beautiful. My aesthetic sense, instead of growing more refined and discriminating, has become catholic and egalitarian. Perhaps this effect arises from my increasing immobility. I can't dash through my surroundings. I can scarcely drag my feet along, and even in the wheelchair I've been relying on increasingly over the past six years I can't go faster than three miles an hour. Much of the time I don't move at all. Stilled, I gaze and gaze. And, looked at deliberately for long moments, the world always yields up some delight. Really.

I take other pleasures as well. I've got a job I'm good at, which pays me more money than I've ever had before. I've got a pleasant little apartment, really just one huge room and a bath, all that I need. I never set wheel on the freeway, but I learn to navigate the surface streets confidently. I go to the supermarket and the drugstore. I treat myself to *pesto* and the fancier sort of frigid yummies. I buy some pretty clothes. On days when I don't teach,

I sometimes don't use my voice at all, except to sing along with the radio or my tapes. "Heaven," I sing with David Byrne, "Heaven is a place, a place where nothing, nothing ever happens."

I spend six months, almost the same ones I spent in Met State and later in my tiny Tucson apartment, as a recluse. This is the retreat I needed those times, but then I was too crazy to use it. Now I'm not crazy at all. I'm simply a woman alone. Then, I was scrambling as fast as I could away from the stifle of domestic life: the way it seemed to cramp my creativity and deaden my sexuality. I thought I would die of suffocation. Now I sense that I was really scrambling out from under the projections of others. I wanted to find the space in which I could become my own creature. Here it is, at last. "And all shall be well," wrote the medieval anchoress Dame Julian of Norwich, another woman alone, "and all manner of thing shall be well." I begin to feel some of her confidence: not that only good things will happen—that's not what she's saying—but that all that happens can be accepted, incorporated, celebrated.

Living alone, having to lug my own laundry, dump my own trash, keep myself in wine and apples and toilet paper, I am desperately aware that good things are not happening to my body. That life-threatening fall at the beginning signaled the deterioration I have time, here in seclusion, to contemplate. If I ran away from home the last time in order to die, I have come here now, after deliberation, in order to figure out just what I need to stay alive. Nothing lofty or glamorous, it turns out after all: help with heavy pots, for instance, and with the vacuum-sealed tops of bottles and with the buttons of my shirt cuffs. A kiss on the back of my neck. A cat to warm the crooks of my knees as I sleep. Someone to laugh at my jokes.

I get what I need most: enough money to write a book without needing an outside job. I resign from UCLA regretfully. I've been happy there, and the teaching life is familiar and rewarding. I have no idea what the writing life will be like. George, his mother, and Anne all fly over and pack the meager trappings of the Great Los Angeles Adventure into boxes, which they load into my old Volvo and a Ryder truck. Then we set out across the desert, through Indio and Blythe and Quartzsite, past the Space Age Lodge in Gila Bend, and on down around the wedge of the Catalinas into Tucson.

"It was about this big." Dr. Johnson forms a circle with his thumb and forefinger about the size of an aggie. "And black." He knows I know what black means: melanoma. "We took out as many lymph nodes as we could, and that was the only black one we saw. The pathologist will look at them more closely, but we hope we've got it." That's what they said with the first one, the mole. The chances were 95 percent that they'd got it all. Somebody's got to fall among the 5 percent.

"And if not?" My tone sounds ridiculously sedate to me, as though I were a little girl imitating what grown-ups sound like, but the only other tone available to me, I'm afraid, is a wail.

"If it shows up again, it will probably be in lung or bone. There's no effective chemo against melanoma. But we'll watch closely, and we'll keep taking out anything we find as long as we can."

"And then?"

"Then we'll let him go." He says it gently but without pity, as though he understands that I need not people who feel sorry for us—we can, and will, find plenty of them—but people who will help us meet our dilemmas and make our choices as honestly as possible.

Out of the recovery room, George sits propped up in a bed in the outpatient surgery ward, struggling to come to. Except for the sunken, purplish flesh around his eyes, he looks much the same as he did five hours ago. I think of him then, the deliberate way he took off his clothes and folded them, slipped his rings over the curled middle finger of my left hand for safekeeping, his face perfectly composed. But his cock gave him away. It crawled all the way up into the bush between his legs, almost out of sight. I was shocked. I'd never seen it like that. I want to reach up under the sheet now and feel whether it's come back down, but there's a nurse hovering around, feeding him sips of cranberry juice, and the gesture doesn't seem quite proper.

He keeps dozing off. I sit on the orange molded plastic chair, my chin barely reaching over his mattress, and read in snatches. I've brought P. D. James's *A Taste for Death*, something to hold my attention, and it is awfully good. Even so, I can't read more than a page before looking up. His eyelids flutter groggily. His mouth sags, the lips dried whitish. When I put my hand on his, he stirs but doesn't quite rouse.

I feel strange, as though I'd slipped into someone else's life, into one of Susan Kenney's novels. Except for the colds and stomach flus a teacher's flesh is heir to, and an awful case of chicken pox he caught from Anne, George has never been sick. He's the sort of person whose head never aches, whose bowels evacuate smoothly at the same time every day, who still has all his teeth. Even the first melanoma seemed like nothing to really worry about. Jesus, I didn't even go with him when he had it cut out. Now, suddenly, here I am keeping bedside vigil. And it occurs to me for the first time that this might be the pattern of my future. I could be sitting just like this, chin propped on mattress, hand cupping dry fingers, the last time he breathes. He's not playing by the rules: I was supposed to go first. *Don't go!* I want to cry out to him. *We've been through so much. We've come so far. Don't leave me!*

For now, he hears me. For now, he stays. Threatening him with an overnight stay if he doesn't wake up, the nurse and I get him dressed, into a wheelchair, down to the parking lot. I drive him home and steer him into bed. Later, I crawl in beside him and lie weeping those tears which run, at midnight, into your ears just the way Dorothy Parker said they do.

Our house is emptying. George's mother, who, newly widowed, has taken care of him during my winter in Los Angeles, returns to Vermont. Matthew graduates from high school, and he and his girlfriend, Poppy, who've been living in the little house in our backyard, move a few blocks away. Taking some music courses at the local community college and trying to establish himself as a rock bassist, Melvin Beastly by name, he pops in now and then to play some Bartók on our piano. Anne graduates from Smith and volunteers for the Peace Corps fisheries program in Zaïre. "Dear Mom and Dad," she writes from her first *sortie en bousse*, "not much happening here. Ate grasshoppers for lunch the other day. . . ."

For the first time, we are living, day after day, alone. No more radar pickets. No more infant wails in the night. No more Big Wheels and ten-speeds and skateboards. No more galloping hooves and rebel yells. The telephone seldom rings. When George is home, the stereo trills a Brandenburg Concerto, though when I'm there it's still apt to blare the Boomtown Rats. We've taken to eating dinner in front of MacNeil/Lehrer, although mealtime television was strictly forbidden while the children lived here. We shout out when we make love. It makes Vanessa Bell, the little sleek black cat who likes to sleep between us, leap straight into the air, but no one else is disturbed.

This house, more graceful than the Chinese grocery, envelops us in filtered light. Sometimes I totter from room to room just to celebrate it. I love the rose and white kitchen and the blue chintz couch with day lilies printed on it in the family room, where Winchester, the gargantuan fuzzy white cat, lolls with his feet in the air, his green eyes slitted, drooling and sometimes sneezing. We think he's allergic to himself. I love the real day lilies, grown from Farm seed, blooming in the whiskey barrel on the front porch. The Mexican tin cross above the fireplace, and the Scheier pots. The marble-topped dresser and commode from my room at 236. The finny, yet another Alpha in our long string of bettas, circling his clear bowl. My Ecstasy mug on the sideboard. The funny bathroom, all archways and alcoves like an Escher print. I don't love the bathroom floor, covered with blue and white tiles like a YMCA locker room, but I can live with it. These days, I can live with a lot.

The National Multiple Sclerosis Society invites me to speak at their leadership conference in Seattle, and I fly up ahead of George. That night, instead of ordering from room service as is my habit, I decide to go down to the restaurant. I've often enough grabbed lunch here or there by myself, but I've never dined alone in public. I have a lovely time. I order *linguine* with smoked salmon and fresh asparagus and a glass of Chardonnay. I eat a miniature éclair for dessert. I catch the glance of a man eating alone at the next table and we both smile in the way that people have of according each other attractiveness without inviting contact. Afterward, I sit in the lounge and drink coffee and Drambuie before going up to bed.

Describing the evening to George later, I try to puzzle out the unwonted boldness of these behaviors. "I felt sure of myself," I say, "in a way I never have before. I'd just arrived and hadn't yet registered at the conference, so I didn't have a name tag and no one could possibly have known who I was. Anyway," I laugh, "my name isn't exactly a household word. But that didn't seem to matter. I still felt like somebody."

Only later do I sense the significance of my words. I am

some*body*. A body. A difficult body, to be sure, almost too weak now to stand, increasingly deformed, wracked still by gut spasms and headaches and menstrual miseries. But some *body*. Mine. Me. In establishing myself as a writer, however modest my success, I have ceased to be no*body*. I have written my way into my embodied self, and here I am at home.

I press my breasts and belly against George's back, my pubis against his buttocks, my knees against the backs of his knees. Reaching over his hips, I take his limp cock in my hand and rub the tip with my thumb. This must be why I love to wear silk above all other fabrics, its slip against my skin the nearest I can come to this softness.

We've been trying to have intercourse. No use. Stroking, squirming, tongue-thrusting, murmuring. But he couldn't get hard. "I want you," he whispered against my face. Twice he rolled between my legs and tried to coax his cock into me, but it flopped in his fingers. Usually it pops up hard at the first caress, but today he's had an upset stomach and no amount of willpower has overcome the effects of queasiness. I climbed into bed planning on a quick good-night kiss and sleep, but he reached for me and held on.

I've caressed him with my fingers, my tongue, my words: "I wish I weren't crippled." Murmuring. "I wish I were still strong enough to kiss you, starting at the top, all the way down, then up the other side." Nothing. He laughed a little at himself, but his gestures felt impatient.

"Roll over," I said to him finally. He turned his back to me and curled up. Now I have his recalcitrant cock cradled in my palm. It moves a little at my touch, and the tension of desire his stroking and sucking have aroused starts beating between my legs.

"Oh God, I'm coming just by touching you," I breathe. He reaches back and slides his finger into the slit between my legs and I push at it hard. Tonight, wouldn't you know, I want his erection inside me, pushing through the tunnel and against the arch of my vagina. This is the image of my insides I get during lovemaking: a tunnel through a dark and reddish arch, like some street in Casablanca, maybe, though of course I've never been there. But I'm not going to get that. Still, I'm getting a lot.

His cock is stiffening. I feel for the drop of fluid at the tip and smooth it all over the silky swelling head. I stroke his foreskin forward, pull it back. Forward. Back. His breathing thickens. His buttocks thrust back into my pelvis. I keep coming in sporadic soft bursts, stroking, squeezing, stroking. All of a sudden I know he's made it.

"Here I come again," I gasp. Fluid wells out of his cock and I catch it in my palm to lubricate the whole shaft. Shudder. Shudder. Sweet slippery semen. Breath trembling, slowing.

"For once I've got the wet spot on my side," he laughs.

"Oh, it's not so bad." I stroke his buttock with my wet hand. "Actually, come feels kind of nice, see?"

"Till it gets cold."

For writing, I have a room of my own. When I first mention renting a separate space, George balks, thinking of my other Tucson apartment.

"Not like that," I tell him. "Not a place to sleep. Just somewhere I can go to work." If I stay at home, I'm inclined to do the laundry. That's the sort of writer I am.

I rent a casita in a little complex called Ramona Court, downtown, across from the police station, a block south of San Agustín Cathedral, between Midtown Liquors, where I buy my smokes and hang out with the tramps, and the now defunct Temple of Music and Art, on the edge of the barrios. It has a bedroom, which I don't need for sleeping but can use as Anne's attic while she's off in Africa, a little bathroom, a kitchen painted searing turquoise. I know turquoise is supposed to be a cool color, but this is searing, believe me. The room I work in has a dark red floor and white plaster walls with glass and tin sconces. Above the pointed arch of the fireplace, in a pointed niche, a statue of Our Lady of Guadalupe stands on her crescent moon. The furnishings are rudimentary: a table for my computer and a flush door on filing cabinets as a desk, with an orange office chair to roll between them; a bookcase; a low table for my dictionary; an easy chair for reading, with most of its stuffing still inside. In the kitchen, at a glass-topped, white wrought-iron table with matching chairs, George and I eat lunch every day. The rest of the time, I'm alone here. With you.

One morning before leaving for work, I am sitting on my screened porch, in my white director's chair with the pink polka-dotted canvas, idly tossing a Wiffle ball for my indefatigable comic terrier, Pinto, and reflecting with alarm, as I often do these days, on my body's steady deterioration. For a long time, my disease, the chronic progressive type of MS, was marked by lulls between the appearance of fresh symptoms. I would get no better, but neither would I get markedly worse. In the past couple of years, I've gotten relentlessly weaker. I can hardly drag myself from one piece of furniture to the next. I've taken several damaging falls, and every footstep now brings the terror of another. I may not be able to put off much longer using a wheelchair all the time. No end to my degeneration is in sight. I'm afraid. I'm afraid. I'm afraid.

And yet, as I sit here in Anne's old UCLA nightshirt, wondering how I will ever summon the strength to put on some clothes and drive the ten minutes to my studio for a day's work, I am washed, suddenly and utterly, by satisfaction. Odd, that as my physical space contracts to the span of a few staggering steps, the inside of my head should grow thus light and large. I am happier now, like this, than I have ever been before.

Such episodes tend to be fragile and transient. If this sense of serenity and fulfillment vanishes, as forty-five years have taught me it is likely to do time and again, I hope I'll at least remember—while lamenting a child's long absence, maybe, or grieving at the death of a parent, bemoaning the failure of a book, sitting at George's deathbed, confined myself to a bed in a nursing home—that I have been, at least once, and in truth many times, happy clear through to the bone.